# Philosophical Principles of the History and Systems of Psychology

Frank Scalambrino

# Philosophical Principles of the History and Systems of Psychology

## Essential Distinctions

palgrave
macmillan

Frank Scalambrino
Department of Philosophy
John Carroll University
University Heights, OH, USA

ISBN 978-3-319-74732-3          ISBN 978-3-319-74733-0    (eBook)
https://doi.org/10.1007/978-3-319-74733-0

Library of Congress Control Number: 2018936139

Cover illustration: Brain light / Alamy Stock Photo

Printed on acid-free paper

This Palgrave Macmillan imprint is published by the registered company Springer International Publishing AG part of Springer Nature.
The registered company address is: Gewerbestrasse 11, 6330 Cham, Switzerland

*To psychē (ψυχή)*

# Preface

As a kind of epigraph, toward contextualizing the central concern of this book, I would inscribe, as still pertinent for contemporary psychology, the following quote from William James' *The Principles of Psychology*:

> The fundamental conceptions of psychology are practically very clear to us, but theoretically they are very confused, and one easily makes the obscurest assumptions in this science without realizing, until challenged, what internal difficulties they involve. When these assumptions have once established themselves (as they have a way of doing in our very descriptions of phenomenal facts) it is almost impossible to get rid of them afterwards or to make any one see that they are not essential... (1918: 145)

This Preface is divided into three (3) parts. First, a general characterization of the structure, function, and content of this book. Second, a brief characterization of some of the motivation for writing this book. Third, a general overview of the book.

(1) This book may be of interest to anyone who wishes to "think through" the history of Western psychology. In fact, its original title was: *Philosophical Principles of the History and Systems of Psychology: Essential Distinctions for Thinking Through Psychology*. Specifically, this book is intended as supplementary for History and Systems of Psychology courses. It "fills a gap" in the literature, so to speak, in that though there

are many excellent "history of psychology" textbooks available today, a gap exists which may be traced to two aspects of the very nature of such books. First, the sheer amount of information contained, necessarily, in history of psychology textbooks makes it difficult for students to hold all the information in mind. Second, history of psychology textbooks are, of course, organized in relation to the vastness of the past, despite the historiographic choices faced by the historians who construct them.

Hence, it should be emphasized that this book is not a history textbook. If it were a history textbook, then it would be missing a good amount of information, for example compared to books produced by the likes of Sahakian (1975), Brennan (2003), Hergenhahn and Henley (2013), or Walsh et al. (2014). Keeping with the reference to the History and Systems of Psychology course, it would be more accurate to say this book is a systems textbook. Thus, on the one hand, this book is able to be manageably concise for students to hold in mind; in this way our focus on principles and essential distinctions may function as mnemonic devices for students. On the other hand, this book is organized in terms of principles and "systems," understood as constituted by clusters of principles. Moreover, after reviewing countless textbooks for, and teaching multiple sections of, the History and Systems of Psychology course, it seems clear that the structure and function of this book may be seen as "filling a gap" in the available literature.

Further, regarding the content of this book—forgive me for pointing it out—the authors of textbooks for the History and Systems of Psychology course have all been trained as psychologists. The value added of having someone with a PhD in philosophy construct a book for thinking through the history and systems of Western psychology will hopefully be evident after reading this book. Historians of psychology, philosophical psychologists, and psychologists with a desire for a panoramic view of their discipline have an understanding that Aristotle and Kant, for example, have been quite influential in the history of psychology; however, it is rare to find a rendering of the history of philosophy sufficient for students studying the history of psychology. The intention written into this book is that readers will invoke history while thinking through systems, whether it be in terms of a genealogy or history of contemporary psychology or in terms of an examination of the historicity of the principles and commitments which have constituted the study of psychology throughout Western history.

A characterization of this book in terms of the technical vocabulary of historiography may be helpful for some readers. Thus, invoking Richard Rorty's (1984) "Four Genres" of historiography—discussed in Chap. 2— this book may be understood as engaged in "rational reconstruction," as opposed to "historical reconstruction," "canon-formation," or "doxography." Yet, the "rational reconstruction" here is directed at the philosophical principles out of which selections constitute the systems of psychology. As a result, such a "reconstruction" may be seen as a point of departure for a "revisionist canon-formation," in Rorty's terminology; however, a better—and a more readily understood—characterization of this book for the purpose of a Preface may come from saying: this book re-orients psychologists to the way the systematization of the history of psychology relates to philosophy, that is, to psychology's unavoidably "underlying" philosophy. Previous books in regard to the History and Systems of Psychology tend toward doxography and to deemphasize the constitutive role of philosophical principles, especially for contemporary psychology, as if psychology's relation to philosophy were merely an aspect of an intellectual historiography.

(2) As a result, this book contributes a statement of the principles from which the history of psychology may be systematically examined, and then works toward showing the differences across the major systems, which have manifested in the history of Western psychology, toward a starting point and orientation for further critical thinking. One of the problems plaguing contemporary psychologists in regard to theorizing psychology may be characterized as a "confusion of levels." On the one hand, many psychologists embrace the political principles of equality and cultural diversity. In terms of theory this is standardly characterized as a "commitment to pluralism." Of course, one of the signs of such pluralism is the agreement to civility despite disagreement. All this is good. However, on the other hand, this commitment has been erroneously embraced by many a graduate student—and, unfortunately for those they serve, some clinical psychologists—such that a kind of "anything goes" attitude may emerge. The actions brought-forth under the sway of such an attitude may or may not be labeled with the technical terms of "eclecticism" or

"anarchism." Yet, in either case, the erroneous embrace of pluralism entails coopting the ideal of pluralism for the sake of excusing oneself from thinking critically and self-reflectively in regard to the practice of psychology. The idea which is absolutely necessary for practitioners so they may emerge from such confusion is: *Incommensurability*. The idea is reflected in this book's subtitle: *Essential Distinctions*.

That is to say, we should recognize that there truly are essential distinctions between the various systems which throughout history have been used to characterize and identify the practice and study of psychology. Perhaps nowhere is such lax as irresponsible as it is in the field of psychotherapy. Some psychologists in the mere description of the services they provide—because they ignore or do not understand incommensurability—illustrate not a commitment to pluralism (again, forgive me for pointing it out) as much as an incompetence regarding the history and systems of psychology, which means an incompetence regarding the theory of their practice. It is as if they advertise: I will be a "blank screen" and provide you with "psychoanalysis," while I share personal information with you and transfer all sorts of "caring" feelings toward you through my office environment and personal comportment. We should have the courage to stand by our convictions (*and commitments*) and agree to disagree. Such a stance signifies a *real commitment to pluralism*.

This book should orient readers to the principles, the constellations of which constitute different systems of psychology, and to the essential distinctions between the different systems which emerge from their differently principled constitutions. That is to say, we can think through psychology by way of the innumerable persons, events, and facts which constitute its history, or we can think through psychology by way of the logic of its systems. This book takes the latter approach. In doing so, what a system rejects is often of more importance than what it affirms. In other words, when we find the points at which a system (personifying it for the sake of illustration) would say: "That is not, and cannot be, me," then we have made true gains toward understanding the activities and applications appropriate for such a system. In other words, true pluralism accepts that "psychology as the Behaviorist views it" is not "psychology as the Psychoanalyst views it," and neither is "psychology as the Existentialist views it."

(3) The Introduction of this book provides an understanding of the notions of "history" and "system" operable for the History and Systems of Psychology. Whereas the principles and distinctions enumerated and explicated in the Introduction are of a generally philosophical nature, the principles and distinctions of Chap. 2 are specifically oriented toward gaining an understanding of the science of psychology in regard to both its natural science (*Naturwissenschaften*) and its human science (*Geisteswissenschaften*) expressions. Further, the discussion of Aristotle on "univocity" provides a helpful bulwark against Postmodern readings of the kind of systematization of psychology for which this book advocates. On the one hand, we may say that the systematization is intended "pragmatically" or for "regulative," rather than reifying, purposes. On the other hand, just as Aristotle pointed to the requirement of univocal meaning as necessary for any scientific endeavor, so too against the Postmodern aversion to systematization we may modestly suggest that our approach is better on, at least, pedagogical grounds; otherwise, the *reductio ad absurdum* to which the Postmodern alternative amounts leads us into an educational situation in which we can no longer discern why plumbing and sandwich-making should not be included in the curriculum for psychologists.

The rest of the book—Chaps. 3, 4, 5, and 6—discuss the philosophical principles of the History and Systems of Psychology beginning with Socrates and Plato and moving into our contemporary situation. By examining the Pre-Modern to the Modern Periods, Chap. 3 discusses the principles of psychology during a time in its history when a sharp distinction was not made between the principles of psychology and the principles of ethics or morality. The period of Western history discussed in Chap. 4 amounts to a smorgasbord of methodological principles which have been carried forward and still influence the study of psychology today. Chapter 4 takes the Renaissance and the Modern Scientific Revolution as its point of departure. With emphasis on Descartes and Early Modern philosophers up to and including Kant, this chapter illustrates the search for a method on which to base, what was at the time called the "new philosophy." In a remarkably direct analogy, the "new psychology" based on the experimental method and modeled after the natural sciences is discussed in Chap. 5.

Beyond a discussion of the influence of "post-Kantian" principles found in the theorizing of Hegel, Darwin, and Marx, for example, Chap. 5 discusses the influence of Wundt and Titchener and the manner in which the principles understood as methodological innovations provided the context within which contemporary psychology emerged. This chapter includes heuristics standard for History and Systems of Psychology, for example the essential distinctions between *Naturwissenschaften* and *Geisteswissenschaften* and the "Four Forces" of contemporary psychology. Moreover, special effort is made throughout this book to organize the discussion of principles around a tripartite distinction between "structure," "function," and "method." Thus, the principles constituting the incommensurability between each of the Four Forces is also presented in terms of this tripartite distinction.

Finally, this book concludes with a discussion of essential distinctions between "Turns," often understood as "Cultural Turns" in the history of Western psychology. This includes the "Linguistic Turn," "Postmodernism," the "Cognitive Turn," aka the "Cognitive Revolution," and the "Historical Turn," aka the "Historic Turn" (for symmetry with "Linguistic"). On the one hand, this chapter functions as the conclusion of the book by providing an illustration—whether understood in terms of progress or not—of the contemporary state of the previously operable principles. On the other hand, it seeks to provide a discussion toward the principles constituting the current state of Western psychology from a systems perspective. In this way, just as one may find persons today who understand and practice psychology from the point of view of any of the Four Forces, so too each of the different "Turns" still stand as viable ways to contextualize contemporary psychology. Therefore, all of these essential distinctions have the potential to be used by the reader toward systematically thinking through the history of Western psychology.

University Heights, OH, USA                                    Frank Scalambrino

# Bibliography

James, William. 1918. *The Principles of Psychology*. Vol. 1. New York: Dover Publications.

Sahakian, William S. 1975. *History and Systems of Psychology*. London: Wiley.

Brennan, James F. 2003. *History and Systems of Psychology*. Upper Saddle, NJ: Prentice Hall.

Walsh, Richard T., Thomas Teo, and Angelina Baydala. 2014. *A Critical History and Philosophy of Psychology: Diversity of Context, Thought, and Practice*. Cambridge: Cambridge University Press.

Rorty, Richard. 1984. The Historiography of Philosophy: Four Genres. In *Philosophy in History: Essays on the Historiography of Philosophy*, ed. R. Rorty, J.B. Schneewind, and Q. Skinner, 49–76. Cambridge: Cambridge University Press.

Hergenhahn, B.R., and Tracy Henley. 2013. *An Introduction to the History of Psychology*. Stamford, CT: Wadsworth Publishing.

# Acknowledgments

I would like to thank the Drs. Nicholas and Dorothy Cummings Center for the History of Psychology for allowing me access to their archives and special collections at the University of Akron.

I would like to thank Dr. Dawn Mitchell, Psy.D., Dr. Stephen T Penepacker M.D., Dr. Elizabeth Aram, Psy.D., Dr. James Swindal, Dr. Jim Collier, Dr. Steve Fuller, Dr. Todd DuBose, Dr. Stephen A. Minnick, and Dr. Robert Arp. I would like to thank my "Deleuzian" friend Beth Metcalf for our recent conversations regarding Deleuze and for her encouragement and affirmation. I would also like to thank Carter, Taylor, and Lexie, Elisa, Hannah, Jonathan, Nate, Ryan, and Zachary for their continued encouragement and friendship. I would like to thank my former students, especially those from The Chicago School of Professional Psychology, Kent State University, the Illinois College of Lake County, Walsh University, Duquesne University, the University of Dallas, and the University of Akron. I would like to thank all those patients and clients who inspired me to continue to study psychology while I was working in multiple capacities, from my time answering suicide hotline calls to doing chemical dependency counseling, to working as a forensic monitor of persons NGRI, to doing pre-hospital admission screening, and to working as the Director of Emergency and Community Psychiatric Services at the Community Mental Health Suicide Prevention Respite Unit and Clinical Intervention Center, which I founded in Ohio

xvi    **Acknowledgments**

in 2003. Lastly, I would like to thank my psychology professors from Kenyon College: Dr. Lecesse, Dr. Levine, Dr. Murnen, Dr. Smolak, Dr. Stolzfus, and Dr. Williams.

I received no outside funding or sabbatical with which to write this book.

# Contents

# 1

# Introduction: The Project of the Philosophical Archeology of the History and Systems of Psychology

The intention of this project is to furnish us with a principled systematic understanding of essential distinctions with which to think through the history of Western psychology. Throughout the course of this book terms such as "principle," "system," "history," and even "psychology" will be further clarified. The following terms have been selected for clarification in the introduction because they will be essential and fundamental in clarifying terms later in the book. Moreover, it is important to keep in mind that the material with which we are dealing is *history*, that is, the history of Western psychology. Thus, we will begin by taking into consideration the principles of historiography—the study of the writing of history; the principles according to which historians inscribe events from the past into historical narratives.

Ultimately, a system dealing with history, especially in the light of historiography, must be philosophical. This is the case because there is too much disagreement as to what "psychology" refers to—especially when considered across the history of Western psychology. In other words, when different participants in the history of a discipline disagree regarding the very elements of what constitutes participation in that discipline, then there is too much essential disagreement, that is, disagreement about the essence of the discipline, to suggest there is an essential systematic

© The Author(s) 2018
F. Scalambrino, *Philosophical Principles of the History and Systems of Psychology*,
https://doi.org/10.1007/978-3-319-74733-0_1

order to the elements constituting the discipline. Rather, what is needed is an explication of *the choices* being made by participants in the history of such a discipline.

Just as a discipline can tolerate a plurality of choices constituting its practice, the distinctions regarding which such choices are being made may be understood as constituting a systematic understanding of that discipline in general. For example, throughout the history of psychology, including today, we find essential disagreement as to what "psychology" is even supposed to be the study of; is psychology the study of biology, spirituality, behavior, mind, unconscious drives and motives, or the use of freedom? Though it may be tempting to say "all the above," some understandings, as the history of psychology illustrates for us, of what constitutes the elements of psychology are essentially distinct from other understandings—we will clarify this later in the book in terms of "incommensurability."

Thus, choices—and commitment to those choices—constitute the activities of the discipline of psychology from out of the potential ways psychology *can* be practiced, and the best indicator of how psychology can be practiced is how psychology has been practiced, that is, its history. What is more, the choices and commitments which constitute the discipline of psychology are made from within a system of distinctions. Now, though it may not be possible to reveal or explicate the entire system of such distinctions, it is possible to become more or less familiar with it. Therefore, (stated in the other direction) by increasing our familiarity with the system of essential distinctions from which choices and commitments constitute the activities of psychology, we increase our ability to think through the activities of contemporary psychology *and* the history of Western psychology.

## 1.1   What Is History?

In regard to the study of history, there are several standard distinctions which are essential for our understanding of the history of psychology. We will discuss the following distinctions: (a) distinct understandings of "History," that is, "History v. the Past," (b) "Original v. Reflective v.

Philosophic History," and (c) "Understandings of the Past: Cyclical v. Linear v. Chaos," (d) distinct understandings of "Historiography," that is "Presentism v. Historicism," (e) "Western Historical Periodization," (f) "Sacred v. Profane History," (g) "Internal v. External History," (h) "Primary v. Secondary Sources," (i) "Witting v. Unwitting Testimony," (j) "Salient v. Deterministic Selection," (k) "Author Intent v. Reader Utility."

(a) "History" refers to the re-presentation of the past, or, as historians like to say, "History" refers to "what historians do." "The Past," then, is supposed to refer to everything that has already happened. This initial distinction points to the importance of historiography, that is, the "writing" or activity of constructing the narratives which constitute history. (b) G.W.F. Hegel (1770–1831), in his *Philosophy of History*, provided the following distinctions. "Original History" refers to simply recording events from the past; the best practice of which being "the annals of history" or recordings of events as they transpire. "Reflective History" refers to re-presenting history with importance placed more on the Present time in which the history is being re-presented than on when the events occurred. Hegel divided "Reflective History" into "Universal," "Pragmatic," and "Critical" history.

Whereas "Universal History" aims to re-present an entire history of, for example, some movement, culture, people, or nation, "Pragmatic History" re-presents historical events as if they were presently happening, that is, making them "Virtually Present". Hegel characterized "Critical History" as a "History of History," that is, "a criticism of historical narratives and an investigation of their truth and credibility" (Hegel 1901: 50). Finally, "Philosophic History" refers to the "thoughtful consideration" of history. In other words, according to Hegel., when historians seek to identify the presence of "universal laws" to which historical narratives may be subordinated, then the resulting narrative may be called "philosophic." Thus, philosophic history may be understood as the decoding of original and universal history to identify the presence and development of various socio-cultural and economic evolutions, which original and universal histories leave concealed.

(c) Our initial distinction between history and the past, should cast the cliché "history repeats itself," in a more complicated light. That is to say, we are not as concerned with the habitual tendencies of historiographers as we are with witnessing patterns repeating throughout the past. Thus, the past may be characterized according to different principles. Understanding the past as "Cyclical" when writing historical narratives, especially reflective and philosophic narratives, means that patterns discernible in the past may be found endlessly repeating across histories. In the West the Cyclical understanding of the past is often associated with ancient Greek cosmological thinking and historians who limit the influence of technology to "change our cycle," while also discerning endless repetition given the potentials of "universal human nature" (cf. Deleuze 2006; cf. O'Brien 1969; cf. Sarno 1969; cf. Vico 2002). A "Linear" understanding of the past provides a different principle for historical narratives. If the past has a linear character to it, then it is headed toward some culmination. When traversing the line is thought to provide a culmination better than the line's point of departure, then the linear historical narratives are construed as "Progressive," and when the line is conversely understood, then they are considered "Regressive."

It is important to note, a number of historians and philosophers of history articulate their historical understanding of our own presence in history as at the conclusion of a Progressive Linear understanding of the past, for example Francis Fukuyama (1952–) and Jean Baudrillard (1929–2007). Thus, Fukuyama speaks of "the end of history" as the end of the idea of historical progress (1992). Similarly, Baudrillard saw Progressive Linear understandings of the past as "utopian-based," and with the failure of economies and politics to accomplish such a utopia has come the collapse of the idea of progression toward such a goal; for example, Baudrillard points to several moments in history each of which he declares to be "the illusion of the end," such as the "World Wars," the "Cold War," and "Y2K" (1994; cf. Baudrillard 2006).

Finally, some historians characterize the past in terms of Chaos, rather than a cycle or a line. The following quote from Richard Rorty (1931–2007) provides an excellent description of the writing of history in regard to the past as Chaos, especially with its reference to Pragmatic history.

The final stage of the Pragmatist's Progress comes when one begins to see one's previous peripeties [reversals of condition or fortune] not as stages in the ascent toward Enlightenment, but simply as the contingent results of encounters [e.g.] with various books which happened to fall into one's hands. This stage is pretty hard to reach, for one is always being distracted by daydreams: daydreams in which the heroic pragmatist plays a Walter Mitty-like role in the immanent teleology of world history. But if the pragmatist can escape from such daydreams, he or she will eventually come to think of himself or herself as, like everything else, capable of as many descriptions as there are purposes to be served. There are as many descriptions as there are uses to which the pragmatist might be put, by his or her self or by others. This is the stage in which all descriptions (including one's self-description as a pragmatist) are evaluated according to their efficacy as instruments for purposes, rather than by their fidelity to the object described (Rorty 1999: 92)

The past characterized. as Chaos, then, not only casts historical narratives in the light of contingency, it completely undermines the idea of progress. In other words, whereas historical events may be contingently determined and yet indicate progress toward a goal in a (cyclically or linearly) unfolding past, this understanding of Chaos characterizes the past as neither progressing cyclically nor linearly.

(d) As will become clear by the end of the book, the distinction between "Presentism" and "Historicism" is essential for thinking through a number of the systematic aspects in the history of Western psychology. There is much to be said about this distinction; to start with, we can recognize its affinity to the distinction between Original and Reflective history, especially the Pragmatic and Critical types of Reflective history. That is to say, "Historicism" refers to the study of the past in the past's terms. In other words, insofar as it is possible to "fuse" the horizon of our understanding with the horizon of the understanding of the past in question, Historicism seeks to understand the meaning and value of the past as it would have been understood at the time it happened. Thus, Historicism holds an affinity to Original History.

Conversely, writing history from the perspective of "Presentism" means interpreting and evaluating the past in terms of presently accepted values and understanding. We may distinguish between mild and strong versions of Presentism. Mild Presentism holds an affinity to Reflective

History in that viewing the past from the position of mild Presentism means interpreting the past from within our present horizon. As we will see, the word "our" in the previous sentence will be seen as relative to culture by some contemporary psychologists. For now, the position of strong Presentism suggests it is not possible to "fuse" the horizon of our present understanding of values and meaning with a past horizon. Much hinges on this distinction since nowadays it is commonplace to pass judgment on actions performed in the distant past; however, from the position of strong Presentism such judgments may amount to mere opinion, since it is as if to not have "been in the shoes of" those involved in the past may mean to not be able to truly evaluate or appropriately understand the past situation in question (cf. Clark 2004; cf. Gadamer 1989; cf. Gergen 1985; cf. Stocking 1968).

To illustrate this important distinction further, note how the historian Herbert Butterfield (1900–1979) defined Presentism as "the tendency in many historians … to praise revolutions provided they have been successful, to emphasize certain principles of progress in the past and to produce a story which is the ratification if not the glorification of the present" (Butterfield 1931: 5). Further, he criticized the Presentist practice of

> abstracting things from their historical context and judging them apart from their context … [to] study the past with one eye … upon the present is the source of all sins and sophistries in history, starting with the simplest of them, the anachronism … [it is] what we mean by … "unhistorical".
> (Butterfield 1949: 11–12)

Whereas Butterfield may be seen here advocating for Historicism, advocates for Presentism, in response—especially those affirming a Linear Progressive understanding of the past—point to "the privilege of retrospection," noting: "In history *we know what happened afterwards, and the actors don't.* The arrow of time makes our knowledge *intrinsically* superior to that of the actors …" (Tosh 2003: 653).

On the one hand, then, notice how advocates draw on other distinctions for support. That is, emphasizing a Progressive understanding of the past undermines the idea that we would want, or need, to know the past "for its own sake." On the other hand, notice how advocates of either position can move toward stronger/more extreme versions to defend their position. In this way, for example, strong Presentism developed into "social constructionism" (cf. Berger and Luckmann 1966) by emphasizing the socio-cultural-economic forces influencing the construction of historical narratives, including our historical understanding of our own presence in history. In other words, it is not a big leap to go *from* the idea that socio-cultural-economic forces determine our view of the past *to* the idea that socio-cultural-economic forces determine our view of the present. Thus, despite its critical stance toward previously constructed historical narratives, it is as if strong Historicism attempts to use the principle of strong Presentism against Presentism by suggesting our historical understanding of our presence in history is itself historically conditioned. That is to say, strong Historicism is critical of a view which may be associated with Presentism, namely that we have progressed to a point in history in which we presently embody the truth toward which the past was striving, so to speak, such that we can now criticize past historical narratives as biased.

(e) Given our discussion thus far, it should be clear that there are many ways to characterize the past, in the West, into historical periods. The following Western Historical Periodizations have been selected, then, for the pragmatic reason that they essentially embody the traditional standard in Western scholarship. The following Periodizations may be referred to as the Threefold, Fourfold and Ninefold models, respectively. The three (3) historical periods of the Threefold division and the spans are as follows:

1. **Pre-Modern** (600 BC–1600)
2. **Modern** (1601–1972)
3. **Post-Modern** (1973–Today)

Note that the Post-Modern historical period contains a hyphen. It is not uncommon to see the word written in one of three ways: Postmodern, Post-Modern, or (Post)Modern. Whereas the first version is technically an "art term," the second refers to a period of history, and the third is used to emphasize that whatever is being described as "Postmodern," is merely a continuation of the Modern. Thus, the philosophical movement titled

"Postmodernism"—to be discussed later—originates from an attitude of "widespread disillusionment." In other words, a suspicion of all "meta-narratives," justifying value-systems and truths. For example, a Postmodern attitude toward institutionalized psychology may call the various values and truths of "the clinic" into question by, for instance, questioning whether clinical activities such as current prescription practices regarding psychiatric medication are influenced by pharmaceutical companies, especially through their "reps," or by insurance-reimbursement policies.

Moreover, it may help in terms of a cultural contextualization to note that the birth of Post-Modernity coincides with the release of the band Pink Floyd's album *Dark Side of the Moon*. Whereas the Sixties are seen by many as a kind of culmination—whether Progressive or Retrogressive, the Seventies are usually depicted in terms of peripeties pointing to widespread disillusionment with, and attempts to "contradict," traditional aspects of Modernism. This included not only notions of the "nuclear family," but also notions of socio-cultural historical progress in general.

The four (4) historical periods of the Fourfold division and their time spans are as follows:

1. **Ancient** (600 BC–400)
2. **Middle Ages** (401–1600)
3. **Modern** (1601–1900)
4. **Contemporary** (1901–Today)

Whereas the Fourfold division tends to be used to refer to philosophical and psychological movements in general, the Ninefold division enters into more specificity. On the one hand, though culture influenced the designation of periods in the Ninefold division, for example the Renaissance, it does not attempt to indicate nor exhaustively represent a cultural periodization, which would inevitably include the "Romantic Period" (c. 1800–1850) and the "Victorian Era" (1837–1901). On the other hand, of course significant events from within such time spans, despite not being listed in the Ninefold division, hold influence and relevance for the history and systems of Western psychology.

1. **Pre-Platonic** (600 BC–300 BC)
2. **Hellenistic** (301 BC–100 BC)
3. **Roman** (101 BC–400)
4. **Medieval** (401–1400)
5. **Renaissance** (1401–1600)
6. **Early Modern** (1601–1800)
7. **Nineteenth Century** (1801–1900)
8. **Twentieth Century** (1901–2000)
9. **Twenty-first Century** (2001–Today)

(f) The remaining distinctions all pertain to the writing of history in that they characterize the various kinds of decisions made in regard to what counts as history. The first of these distinctions is between "Sacred" and "Profane" history. Whereas Sacred history takes the Bible as its point of departure for understanding history, Profane history is more concerned with "secular" events and secular interpretations of events when writing and understanding history. In other words, should the past event in question be understood in terms of a religious tradition and its documents, or not? Be sure that the simplistic and straightforward nature of this distinction does not conceal its importance for thinking through the history and systems of psychology. In this regard, a few words of explication may be of value here.

There is a tendency, especially among twentieth-century textbooks regarding the history and systems of psychology, to consider—what in the twenty-first century is now called—the "new psychology" as legitimate psychology and everything prior to the "new psychology" to be philosophy merely progressing toward a stage in which psychology becomes scientific. Despite this tendency to distinguish between "old" and "new" psychology and, then, to consider "old" psychology outdated and obsolete, many people today still adhere to the principles and, thereby, sustain a psychological worldview in terms of the so-called "old" psychology. Therefore, the distinction between Sacred and Profane history remains viable for thinking through the history and systems of psychology.

The Modern version of the question of the Sacred and the Profane is cast in terms of whether psychology should consider questions of morality within its domain. Like the separation between Church and State, these domains may be seen as essentially distinct. To illustrate, consider the following quote from Antonio Gramsci (1891–1937).

> A distinction must be made between civil society ... (i.e. in the sense of political and cultural hegemony of a social group over the entire society, as ethical content of the State), and on the other hand civil society in the sense in which it is understood by Catholics, for whom civil society is instead political society of the State, in contrast with the society of family and that of the Church. (Gramsci 1971: 447–448)

Similar to the distinction between the past and history, it is possible to understand one-and-the-same "civil" action in accordance with different principles and worldviews. At the same time, there will be points of irreconcilable difference regarding one-and-the-same action; for example, some action acceptable, or at least not illegal, within civil society, the Church may consider a sin. Thus, when considering the passing of time in writing and understanding the history and systems of psychology, the distinction between Sacred and Profane allows for a deeper appreciation, for example in terms of multiple viewpoints and in terms of irreconcilably different interpretations.

(g) "Internal History" considers events in the passing of time only insofar as they influenced the discipline whose history is in question. Conversely, "External History" refers to events considered peripheral and, though perhaps historically contextualizing, of little to no influence on the discipline whose history is in question (cf. Richards 1987). Again, just like with (f), there is potential for this distinction to be complicated. That is to say, especially regarding Postmodernism in psychology, if one understands socio-cultural and economic influences to determine, to some extent, the writing of psychology's history, then it may not be immediately clear that events seemingly External to the discipline of psychology have not influenced the writing of its history. Recalling Hegel's distinctions above, Critical history of psychology may largely be understood as engaged in the practice of providing a history of the history of psychology for the purpose of uncovering the seemingly External events influencing the history of psychology.

(h) Anyone researching in the Humanities should already know the distinction between "Primary" and "Secondary" sources. An interesting question that comes from historian discussions of the distinction: Are translations of Primary texts Secondary sources? If we were to think of the *original* work as the Primary source, then it follows that translations are, by virtue of being translated, Secondary sources. According to historian Arthur Marwick (1936–2006), "Primary sources, as it were, form the basic 'raw material' of history; they are sources which came into existence within the period being investigated." (2001: 26). Keeping in mind the distinction between Presentism and Historicism, notice Marwick was careful to point out that a Primary source belongs to the historical period in which it "came into existence" (cf. Kragh 1989). That is to say, "The articles and books written up later by historians, drawing upon these primary sources, converting the raw material into history, are secondary sources" (Marwick 2001: 26).

(i) The distinction between "Witting and Unwitting Testimony" originated from the historian of science Henry Guerlac (1910–1985). According to Marwick, "'Witting' means 'deliberate' or 'intentional'; 'unwitting' means 'unaware' or 'unintentional' [and] 'Testimony' means 'evidence'." (2001: 172). Therefore, "'witting testimony' is the deliberate or intentional message ... of a document or other source; the 'unwitting testimony' is the unintentional evidence (about for example, the attitudes and values of the author, or about the 'culture' to which he/she belongs) that it contains." (Ibid: 172–173). Notice that this distinction may apply to the "Primary source" itself, or it may apply to the historian constructing a "Secondary source." For example, "Witting testimony" may be "the information or impression that the person or persons who originally compiled the document or source intended to convey ... or record." (Ibid: 173).

(j) The distinction between "Salient and Deterministic Selection" refers to a series of standard principles in the writing of history. These principles are: *Zeitgeist*, *Ortgeist*, Great Person Theory, Artifacts, Wars, and Worldview Shifts. Whereas "Salient" suggests a person, thing, or event is particularly noticeable on its own, "Deterministic" suggests a threshold such that some person, thing, or event becomes history-worthy, so to speak, by differing from other persons, things, or events in regard to the feature in question. In other words, many people performed actions today, however, unless those actions exceed threshold-levels regarding some feature, historians may not consider the actions as having "made history" (cf. Marwick 1993). It is worth pointing out that the features and thresholds vary across cultures, economies, and historical periods, and, therefore, may be understood as dependent variables.

All histories, then, may be analyzed in regard to how these principles influenced their writing. Whereas *Zeitgeist* means "spirit of the time," *Ortgeist* means "spirit of the place." Thus, these principles function as potential justifications for writing some activity into history. For example, consider how original documents are, of course, produced in some language. Some key examples may be the "New Testament" of the *Bible* being written in Greek or Immanuel Kant's *Critique of Pure Reason* being written in German. Some argue that these documents in some way required the languages in which they were written. It is as if, were Kant writing in some language other than German, then perhaps he would not have come to realize the ideas presented in the *Critique of Pure Reason*. Along these same lines, historians sometimes suggest it was the *Zeitgeist*, "the spirit of the time," or the *Ortgeist*, "the spirit of the place," which is ultimately responsible for determining, or constituting as salient, some thing or event as history-worthy. As may be expected, these two principles are often contrasted with the "Great Person Theory," which—remaining with our example—might suggest that Kant could have produced his book regardless of his language, nationality, or historical period (supposing someone else did not write it before him).

Of course given the present ubiquity of historical narratives, it is perhaps commonplace to notice that histories seem to be written around Wars, artifacts, and worldview shifts. To be clear, "artifacts" may include technological inventions, laboratory and medical devices, and books. On the one hand, an examination of the histories of Western psychology illustrates the point. On the other hand, as noted above, all of these principles can be "played-off" one another, so to speak, such that, for example, various artifacts or Wars may be understood as responsible for a *Zeitgeist*, *Ortgeist* or worldview shift. Keeping this in mind allows for Critical and Philosophic thinking through the history of psychology. Moreover, the various systems of psychology may be understood as so many worldview shifts in the history of psychology. Thus, the relations between the various systems may be Critically and Philosophically examined in regard to, for example, logic and history; that is, not just why is this system supposed to be better than its competitors, but what were the conditions which led to its formation; and, how might it best suit this *Zeit*, *Ort*, Person, War, artifact, etc?

(k) Finally, the distinction between "Author Intent and Reader Utility" helps provide clarification and lends itself to Critical and Philosophic thinking in the history of psychology. Like the distinction between Internal and External History and Witting and Unwitting Testimony, there will be times when the difference between Author Intent and Reader Utility is significant. Perhaps the three most common: First, when the Author is understood as a Primary source and the historian constitutes the Reader. In such cases, the Reader need not be understood as merely passively receiving the Author's Intention. For example, a Reader's focus may be on Unwitting Testimony or may be strongly determined by Historicism or Presentism. Second, when the Author is understood as a Secondary source, the Reader may simply disagree with the Author or decide differently in regard to the salience of evidence presented, and not presented, by the Author. Third, when the Author is understood as strongly determined by Historicism, the Reader may understand the Author's comments as historically contextualized, for example in terms of the Author's social, cultural, economic, or political context. In these ways, we may justify significant differences between our interpretation—as the Reader's—of some work, despite its Author's Intent, as we, for example, Critically and Philosophically consider the history and systems of Western psychology.

## 1.2   What Is the Value of Learning History?

Of the perennial questions which emerge when studying the history and systems of Western psychology, the most immediate may be: Why should we study history? In response textbooks in the history and systems of psychology traditionally devote a section to addressing this question. Hence, the content of this section may be understood as an articulation of the traditional approaches toward answering this question: (l) the Poetic Necessity of History, (m) History as Illumination, (n) History as Philosophical Laboratory.

Of course we may be skeptical of the capacity for historical narratives to accurately reflect events of the past. Representing such a position Jean-Jacques Rousseau (1712–1778) infamously suggested:

> the facts described by history are far from being an exact portrayal of the same facts as they happened … and what lessons can I draw from an event of whose true cause I am ignorant? The historian gives me one, but he counterfeits it; and critical history itself, which is making such a sensation, is only an art of conjecture, the art of choosing among several lies the one best resembling the truth. (Rousseau 2010: 392–393)

In fact, Rousseau's is not the only way to cast historical narratives in a skeptical light. Yet, the question of the value of learning history seems to take its foothold before the question of the accuracy of history is even raised. Because we may be motivated to study history even if historical narratives are merely approximate truths, the question of the value of learning history is still a viable question despite Rousseau's insight. In other words, the question of the value of learning history seems motivated such that even if historical narratives are "true," what is the value of learning history. Therefore, the following addresses this latter contextualization of the question. However, there will be more to say about Rousseau's contextualization of the question in discussing Postmodernism.

(l) The "Poetic Necessity of History" is a twofold reference. On the one hand, it refers to the sense in which human creation comes from something, rather than from nothing. That is to say, not only must there have already been something present from the past that individuals must use as material with which to create, but also, collectively, as humans endure the process of existence the various states of creation necessarily have a past by being part of that process. Thus, "For the historian of Psychology who is also a psychologist, the discipline's history is therefore in itself a psychological phenomenon." (Richards 2002: 7). This is especially the case when history is understood by the psychologist such that "we are looking at Psychology's role in the dynamic psychological process by which human nature constantly recreates, re-forms, and regenerates itself." (Ibid). However, if human nature is not the aim of your investigation, the process may also be examined in terms of our (human) *inheriting* a body of knowledge, a culture, and so forth (cf. Csikszentmihalyi 1996; cf. Harris 2009; cf. Moravcsik 1981; cf. Mumford 2003; cf. Serres 1982; cf. Simonton 2004). On the other hand, the patterns of action applied *to* the past may already—partially or completely—have been applied *in* the past. Thus, the "poetic necessity of history" refers also to an inherent desire to know the past. The phrase comes from historian George M. Trevelyan (1876–1962).

> The dead were and are not. Their place knows them no more and is ours today ... The poetry of history lies in the quasi-miraculous fact that once, on this earth, once, on this familiar spot of ground, walked other men and women, as actual as we are today, thinking their own thoughts, swayed by their own passions, but now all gone, one generation vanishing into another, gone as utterly as we ourselves shall shortly be gone ... (Trevelyan 1949: 13)

What was it like to study psychology in the past? Why were the people studying psychology in the past asking the questions they asked? Was there some aspect of psychology they could see that is presently opaque to us? Imagine the questions you might ask if you were given the opportunity to speak with the likes of Plato, Aristotle, Augustine, Aquinas, Descartes, Kant, Hegel, Kierkegaard, Nietzsche, Heidegger, Freud, Jung, Skinner, Rogers, Satir, or Deleuze, for example.

(m) From historian Will Durant (1885–1981) comes the suggestive metaphor of history as "a lantern of understanding held up to the present and the future." (Durant 1939: 614). The sentiment resonates well with the ancient Greek proverb that "History is philosophy teaching by example." How do psychologists who are also historians of psychology understand this "illuminating" power of history? They seem to agree that the value of learning history, at a minimum, consists in: "Knowing how to establish a scholarly project by placing one's own ideas amidst what others have said. Citing sources as both intellectual and social touchstones ... [and] Justifying one's decisions in determining what is important."

(Green 1994: 95; cf. Geuter 1983; cf. Vaughn-Blount et al. 2009). For, as psychologist and historian of psychology Robert I. Watson (1909–1980) aptly noted: "None of us can escape history … History cannot be denied; the choice is between making it a conscious determinant of our behavior as psychologists, or allowing it to influence us unawares. There is no alternative." (Watson 1966: 64). Thus, learning the history of psychology functions as a kind of increase in illumination in regard to *thinking* in the field of psychology.

(n) Another metaphor that characterizes the remaining traditional responses to the question regarding the value of learning history mentioned here is that of a "philosophical laboratory." The metaphor was emphasized by philosopher and historian of philosophy Étienne Gilson (1884–1978). For our purpose the idea the metaphor invokes may be divided in terms of "progress," "inspiration," and "critical deconstruction." According to the historian Polybius (c. 200-c.118 BC) "there is no more ready corrective of conduct than knowledge of the past." (Polybius 1922: 3). Similarly, George Santayana (1863–1952) famously claimed, "Those who cannot remember the past are condemned to repeat it." (2011: 172; cf. Fuchs et al. 2007). Of course, as noted above, these truisms do not determine whether the past should be understood as Linear or Cyclical.

Be that as it may, historians advocating for an understanding of history as a "philosophical laboratory" often emphasize that history should be understood in terms of progress. Thinking through the question "How is scientific progress possible?" philosopher of science Gaston Bachelard (1884–1962) held that the history of science is an essential component of scientific theory (2016; cf. Bergson 2004; cf. Jones 1991). Simply put, how can there be progress if you do not know from what you are progressing? It is helpful to show a distinction here between what we may call teleological and epistemological "progress." Whereas "teleological progress" suggests that the past, and thereby reality itself, is progressing toward some purposeful end, "epistemological progress" more modestly suggests that progress has been made from an earlier state of knowledge. Epistemological progress need not take a stance in regard to whether the progress is teleological in nature. Thus, historians critical of the idea of teleological progress critique historical narratives for the immodesty of their claims. Such historical narratives are pejoratively called "Whig," or "Whiggish," understandings of history (cf. Butterfield 1931).

Though the idea of history as a "philosophical laboratory" allows for multiple understanding of progress, it is important to stress that even if it were to amount to merely learning a "history of errors," learning history would still be of essential value. Moreover, learning history may be of "inspirational value." Coded in history are the hopes of the previous members of our historical community, so to speak. Just as the activities, that is, the "experimenting," performed in a laboratory by a community of scientists informs the very identity of that community and its understanding of progress, so too as a fruitful and commonly expressed analogy has it: history is to its community what memory is to the individual. Conversely, historians point to the analogous relation between amnesia and not learning history; it is as if without history a community can neither fully understand its own identity nor be positioned to best navigate its future.

In this way, "Thanks to our knowledge of history we find that instead of being totally adrift in an endless and featureless sea of time, we do have some idea at least of where we are and of who we are." (Marwick 1970: 18). Thus, the history of psychology has the capacity to function as a "philosophical laboratory" through which the community of individuals who study and practice psychology may be inspired by the goals of the community, orient to the progress of the discipline's "laboratory," and derive a participatory-identity "within the community," even though that community may be understood as spanning the history of the West.

Finally, it is important to emphasize that it is *from within* such a philosophical laboratory and the progress and hopes of a discipline's historical community that "critical deconstruction" takes place. Otherwise, critical deconstruction "throws the discipline out with the bath water." In other words, those who would have the discipline of psychology totally deconstructed thereafter have no ground upon which to stand as a "psychologist." Lest they be willing to take some other discipline, such as philosophy, as the point of departure for such a devastating deconstruction, then their critical deconstruction must take place within the discipline's laboratory, that is, the history of psychology. Notice, in this way, so long as a separate discipline is not taken as a point of departure, then activities of "critical deconstruction" directed at the history of a discipline may be—perhaps ironically—understood as contributing to "progress" for the discipline.

In order to clarify, before concluding this section, briefly consider three terms and an example. The three terms are: Historicity, Genealogy, and Hegemony. "Historicity" refers to the actuality and authenticity of some thing or event in the past. Thus, if your claim that some chair is an authentic piece of Victorian Era furniture is to be factual, then the chair must have actually originated—been brought into existence—during the time of the Victorian Era. Notice how the idea of historicity helps us further clarify the distinction between Historicism and Presentism. Historicism holds that things and events both can and should be understood in terms of their historicity. Presentism holds that it is not possible to *understand* some thing or event in terms of its historicity. We may be able to factually date in the past the thing or event in question; however, our understanding of its meaning will be inextricably bound to the present point of departure from which we seek to understand it.

In terms of "critical deconstruction," then, "genealogy" refers to the practice of tracing a thing's or an event's history with regard to the "conditions for the possibility of" the thing or event in question. Genealogy may be considered a methodology of "critical deconstruction" insofar as the genealogy is performed so that the conditions for the historically significant things or events may be accounted for beyond the *present* "standard" historical narrative in which the things or events are considered significant based on our present aims and present understanding. In this way, the goal of genealogy is to criticize and deconstruct the presently accepted historical narrative. Of course, the history of Western philosophy offers a number of ways to characterize the conditions for the possibility of things and events. Therefore, the term "hegemony"—"Episteme" in Foucault's vocabulary (1971)—is helpful here in that it may refer to whatever conditions are presently dominating the historian's construction of narratives. Moreover, because these conditions are actual, they may also condition the birth of various historically significant things or events beyond mere narrative constructions. For example, Michel Foucault's (1926–1984) genealogy of mental health clinics provides an account of the birth of such clinics which—taking philosophy as its point of departure—may be critical of narratives inclusive to the discipline of psychology which otherwise account for the "birth" of the clinics (1988; cf. Foucault 1994). Thus, it may be said that "critical deconstruction" calls the historicity of a thing or an event into question (cf. Barthes 1978; cf. Danziger 1990; cf. Deleuze 2004; cf. Deleuze and Guattari 2004; Derrida 1978; cf. Nietzsche 1989).

Finally, consider the following example of the ways in which the three-fold and fourfold historical divisions of Western philosophy are "standardly" characterized. As preface to discussing the fourfold division, the threefold division consists of: Thinking as aspiring to be the Divine Mirror of God in the Pre-Modern Worldview; Thinking as aspiring to be the Mirror of Nature in the Modern Worldview, and Thinking understood as the Mirror of Culture, that is, influenced, if not fully determined by, social, economic, and historical forces in the Post-Modern Worldview. In regard to the "standard" way to characterize the fourfold historical division of Western philosophy: For the Ancient Period, "philosophy" referred to a "way of living." On the one hand, notice how though we may be able to characterize this accurately in general—be it from primary Original History, etc.—if we take a Presentist stance we may still claim to not fully understand the particularities of the meaning of "philosophy as a way of living" in the way the ancient Greeks, for instance, understood it. On the other hand, despite the possibility of a Presentist critique, when "psychotherapy" is thought to be essentially a synonym for "philosophy," the point of view of ancient Western philosophy is often invoked (cf. Entralgo 1970; cf. Hadot 1995, 2002; cf. Howard 2000; cf. Moes 2000; cf. Szasz 1988, 1997).

For the Middle Ages, "philosophy" was—according to this "standard characterization"—understood as "the handmaiden to theology." This may be variously explicated; however, in brief, it is as if because the Middle Ages had the advantage, over the essentially (retrospectively characterized) "pagan" Ancient Period, of the Christian revelation, the only role thought left to philosophy was the clarification of theology, or "faith seeking understanding." The question of the primacy of theology, then, surfaces regarding this historical period from the point of view of the Presentism/Historicism distinction. That is to say, as will become clearer throughout this book, there is a fundamental and essential distinction regarding philosophy between the first two and the latter two historical periods in the West. The former being essentially "Theo-centric," and the latter "Ego-centric." For instance, just as the Gramsci quote above, in expressing two different understandings of "society," may be understood as characterizing two different worldviews, so too this historical shift may be understood as an essential distinction characterizing different understandings of psychology, especially regarding psychology and the domain of morality. Of course, the consequences of the historical-shift, to which this distinction refers, still ripples through the discipline of psychology and its various ways of being understood.

One of the particularly relevant shifts in worldview which is understood to have occurred in the history of the West from the first two to the second two periods of the fourfold historical division regards the relationship among words, concepts, and things. That is, do words primarily refer to concepts or to things? The "standard" understanding, again in general at this point, holds that the first two periods tended, at least, to understand words as referring primarily to concepts, and the second two periods, especially the Modern Period, tended to understand words as referring primarily to things (Brümmer 1981: 35–64; Cunningham 1988: 22–46; Petit 1977: 5; Wehrle 2000: 175–177; cf. Foucault 1971; cf. O'Callaghan 2003; cf. de Saussure 2011). As will be clear later in the book during a discussion of different theories of truth, the very identity of philosophy, and thereby psychology, is seen as at stake here in the history of philosophy. In other words, is philosophy ultimately semantics, metaphysics, or theory of knowledge?

For the Modern Period, "philosophy" was—according to this "standard characterization"—understood as "the handmaiden to science." Whereas the aim of a philosophical worldview from the first two periods of the fourfold division may be understood as attempting to understand nature, and the place of humans in it, the Modern Period is characterized by Descartes', perhaps infamous, declaration from his 1637 *Discourse on the Method for Conducting One's Reason Well and for Seeking Truth in the Sciences* that—by way of science—humans shall "render ourselves, as it were, masters and possessors of nature" (Descartes 1998: 35). Thus, Modern philosophical thinking is historically characterized in terms of a shift *from* the project to achieve—to whatever extent possible—a "God's eye" view of nature, *to* the project to bend "the will," so to speak, of nature to that of our own, that is, from Theo-centric to Ego-centric. That is to say, what is the *method* for discovering how to *control* nature?

For the Contemporary Period, "philosophy" is understood, not surprisingly, in a number of diverse ways. However, an efficient, albeit twofold, way, to characterize philosophy emerges according to this "standard characterization." First, we cannot determine the meaning of "philosophy" in the Contemporary Period, because we are living it presently. Of course, the distinction between Presentism and Historicism may be operable here. Second, "philosophy" in the Contemporary Period refers to the ability to be "critical." Insofar as this is the case, it behooves us to be able to think through the history and systems of Western psychology as a constitutive part of not only the Critical and Philosophical history of psychology but also of the discipline of psychology itself. Thus, an analogy with the night sky may help express a summary statement of the ground covered at this point. Just as over time some stars in the night sky seem more visible than others and just as different constellations are brought into focus by the varying visibility of different stars, so too history provides an important context within which the various shifts in worldviews and systems may be understood in terms of selections among philosophical principles. Of course, the principles, according to this analogy, then, refer to the stars and the visibility of the stars refers to the emphasis and prominence of various principles throughout history.

## 1.3   What Is a System?

When we hear the word "system" it brings to mind the concept of plurality. In other words, "system" implies an interconnection of multiple parts. In fact, because there are many different types of systems and particular ways of systematizing different disciplines, it is helpful to recognize that the study of systems most generally belongs to the field of "mereology." "Mereology," derived from the "study of" the ancient Greek word for "part," refers to the study of parts and wholes, the relationship between parts, and the relationship between parts and wholes. On the one hand, it is important to note that "Mereology is not a logical theory because its terms and axioms cannot be deduced from the principles of logic."

(Sobociński 1984: 42; cf. Peregrin 2001; cf. Von Bertalanfy 1968). On the other hand, every major Western philosopher—beginning even with the Pre-Platonic philosophers—can be seen as having a "mereology." Anticipating what will be considered more fully below, it is important to note that because mereology cannot be simply reduced to logic, mereology often takes precedence when a theorist enters into discussions of "ontology" or the parts of a system a theorist takes to have some kind of being.

Though there is, of course, much more to say about "systems," consider how the following two terms relate to what has already been said: "infinite regress" and "incommensurability." In regard to taking some thing as having a kind of being and, then, considering it as a part in a system, notice how systems may be understood as relating like—as a convenient and popular metaphor states it—a "matryoshka" or "Russian nesting doll." That is, a system may be placed within another system, which may be placed within another, and so on. The idea that such placement within another system may go on endlessly is the idea captured by: "infinite regress." Traditionally, at least, it is seen as a virtue of a theory that it avoids infinite regress. Yet, this gives rise to the problem of "priority" or "privilege" in the sense that—to use the metaphor again—some one of the dolls must be the doll at which we stop, and go no further. Now, with actual physical dolls we could point to the physical constraints, as if at some magnitude it becomes impossible for us to construct a doll, then the last created size of doll would be seen as doll that stopped the infinite regress. However, when dealing with theories—as non-physical beings—it may be much more difficult to recognize "where" the regress stops.

After discussing "incommensurability" we will summarize both of these ideas in regard to mereology and the idea of a "system." Though the term has always been a part of the vocabulary of Western philosophy (cf. Plato 1860: 16d1; cf. Aristotle 1984: 983a16, 1967: 106b1, 1956: 430a31), "Incommensurability" is associated with the philosophers of science Paul Feyerabend (1924–1994) and Thomas Kuhn (1922–1996). The term refers to the sense in which two theories may relate to each other in such a way that they have "no common measure" (cf. Feyerabend 2001: 33; cf. Feyerabend 1983: 211; cf. Kuhn 1996: 4–5 and 37–39).

Now, of all that may be said regarding the work of Feyerabend and Kuhn, for our purpose we want to notice how incommensurability can be explained in terms of the difference between, for example, two different systems in which each theory may be located. In other words, even though two different theories may—on the surface—appear to be about the same thing, concept, or word, it is possible for the theories to be incommensurable with one another insofar as their systems do not allow for a "common measure" of the thing, concept, or word in question. This is easier to see when it is spread across history; for example, think of the difference between the night sky in the Ptolemaic system and in the Copernican system. However, as we will see, it is even possible to have incommensurability between two psychologists viewing, at the exact same time, the ostensibly same psychological phenomenon.

Due to opposition to the work of Feyerabend and, especially, Kuhn, some historians have attempted to strip their special vocabulary terms of meaning; therefore, rather than emphasize, for example, Kuhn's notion of a "paradigm" and a "paradigm-shift" we will use these words, in this book, as essentially synonymous with the terms "worldview" and "worldview-shift." An even better expression, were it not more cumbersome, would be "system-view" and "system-view-shift." However, for the context, consider the following from Kuhn regarding the historicity of such distinctions.

> As a former physicist now mainly engaged with the history of that science, I remember well my own discovery of the close and persistent parallels between the two enterprises I had been taught to regard as polar. A belated product of that discovery is the book on Scientific Revolutions ... Discussing either developmental patterns or the nature of creative innovation in the sciences, it treats such topics as *the role of competing schools* and of *incommensurable traditions*, of *changing standards of value*, and of *altered modes of perception*. Topics like these have long been basic for the art historian but are minimally represented in writings on the history of science [emphases added]. (Kuhn 1969: 403)

Regarding systems, then, in the history of Western psychology, it is clear that different systems, or "schools," compete with each other, that they have different standards of evaluation, and that taking a point of view from within different systems actually involves a "shift" in one's mode of perception. That is to say, two different psychologists viewing, at the exact same time, the ostensibly same psychological phenomenon may actually *perceive* it differently.

This is to be understood in terms of theory more than, for example, two different subjective perceptions of, say, the color blue. In other words, the same behavior may be perceived as an expression of resistance to unconscious forces, a habitually instantiated reaction, the result of a misapplied pattern of past coping, or the action of a free agent; moreover, were we to examine the principles constituting each of the different systems from which such theoretical characterizations would be a consistent depiction of the behavior, then we would see these theoretical characterizations may, in fact, be incommensurable. For instance, insofar as unconscious forces are *deterministic*, then the system from which such a view is produced would be incommensurable with the system which views the action as involving *free agency*. Moreover, just as two different observers of the same star in the night sky may perceive that star as being in different constellations, it would still be possible for a philosophical characterization of the primary constellations in which the star could be, or has been, seen, and to illustrate the styles of clustering stars (principles) which determined the different constellations. Note well, however, that such an activity is a theoretical activity, and, therefore, it is essentially different from the practical activity of applying some particular location of the star in a constellation to a reading (keeping with the analogy) in regard to someone's birth chart. In other words, a philosophical "meta-view," so to speak, of the systems of psychology does not relieve a practitioner of selection and commitment of a particular system at the point of application.

Consider how psychologist and historian of psychology Robert I. Watson discussed Kuhn's innovative vocabulary. "In one of its meanings a paradigm is a contentual model, universally accepted by practitioners of a science at a particular temporal period in its development … Illustrative in astronomy is the Ptolemaic paradigm which gave way to the Copernican paradigm" (Watson 1967: 435). Notice, Watson's use of the term "contentual" to attempt to capture what has been discussed thus far in this section; that is, a "paradigm" or "worldview" is "contentual" because it is a *system* for understanding the content, taking the content to be parts of a whole system. In other words, we have this information and these facts (though even such perceptions may be contested from the perspective of some worldviews in psychology)—such as the observation of some behaviors, and in comprehending the observation in terms of some system, we may ask how do these parts relate to each other in a whole? Often the whole would include theories that are fundamental to the system-view being worked out. Put another way, what theories should we use to constellate the parts? Thus, the selection between principles— such as, for instance, between determinism and free agency—constitutes a system by limiting what counts as other parts of the whole and by limiting how the rest of the parts may be constellated. This is an important insight because it allows us to *think through* incommensurable "paradigms," "worldviews," or systems by examining the *essential distinctions* across which various selections have comprised *the principles of the systems*.

On the one hand, then, it is important to note regarding systems in psychology that they serve a "guidance" or "regulative" function. That is, a system "functions as an intellectual framework, it tells [psychologists] what sort of entities with which their scientific universe is populated [i.e. the parts of a system a theorist takes to have some kind of operative being] and how these entities behave, and informs its followers what questions may legitimately be asked" (Watson 1967: 436). On the other hand, what every psychologist and historian of psychology should recognize in the twenty-first century is that there is no

> universal agreement about the nature of our contentual model ... In psychology there is still debate over fundamentals. In research, findings stir little argument but the overall framework is still very much contested. There is still disagreement about what is included in the science of psychology. (Watson 1967: 436)

Moreover, there are some historians of psychology who see the suggestion that psychology liberated itself in the nineteenth century, "either from parent disciplines [such as philosophy or biology] or from external social concerns during its formative period" (Woodward and Ash 1982: v), as merely a popular narrative among psychologists derived from deliberate historiographical choices (cf. Feigl 1959; cf. Klein 1970; cf. Rachlin 1994; cf. Van Kaam 1966: esp. 107–109). Were psychology to unanimously adopt a worldview, or paradigm, then the discipline—to use Kuhn's terminology—would be engaged in "normal science," as opposed to a state of "crisis" in which different worldviews may be understood as "battling" or vying to be *the* system of psychology (cf. Slife et al. 2017; cf. Toulmin 1972). When either a system becomes *the* system for a time or when some major shift occurs in the understanding of the set of principles involved in the crisis of vying systems, then a "revolution" may be said to have taken place; otherwise, when different systems or clusters of principles alternate emphasis over time it is called a "turn," not a revolution.

To sum thus far, then, notice that it becomes highly unproductive and unhelpful for us to understand systems in terms of an infinite regress. This is because it would be as if there were no "traction." We could point to one "level" of system and our interlocutor could simply point to a different level, then we could follow suit, and it would be as if we were both caught in an endless freefall. As a result, history and systems of psychology rightfully uses *history* to stop an infinite regress of systems; that is to say, these are the systems (constituted by principles chosen across essential distinctions) from within which persons during this particular period of time understood their point of view. Whereas advocates of some historically based system may, of course, understand psychology solely in terms of that system, given the twenty-first-century state of the discipline, such activity is inevitably part of the vying for their chosen system to be taken on as the "norm" or considered presently the best (cf. Mandler 1996). Ultimately, being able to think through the multiple systems in the history of psychology is the purpose of this book. Of course, our purpose may also be understood as allowing for psychologists to better advocate for whichever system they presently privilege, for example, by being able to understand multiple worldviews and the essential differences across worldviews. In this way, the notion of "incommensurability" reiterates the importance of learning how to think through the history of psychology, so as to be able to think through the relations within and between different systems.

For instance, this notion reminds us that we are not simply talking about different points of view throughout the history of Western psychology; rather, we are talking about different points of view from within different contextualizations and constellations of principles. Thus, some of the points of view cannot simply resolve into one another, since the "worlds" within which each constitutes a different worldview are simply too different from one another. By understanding systems in regard to psychology this way—as constituted by principles selected in regard to essential distinctions—the notion of an "eclectic" system is undermined, or rather "eclectic" merely becomes the name given to a system before it receives a historically designated name. Ultimately, this is because the essential distinctions—whether they can all be enumerated or not—remain sufficiently constant; if they were to change too much, then we would no longer be considering systems of *psychology*, since the distinctions and principles would pertain to some other topic. For example, it is surely a confusion to think it necessary that psychologists learn the principles of plumbing. Orienting oneself to those principles provides one with a worldview specific to the profession of plumbing, etc. not psychology.

Though this understanding of the idea of a "system" is not novel, its application in terms of this book may be. In fact, a seminal article published in 1933 in *The Psychological Review* titled "The Formal Criteria of a Systematic Psychology" written by John A. McGeoch (1897–1942) is worth quoting here at length.

> as one reads the eclectics themselves, one is struck by the fact that what they are trying to do, in their escape from the bonds of existing systems, is to erect another, less *a priori* and less "finished," perhaps, but still *a system, out of the principles which have been found to be most adequate in preceding systems* [emphasis added] … It is better, therefore, to attempt to systematize admittedly and rationally. One need not, as a result, found a "school" or nurture a cult. It is possible to be a *psychologist*, not a defender of a school, and yet to attempt to order constructively the field one studies. (1933: 4)

It is interesting to note that the article from which this excerpt comes was written before the canonization and popularization of Kuhn's notion of "incommensurability." In the wake of Kuhn, whereas McGeoch enumerates "principles of connection" and "principles of selection," in this book we consider principles of selection primal and constitutive in regard to the constructive ordering of systems. For the remainder of this section we will briefly examine some traditional characterizations of "systems" articulated in textbooks and other sources used in the study of "the history and systems of psychology." These include five (5) entries from the *American Psychological Association Dictionary of Psychology* (2007) and two History and Systems of Psychology textbooks which take McGeoch's principles as a point of departure, that is, *Systems and Theories in Psychology* (1963) and *Theories and Systems of Psychology* (1972 & 1979).

According to the *American Psychological Association Dictionary of Psychology*, "system" means:

> (1) any collective entity consisting of a set of interrelated or interacting elements that have been organized together to perform a function. (2) an orderly method of classification or procedure. (3) a structured set of facts, concepts, and hypotheses that provide a framework of thought or belief, as in a philosophical system. (VandenBos 2007: 918)

Because this definition of "system" invokes the notions of "structure," "function," and "frame" it will be helpful to see how these terms are defined. On the one hand, "structure" means: "a relatively stable arrangement of elements or components organized so as to form an integrated whole. Structure is often contrasted with function to emphasize how something is organized or patterned rather than what it does." (Ibid: 901), and "function" means "the use or purpose of something" (Ibid: 392). Moreover, notice from the definition of "system" how "function" and "performance" belong together. On the other hand, "frame of reference" means "the set of assumptions or criteria by which a person or group judges ideas, actions, and experiences." (Ibid: 388), and "cognitive system" is defined as "a set of cognitions that are organized into a meaningful complex with implied or stated relationships between them." (Ibid: 191). Now, we should draw two conclusions here. First, the answer to the question "What is a System?" given in this section is perfectly consistent with answers considered "standard" both presently and historically. Second, insofar as "system" is associated with "structure," then, "system" may be standardly contrasted with performance. The relevance of these conclusions will increase by the end of this book.

There have been prior attempts to apply a "principles" approach to the History and Systems of Psychology, such as the ones based on McGeoch's work in *Systems and Theories in Psychology* (1963 & 1987) and *Theories and Systems of Psychology* (1972 & 1979). By the 1979 publication of Lundin's *Theories and Systems of Psychology*, he had incorporated a way of viewing the above criteria as establishing the *structure* of a system and the following criteria toward expressing the *function* a system should serve. Thus, we have the following two lists of criteria.

Criteria regarding the "structure of a system:

(1) **Definition**. The system must contain a definition of the field of psychology;
(2) **Postulates**. The system must make its postulates explicit;
(3) **Data Selection**. The nature of the data to be studied must be specified;
(4) **Mind-Body Interaction**. A mind-body position must be taken;
(5) **Principles of Organization**. A system should account for the principles according to which it organizes data.
(6) **Principles of Selection**. A system should account for the principles according to which it selects data, i.e. considers data salient. (Adapted from Marx and Hillix 1963: 49 and Lundin 1972: 2–3).

Criteria regarding the "function" of a system:

(1) **Organization**. A system should be able to organize diverse facts and *principles*, relating them in a way that is meaningful. A haphazard accumulation of data will lead only to confusion, disorder and misunderstanding [emphasis added].
(2) **Inference**. Along with the observed data, theoretical propositions may be included so things fit together in a meaningful whole.

(3) **Heuristic function**. A system or theory which leads to the discovery of new findings, experimental or otherwise is said to have a heuristic function. The theory's propositions allow for the generation of new research.

(4) **Interpretation**. Whereas the Heuristic function of systems point us in new directions and the Inference function of systems allow us to fill-in missing information regarding data and observations, the Interpretation function provides us with a framework or frame of reference for understanding the meaning of data and observations.

(5) **Morale function**. Ordinarily, systems and theories are developed by people either working alone or in a group. These people share *basic convictions* and profit from interaction with each other [emphasis added].

(6) **Limiting function**. This refers to what is going to be included or left out, for example, in regard to theoretical innovations or potential data to be examined. (Adapted from Lundin 1979: 8; cf. Lichtenstein 1967).[1]

There are only three points to be made here, beyond the value of merely presenting these lists. First, despite these excellent insights expressed in the journal literature and textbooks regarding the History and Systems of Psychology, no one had combined these insights with those expressed by Kuhn. Second, emphasis was added to the term "principles" to highlight how the term was relegated to the content being organized, as opposed to the very principles in accordance with which the organization of content is performed; rather, the term "basic convictions" was used to refer to the shared principles from which the shared practices flow, thereby constituting a community of practitioners or school of thought. Third, reading the above lists from a philosophical perspective, the first question which comes to mind is: Why were they trying to recreate the wheel? That is, just as the APA definition stated, "as in a philosophical system," the systematic articulation of the work of philosophers has a long history, and it does not use these lists of criteria to *organize* the information. In other words, we should use the philosophical principles according to which philosophy itself is standardly organized, for example in regard to the "criteria regarding structure" list. Moreover, the "criteria regarding function" list directly relates to the former list in that it refers to the function of a structure constructed in accordance with the "criteria regarding structure." Put bluntly, the systems of psychology have their own ontologies, epistemologies, and theories of predication, by way of which they may by differentiated; moreover, by thinking about them in these terms, one is able to "think though" the history and systems of Western psychology without privileging any one system *of psychology* over another.

Some further clarification regarding the second and third points will prove helpful. As has been clear since the time of Aristotle, "philosophy" transcends the classification of the sciences. Of course this may be easily understood by simply realizing that the sciences are classified according to some philosophy. When the physical eye sees, it does not see itself seeing. However, as should be common knowledge among those who study the history of psychology, psychologists in the twentieth century, especially, seemed quite eager to establish their "independence" from philosophy, for example as the "new psychology." This is usually cast in terms of psychology as a separate discipline from philosophy, and if when you hear "discipline" you think of offices occupied by people, then you may not take issue with the idea expressed. Yet, if you understand that philosophy is not a separate "discipline" from which psychology *can* be separated, then the eagerness seems more culturally and politically (not to mention probably economically) motivated. This issue—figuratively call it "psychology's anxiety to establish its 'independence'"—may account for the desire to "recreate the wheel," so to speak (cf. Finkelman 1978).

## 1.4   What Are Principles & Distinctions?

To begin, it is helpful to notice the difference between two easy to confuse terms. The term "principal" can be used as either a noun or an adjective; as a noun it means a person or property of a specified rank or type, and as an adjective it means that whatever it describes is first or most important in rank. The term "principle" is a noun, and it refers to "that from which anything in any way proceeds; a starting point of being, or of change, or of knowledge, or of discussion." (Wuellner 1956: 4). Thus, a "principle" may function as a foundation for a system of thinking, understanding, or behaving. These terms may be easily confused, since using the former as an adjective we may correctly refer to principles as principal. However, it is, of course, the term "principle" which interests us in this book, and because the ancient Greek term for "principle" was "*archē*" or "*archai*" in the plural, the project of uncovering the principles of the systems of Western psychology may be referred to as an "archaeology."

Traditionally, principles may be divided into principles of reality (or "ontological" principles) and principles of logic (or "mental" principles). In regard to the former, a being or some part of a being may be considered a principle of being or principle of reality, and if some other being comes from the principle, then the principle may be called a principle of change. In regard to the latter type of principles, they refer to "a source of knowledge or of thought; especially a truth from which another truth or truths proceed." (Ibid: 5) The relationship between order and principles provides additional illumination for the relationship between principles and systems. Notice, "The means precede the end in the order of execution." (Ibid: 39). That is, "The end is the correct principle of the selection, direction, order (arrangement), and subordination of the means." (Ibid). In this way, terms "selection" and "order" should recall "principles of organization" and "selection," noted above, with the end being the truth, or identity of the system of "psychology" with which the practitioner is operating.

In order to appreciate the value of explicating the principles operable regarding the systems of psychology throughout history in the West, we will enumerate a few principles and an example here. First is the "principle of identity," which in its ontological formulation holds, "Whatever is, is", and in its logical formulation holds "The true is true; the false is false." (Ibid: 14–15). Next is the "principle of non-contradiction," which in its ontological formulation holds, "A thing cannot both be and not be at the same time in the same respect or relation," and in its logical formulation holds, "The same judgment cannot at the same time in the same meaning be both true and false." (Ibid). Two more. The "principle of causality" holds "Every physical change requires a cause distinct from the subject changed, and the new form arising in the subject" and "Whatever comes to be comes to be from another being." (Ibid: 30). Lastly, the "principle of finality" holds "Every agent or nature in acting must act for an end." (Ibid: 38).

Notice the power of these principles for ordering knowledge. For example, consider the principle of non-contradiction (PNC). The PNC is the motor force behind alibis. If you know where a person was at the time some crime was committed (and that place was not the place where the crime was committed), then you know the person in question is not guilty of the crime. Moreover, you know the person *is not* guilty of the crime even though you do not know who *is* guilty of the crime. In fact, Aristotle called the principle of non-contradiction "the most firm of all first principles." (1984: 1005b11–23).

Thus, it was through the power of articulating these principles that Aristotle was credited with originating "science" in the West. His description of science in general from the beginning of his *Physics* (184a10–21) points to the value of principles, as he understood them.

> In every systematic inquiry where there are first principles, or causes, or elements, knowledge and science result from acquiring knowledge of these; for we think we know something just in case we acquire knowledge of the primary causes, the primary first principles, all the way to the elements. It is clear, then, that in the science of nature as elsewhere, we should try first to determine questions about the first principles. (Irwin 1990: 3)

The idea here is that if we were to encounter some random thing and were to provide a systematic inquiry into it, then we would be hoping to uncover the principles, causes, and elements which would constitute "scientific" knowledge of the thing in question.[2] Conversely, to the extent that "science," or our systematic inquiry, can uncover the truth of reality, then we will come to understand that reality in question in terms of "first principles." It is because these principles are the ultimate first principles from which knowledge proceeds that Aristotle thinks them constitutive of "science."

Notice, then, because the systems of Western psychology which we will be examining all purport to be accurate approaches to that to which "psychology" is supposed to refer, the standpoint of principles is a good position in relation to the approaches. That is to say, our aim is to find some common ground on which to compare and contrast the different systems; though each system may be radically different from one another, each system is still a system. In this way, going back to the example of "encountering some random thing" from the previous paragraph: there may be several different ways to engage in the systematic inquiry of the random thing we have encountered, and, in fact, the random thing may in the light of each system seem different; however, insofar as each of those systems is aiming to produce true knowledge of the thing, then ultimately each of those systems will be articulated in terms of first principles which will be the same for them all. For example, each system will *identify* what is to be examined. Each system will direct its inquiry at some *reality* and articulate its findings *logically*. Even in extreme examples like the "Freudian Unconscious," which is supposed to not operate in accordance with—or be constrained by—the principle of non-contradiction, Sigmund Freud, of course, was constrained by the principle of non-contradiction when articulating his psychoanalytic system of which the Unconscious is a *part*.

As a transition, then, from discussing principles to discussing distinctions, consider the following distinctions Aristotle made in regard to the principle of causality. As the following makes clear, Aristotle understood the principle of a thing's identity—the type of being it is—to be intimately related to the principle of causality.

> Knowledge is the object of our inquiry, and men do not think they know a thing till they have grasped the 'why' of it (which is to grasp its primary cause). So clearly we too must do this as regards both coming to be and passing away and every kind of natural change, in order that, knowing their principles, we may try to refer to these principles each of our problems. (1950: 194b17–23)

Notice how this quote from Aristotle echoes the strategy of discovering the principles so that the "problems" encountered in the course of systematic inquiry can be "referred to these principles." Of course, the principles in this case are more commonly known as Aristotle's "Four Causes." Whereas knowing the Four Causes constitutes knowing "the why" of a thing for Aristotle, it is the distinctions among the causes which allow us to think of each as a separate principle, and they are: "the Material Cause," "the Formal Cause," "the Efficient Cause," and "the Final Cause."

The "Material Cause" refers to "that out of which a thing comes to be," for example, "the bronze of the statue, the silver of the bowl, and the genera of which the bronze and the silver are species." (Aristotle 1950: 194b23). In order to more easily understand the "Formal Cause," it may be helpful to recall, as mentioned in general above, Aristotle's "word-concept-thing" understanding of signification. As noted by Thomas Aquinas (1225–1274), "Since according to [Aristotle], words are signs of ideas, and ideas likenesses of things, evidently words refer to things signified through the medium of an intellectual conception." (Aquinas 1920: 150/ST Ia, 13, 1). In this way, "Formal Cause" refers to "the form or the archetype, i.e. the statement of the essence and its genera, are called 'causes' ... and the parts of the definition." (Aristotle 1950: 194b26). Since the concept "human" belongs to the genus "animal" with the specific difference being "rational," the definition of "human" would be "rational animal," this states the essence of the being, then, that is human. To attempt to define "human" merely as an "animal" would be an insufficient definition, as it would merely invoke the "Material Cause," in terms of the genera, out of which the "human" is made. Moreover, it would not be a good definition in that with such a *concept* you could not tell the difference between cats and humans.

The "Efficient Cause" refers to "the primary source of the change or coming to rest ... and generally what makes of what is made and what causes change of what is changed." (Aristotle 1950: 194b30). In the sculpture example, the sculptor is the Efficient Cause. We may even go so far as to say that the sculptor had the idea of the shape into which the Material would be placed, and placing the Material in that Form makes the sculptor the Efficient Cause. Finally, the "Final Cause" refers to "the sense of end or 'that for the sake of which' a thing is done, for example health is the [Final] cause of walking about." (Ibid: 194b34). In this way, the "Final Cause" refers to the purpose for which the Efficient Cause put the Material in the Form; thus, recalling the "principle of finality," the Final Cause stands out as the ultimate reason which unites the other causes. Final translates the ancient Greek "*telos*," and so "teleology" refers to the study of a thing's development toward its end.[3]

"Distinction" invokes the ontological formula of the "principle of identity and difference," which may be articulated as:

> Things, or objective concepts, which are the same as a third thing, or objective concept, are the same as each other [—identity]. But if one of them is the same as a third and the other is different from that same third, these two are different from each other [—difference]. (Wuellner 1956: 25)

There are three major types of distinction to discuss here: real, virtual, and purely rational. There is a real distinction between two individually existing things; that is, the table and the chairs are really distinct, and two different chairs are really distinct. Next, consider how it is possible to conceptually differentiate between "human" and "rational animal," that is, they are two different concepts; however, the distinction does not pertain to any real difference. Thus, though the concepts are distinct, it is a purely rational distinction since it has no grounding in reality. Lastly, a virtual distinction is a rational distinction, which does have some basis in reality. Whereas there is no difference in reality between a thing and the qualitative aspects to the material of which it is made, it is possible to identify a conceptual difference. For example, we may talk about the difference between this chair and the wood of which it is composed; however, in reality, there is no difference between this chair and the wood of which it is composed.

Anticipating what will be considered more fully below, when regarding a plurality of concepts or things it is not enough to merely point out differences among the plurality, if we hope to gain, or sustain, a systematic understanding of the plurality. Rather, principles are needed in addition to distinctions. Unfortunately, articles and textbooks regarding the systems in the history of Western psychology have a tendency to merely list distinctions, as if they are merely a haphazard rhapsody of binary oppositions. For instance, though not worth reproducing in its entirety here, R. I. Watson's list of eighteen (18) binary oppositions also appears in James F. Brennan's celebrated textbook *History and Systems of Psychology* (2003: 133). The list includes:

"Conscious mentalism v. Unconscious mentalism; Mechanism v. Vitalism; Determinism v. Indeterminism; Empiricism v. Rationalism;

Functionalism v. Structuralism; Monism v. Dualism; Quantitativism v. Qualitativism," and so on. (cf. Watson 1967: 436–437). However, by the end of the next chapter we will have an idea of the principles by way of which the organization of these distinctions provides for a more systematic understanding of the various patterns of selection exemplifying the various systems of Western psychology.

## Notes

1. I constructed both of these lists by initially inserting them as quotes; however, upon further reflection, I corrected the grammatical structure of some of the locutions and added clarifying articulations. Therefore, I take credit for the lists as a totality—especially insofar as they cannot be found elsewhere in this form; however, the lists do contain partial, and at times completely verbatim, quotes from the cited authors. Readers are encouraged to look at the primary sources if they would like to determine the exact differences between my presentation of the lists here and information presented in the cited sources.

2. At this point we need not concern ourselves with different historical understandings of "science," we will address the difference at a later point. Moreover, "systematic knowledge" would be a suitable substitute for "scientific knowledge" in either case.

3. Though Aristotle is, of course, credited with systematizing the Four Causes, it is worth pointing out that they can be found already stated in Plato's dialog *Timaeus* (30a).

## Bibliography

Aquinas, Thomas. 1920. *The "Summa Theologica" of St. Thomas Aquinas*. Trans. Fathers of the English Dominican Province. London: Burns Oates & Washbourne.

Aristotle. 1950. *Physics*. Trans. W.D. Ross. R.P. Hardie and Revised by R.K. Gaye (Rev.). In *The Complete Works of Aristotle: The Revised Oxford Translation* (1995), ed. J. Barnes, vol. I, 315–446. Princeton, NJ: Princeton University Press.

————. 1956. *On the Soul*. Trans. J.A. Smith. In *The Complete Works of Aristotle: The Revised Oxford Translation* (1995), ed. J. Barnes, vol. I, 641–692. Princeton, NJ: Princeton University Press.

————. 1967. *Topics*. Trans. J. Brunschwig. In *The Complete Works of Aristotle: The Revised Oxford Translation* (1995), ed. J. Barnes, vol. I, 167–277. Princeton, NJ: Princeton University Press.

————. 1984. *Metaphysics*. Trans. W.D. Ross. In *The Complete Works of Aristotle: The Revised Oxford Translation* (1995), ed. J. Barnes, vol. II, 1552–1728. Princeton, NJ: Princeton University Press.

Bachelard, Gaston. 2016. *The Dialectic of Duration*. Trans. M.M. Jones. London: Rowman & Littlefield International.

Barthes, Roland. 1978. Death of the Author. Ed. and Trans. S. Heath, *Image, Music, Text*, 142–149. New York: Hill and Wang.

Baudrillard, Jean. 1994. *The Illusion of the End*. Stanford, CA: Stanford University Press.

————. 2006. The Precession of Simulacra. In *Simulacra and Simulation*, ed. and trans. S.F. Glaser 1–42. Ann Arbor, MI: University of Michigan Press.

Berger, Peter L., and Thomas Luckmann. 1966. *The Social Construction of Reality: A Treatise in the Sociology of Knowledge*. New York: Anchor Books.

Bergson, Henri. 2004. *Matter and Memory*. Trans. Nancy Margaret Paul & W. Scott Almer. New York: Dover Publications.

von Bertalanffy, Ludwig. 1968. *General Systems Theory: Foundations, Developments, Applications*. New York: Braziller.

Brennan, James F. 2003. *History and Systems of Psychology*. Upper Saddle, NJ: Prentice Hall.

Brümmer, Vincent. 1981. *Theology & Philosophical Inquiry: An Introduction*. London: The Macmillan Press.

Butterfield, Herbert. 1931. *The Whig Interpretation of History*. London: George Bell.

————. 1949. *Christianity and History*. London: George Bell.

Clark, Jonathan. 2004. *Our Shadowed Present: Modernism, Postmodernism, and History*. Stanford, CA: Stanford University Press.

Csikszentmihalyi, Mihaly J. 1996. *Creativity: Flow and the Psychology of Discovery and Invention*. New York: Harper Collins.

Cunningham, Francis A. 1988. *Essence and Existence in Thomism: A Mental Vs the "Real Distinction?"*. Lanham, MD: University Press of America.

Danziger, Kurt. 1990. *Constructing the Subject: Historical Origins of Psychological Research*. Cambridge: Cambridge University Press.

Deleuze, Gilles. 2004. How Do We Recognize Structuralism? (1967). In *Desert Islands and Other Texts, 1953–1974*, ed. D. Lapoujade and trans. M. Taormina, 170–192. New York: Semiotext(e).

———. 2006. *Nietzsche and Philosophy*. Trans. H. Tomlinson. New York: Columbia University.

Deleuze, Gilles, and Félix Guattari. 2004. *Anti-Oedipus*. Trans. R. Hurley, M. Seem, & H. R. Lane. Vol. I. of *Capitalism and Schizophrenia*. (1972–1980). London: Continuum.

Descartes, René. 1998. *Discourse on the Method for Conducting One's Reason Well and for Seeking Truth in the Sciences*. Trans. D.A. Cress. Indianapolis, IN: Hackett Publishing.

Derrida, Jacques. 1978. *Writing and Difference*. Trans. A. Bass. Chicago: University of Chicago.

Durant, Will. 1939. *The Story of Civilization: The Life of Greece*. New York: Simon & Shuster.

Entralgo, Lain. 1970. *The Therapy of the Word in Classical Antiquity*. New Haven: Yale University Press.

Feigl, Herbert. 1959. Philosophical Embarrassments of Psychology. *American Psychologist* 14 (3): 115–128.

Feyerabend, Paul. 1983. *Against Method*. New York: Verso.

———. 2001. *Conquest of Abundance: A Tale of Abstraction Versus the Richness of Being*. Chicago, IL: University of Chicago Press.

Finkelman, David. 1978. Science and Psychology. *American Journal of Psychology* 78 (91): 179–199.

Foucault, Michel. 1971. *The Order of Things: An Archaeology of the Human Sciences*. Trans. A. Sheridan. New York: Pantheon Books.

———. 1988. *Madness and Civilization: A History of Insanity in the Age of Reason*. Trans. A. Sheridan. New York: Vintage Books.

———. 1994. *The Birth of the Clinic: An Archaeology of Medical Perception*. Trans. A. Sheridan. New York: Vintage Books.

Fuchs, Alfred H., Rand B. Evans, and Roger K. Thomas. 2007. History of Psychology: Recurring Errors Among Recent History of Psychology Textbooks. *The American Journal of Psychology* 120 (3): 477–495.

Gadamer, Hans-Georg. 1989. *Truth and Method* (2nd rev). Trans. J. Weinsheimer and D.G. Marshall. New York: Continuum Press.

Gergen, Kenneth J. 1985. The Social Constructionist Movement in Modern Psychology. *American Psychologist* 40 (3): 266–275.

Geuter, Ulfried. 1983. The Uses of History for the Shaping of a Field: Observations on German Psychology. In *Functions and Uses Disciplinary Histories*, ed. L. Graham, W. Leneies, and P. Weingart. Dordrecht: Springer.

Gramsci, Antonio. 1971. *Selections from the Prison Notebooks*. Ed. and Trans. Q. Horare and G. N. Smith. London: Lawrence & Wishart.

Green, Stuart. 1994. The Problems of Learning to Think Like a Historian: Writing History in the Culture of the Classroom. *Educational Psychologist* 29 (2): 9–96.

Hadot, Pierre. 1995. *Philosophy as a Way of Life*. Oxford: Oxford University Press.

———. 2002. *What Is Ancient Philosophy?* Cambridge, MA: The Belknap Press of Harvard University.

Harris, Ben. 2009. What Critical Psychologists Should Know About the History of Psychology. In *Critical Psychology: An Introduction*, ed. D. Fox, I. Prilleltensky, and S. Austin, 20–35. London: Sage.

Hegel, G.W.F. 1901. *Philosophy of History*. Trans. J. Sibree. New York: P.F. Collier and Son.

Howard, Alex. 2000. *Philosophy for Counselling and Psychotherapy: Pythagoras to Postmodernism*. London: Macmillan Press.

Irwin, Terence H. 1990. *Aristotle's First Principles*. Oxford: Oxford University Press.

Jones, Mary McAllester. 1991. *Gaston Bachelard, Subversive Humanist: Text and Readings*. Madison, WI: University of Wisconsin Press.

Klein, D.B. 1970. *A History of Scientific Psychology*. New York: Basic Books.

Kragh, Helge. 1989. *An Introduction to the Historiography of Science*. Cambridge: Cambridge University Press.

Kuhn, Thomas. 1969. Comment [On the Relations of Science and Art]. *Comparative Studies in Society and History* 11: 403–412.

———. 1996. *The Structure of Scientific Revolutions*. Chicago: University of Chicago.

Lichtenstein, Parker E. 1967. Psychological Systems: Their Nature and Function. *Psychological Record* 17 (3): 321–340.

Lundin, Robert W. 1972 [1979]. *Theories and Systems of Psychology*. Toronto, Canada: D.C. Heath.

Mandler, George. 1996. The Situation of Psychology: Landmarks and Choicepoints. *The American Journal of Psychology* 109 (1): 1–35.

Marwick, Arthur. 1970. *What Is History and Why It Is Important*. London: McGraw-Hill/Open University Press.

Marx, Melvin Herman, and William A. Hillix. 1963. *Systems and Theories in Psychology*. New York: McGraw-Hill.

———. 1993. "A Fetishism of Documents?" The Salience of Source-Based History. In *Developments in Modern Historiography*, ed. H. Kozicki, 107–138. London: Macmillan.

————. 2001. *The New Nature of History*. London: Palgrave.

McGeoch, John A. 1933. The Formal Criteria of a Systematic Psychology. *The Psychological Review* 40 (1): 1–12.

Moes, Mark. 2000. *Plato's Dialogue Form and the Care of the Soul*. New York: Peter Lang.

Moravcsik, Michael J. 1981. Creativity in Science Education. *Science Education* 65: 221–227.

Mumford, Michael D. 2003. Where Have We Been, Were Are We Going? Taking Stock in Creativity Research. *Creativity Research Journal* 15: 107–120.

Nietzsche, Friedrich. 1989. *On the Genealogy of Morals*. Eds. and Trans. W. Kaufmann and R.J. Hollingdale. New York: Vintage Books.

O'Brien, Denise. 1969. *Empedocles' Cosmic Cycle*. Cambridge: Cambridge University Press.

O'Callaghan, John P. 2003. *Thomist Realism and the Linguistic Turn: Toward a More Perfect Form of Existence*. South Bend, IN: Notre Dame University Press.

Peregrin, Jaroslav. 2001. *Meaning and Structure: Structuralism of (Post)Analytic Philosophers*. Burlington, VT: Ashgate.

Petit, Philip. 1977. *The Concept of Structuralism: A Critical Analysis*. Berkeley, CA: University of California Press.

Plato. 1860. *Philebus: A Dialog of Plato on Pleasure and Knowledge and Their Relations to the Highest Good*. Trans. E. Poste, Edward. London: John W. Parker and Son, West Strand.

Polybius. 1922. *The Histories*. Trans. W.R. Paton. London: William Heinemann.

Rachlin, Howard. 1994. *Behavior and Mind: The Roots of Modern Psychology*. Oxford: Oxford University Press.

Richards, Graham. 1987. Of What Is History of Psychology a History? *The British Journal for the History of Science* 20 (2): 201–211.

————. 2002. *Putting Psychology in its Place: A Critical, Historical Overview*. New York: Routledge.

Rousseau, Jean-Jacques. 2010. *Emile or On Education*. Trans. C. Kelly and A. Bloom. Hanover, NH: Dartmouth College Press.

Santayana, George. 2011. *The Life of Reason or The Phases of Human Progress*. Cambridge, MA: MIT Press.

Sarno, Ronald. 1969. Hesiod: From Chaos to Cosmos to Community. *The Classical Bulletin* 45 (5): 17–23.

de Saussure, Ferdinand. 2011. *Course in General Linguistics*. Eds. P. Meisel and H. Saussy, Trans. W. Baskin. New York: Columbia University Press.

Serres, Michel. 1982. *Hermes: Literature, Science, Philosophy*. Trans. D.F. Bell. Baltimore, MD: The Johns Hopkins University Press.

Simonton, Dean. 2004. *Creativity in Science: Chance, Logic, Genius, and Zeitgeist*. Cambridge: Cambridge University Press.

Slife, Brent D., Kari A. O'Grady, and Russell D. Kosits. 2017. Introduction to Psychology's Worldviews. In *The Hidden Worldviews of Psychology's Theory, Research, and Practice*, ed. B.D. Slife, K.A. O'Grady, and R.D. Kosits, 1–8. New York: Routledge.

Sobociński, Bolesław. 1984. Leśniewski's Analysis of Russell's Paradox. In *Leśniewski's Systems: Ontology and Mereology*, ed. J.T.J. Srzednicki and V.F. Rickey, 11–44. The Hague: Martinus Nijhoff Publishers.

Stocking, George. 1968. On the Limits of 'Presentism' and 'Historicism' in the Historiography of the Behavioral Sciences. In *In Race, Culture, and Evolution: Essays in the History of Anthropology*. Chicago: University of Chicago Press.

Szasz, Thomas. 1988. *The Myth of Psychotherapy*. Syracuse, NY: Syracuse University Press.

———. 1997. The Healing Word: Its Past, Present, and Future. In *The Evolution of Psychotherapy The Third Conference*. Bristol, PA: Brunner/Mazel.

Tosh, Nick. 2003. Anachronism and Retrospective Explanation: In Defense of a Present-Centered History of Science. *Studies in History and Philosophy of Science* 34 (3): 647–659.

Toulmin, Stephen. 1972. *Human Understanding*. Princeton, NJ: Princeton University Press.

Trevelyan, George M. 1949. *An Autobiography and Other Essays*. London: Longmans.

VandenBos, Gary R. 2007. *APA Dictionary of Psychology*. Washington, DC: American Psychological Association.

Van Kaam, Adrian. 1966. *Existential Foundations of Psychology*. Pittsburgh, PA: Duquesne University Press.

Vaugh-Blount, Kelli, Alexandra Rutherford, David Baker, and Deborah Johnson. 2009. History's Mysteries Demystified: Becoming a Psychologist-Historian. *The American Journal of Psychology* 122 (1): 117–129.

Vico, Giambattista. 2002. *The First New Science*. Cambridge: Cambridge University Press.

Watson, Robert I. 1966. The Role and Use of History in the Psychology Curriculum. *Journal of the History of the Behavioral Sciences* 2 (1): 64–69.

———. 1967. Psychology: A Prescriptive Science. *American Psychologist* 22 (6): 435–443.

Wehrle, Walter E. 2000. *The Myth of Aristotle's Development and the Betrayal of Metaphysics*. London: Rowman & Littlefield.

Woodward, William R., and Mitchell G. Ash. 1982. Preface. In *The Problematic Science: Psychology in Nineteenth-Century Thought*, ed. W.R. Woodward and M.G. Ash, v–vi. New York: Praeger Publishing.

Wuellner, Bernard J. 1956. *Summary of Scholastic Principles*. Chicago: Loyola University Press.

# 2

# Some Historically Based Essential General Distinctions

## 2.1   What Is Psychology?

Etymologically, the word "psychology" comes from the combination of two ancient Greek words: ψυχή and λογός, that is, transliterated as *psychē* and *logos*, respectively. Whereas the latter term means "reason, definition, to give an account of, or study of" (cf. Peters 1967: 110–111), the meaning of the former term has proved more ambiguous. For the ancient Greek philosophers, as we will see, it meant something like "life-principle" or "force that animates." However, it would be inaccurate to equate the ancient Greek thinking of Plato and Aristotle, for example, with an Eastern animism such as the kind found in Japanese Shintōism (cf. Scalambrino 2017). At the same time, the Latinate term *anima* was used to translate the Greek ψυχή, and *anima* is the root of the English "animation." Hence, in the West, beings are said to have ψυχή if they can self-animate.

Of course, following Plato's understanding of ψυχή as divine and immortal, the Modern translation of the Latin *anima* of the Christianized Middle Ages in the West into "soul" tends to carry clear theological connotations, for example souls may go to Heaven or souls were created by God, and so on. Further, many attempts have been made—especially in

© The Author(s) 2018
F. Scalambrino, *Philosophical Principles of the History and Systems of Psychology*,
https://doi.org/10.1007/978-3-319-74733-0_2

the Modern and Contemporary Periods—to "naturalize" ψυχή, which means to account for ψυχή in purely natural or material terms. There will be more to say about this as we proceed through the course of the book; however, it is important to note that much is at stake in regard to how ψυχή is understood. Thus, throughout history in the West there have been many different attempts to account for the "origin" of the term "psychology." Of course because there may be much at stake regarding how we understand ψυχή, we will examine some of the major candidates for the origin of the term "psychology." The convention of continuing to use "ψυχή," rather than "soul" or "*psychē*" has been adopted for this book to function as a reminder to the reader of the historical depth involved in our discussion.

During the time in the West when psychologists were particularly anxious to establish their independence from philosophy, there were philosophers who spoke out against the idea that psychology could be a discipline completely separated from philosophy. For example, Herbert Feigl identified "what is perhaps the most painful philosophical embarrassment of psychology: the definition of its very subject matter. As the well-known saying goes: psychology first lost its soul, later its consciousness, and seems now in danger of losing its mind altogether." (1959: 121). Feigl's notion points to the progressive naturalization of the understanding of ψυχή along the history and systems of Western psychology. It is worth noting a contemporary emergence in the history of psychology which directly relates to Feigl's comment. Though he may have intended the comment humorously, it speaks to the historical-shifts which have occurred from system to system in regard to the ontology—that is, the ontological principles—operable along the history of psychology. Whereas psychologists celebrated such a shift away from philosophy, it is as if, presently, the momentum of the slide threatens to do to "psychology" precisely what the psychologists hoped to do to philosophy. That is to say, "psychology" presently runs the risk of being subsumed by the disciplines of biology and neuroscience (cf. Gazzaniga 2006; cf. Henriques 2004; cf. Kagan 2013; cf. Leonelli 2016; cf. Lilienfeld 2012; cf. Miller 2010).

Of course, as our book emphasizes, thinking and theorizing are them-selves "philosophical activities," and it should be commonly understood among psychologists that

> what is now called the science of psychology used to be called mental phi-losophy. As such it had to do with what many generations of philosophers had been thinking about ... This resulted in the accumulation of a mass of data, both factual and conjectural, pertaining to the realm of the mind. It was this heritage of mental philosophy as it had taken shape by the 1870s and 1880s that the pioneering laboratory psychologies had at their dis-posal. (Klein 1970: viii)

In this way, despite advances in the study of biology and neuroscience, recalling the philosophical nature of "psychology" makes Cambridge phi-losopher of science John Rust's suggestion more palpable, that is: "Where the areas of interest of the two disciplines [philosophy and psychology] overlap, even the established psychologist frequently makes philosophical errors which would be apparent to the first year philosophy student." (1987: 49). Thus, one of the aims of learning the history and systems of Western psychology, and recalling its intimate relation to philosophy, is for psychologists to decrease the number of such "philosophical errors."

A number of studies have been constructed tracing the history of the use of the term "psychology" (cf. Vidal 2011: 25–30; cf. Merz 1965: 200–201; cf. Krstic 1964; cf. Lamanna 2010; cf. Lapointe 1973). In sum, the Middle Ages referred to the studies found in Plato and Aristotle regarding ψυχή as the "*scientia de anima*," and by the 1570s, though apparently used once prior, and on into the Early Modern Period, the term "*psychologia*," that is, "psychology" took its place. Along the lines of this shift from *scientia de anima* to *psychologia* a shift from study of "soul" to study of "mind" occurred. Moreover, anticipating what will be consid-ered more fully throughout this book, it may be said that the conflict between whether to characterize ψυχή in terms of "natural" science or not (cf. Dilthey 1989, 2010; cf. Ladd 1892; cf. Raue 1889; cf. Titchener 1914; cf. Wundt 2014) is as old as the apparent disagreement between Plato and Aristotle on the issue. As we shall see, this issue has manifested in various ways throughout the entire history of psychology in the West.

When considering the history of Western psychology in general across the fourfold historical division (similar to the characterization of philosophy noted above), then, whereas the Ancient Period emphasized a concern for both the structure and function of ψυχή, with the emphasis shift toward morality and the notion that the structure of ψυχή had been sufficiently revealed, the Middle Ages emphasized a concern more for function than structure. Of course, though it is not possible to eliminate one in favor of the other, it is heuristically and mnemonically valuable for us to characterize the fourfold division in this way. Next, with the Modern Period the emphasis shifted to concerns for the best method for examining ψυχή, and—as we will see—Kant's discovery of the "Transcendental Method," had a twofold consequence for the history of psychology at the level of characterizing its emphases in general.

On the one hand, Kant's work is standardly considered "revolutionary." That is to say, the Transcendental Method was supposed to have ended the quest of the Modern Period to discover the best method for examining ψυχή. Of course, what Kant's method revealed is a systematic unity at the heart of ψυχή. In regard to his revolution's value for philosophy we hear talk of the "architectonic" of reason. This discovery illuminates Kant as a kind of "system architect," even though it is the method that reveals, rather than constructs, the architecture itself. On the other hand, Kant's revolution influenced thinking about ψυχή so much going forward in history, that there is a sense in which all the major theorists after him either engage in a kind of architectural design or react strongly against such "systematizing." In this way, again for heuristic and mnemonic value, we may characterize twentieth-century Western psychology in terms of its history and systems as initially attempting to operationalize the Transcendental Method (as it was understood by the psychologists attempting the operationalization), and concluding with reactions against the system-building of the architects, that is, the "Great Men" of Western psychology. Two more points to make regarding this movement across the historical periods.

First, the movement in the history of psychology from system-building to reaction against system-building architects mirrors the same movement which took much less time to play out in the history of Western philosophy. That is to say, whereas German Idealism, especially Kant and

Hegel, represents a zenith of systems-building—philosophers today still marvel at the magnitude and majesty of these "cathedrals"— "existentialism," referring to the philosophical ideas of Søren Kierkegaard (1813–1855) and Friedrich Nietzsche (1844–1900), represents a reaction against what may be characterized as the "oppressive" relation individual existences may experience upon encountering the revelations of such systems and system architects. Second, it becomes possible, then, to retrospectively understand the history and systems of Western psychology in terms of the elements with which we just characterized the fourfold division. That is, whereas writings from the Ancient Period regarding ψυχή certainly seem aware of some sense in which ψυχή may be characterized from the perspective of many different systems and approached by way of many different methods, competition between systems was very much a reality, since each was attempting to articulate *the truth* regarding the structure and function of ψυχή. With the dominance of the Christian Church, then, in the Middle Ages, considering the truth of ψυχή to have been essentially already revealed regarding structure (identity and place in nature) and function (morality), emphasis could be shifted toward articulating the place of ψυχή within a larger system.

Now, just as the system architects of the Middle Ages—Thomas Aquinas towering above the others—constructed systems based on revelation and philosophy (or "faith and reason"), the system architects of the Modern Period constructed systems based on reason and experience. We will discuss the reasons for this shift in more detail below; however, the point to emphasize is that just as the Early Modern thinkers may have considered the faith-based systems and architects "oppressive," the Contemporary Postmodernists and Eclectics find the systems of the Modern Period "oppressive." Moreover, it is heuristically and mnemonically quite valuable to recognize that this movement may be understood in terms of movement along a spectrum from "faith and reason" based to "reason and experience" based to "experience and anarchy" based. Though, it is important to understand that "anarchy" here is used as a technical term. That is, as noted above, *archē* comes from the ancient Greek term for "principle," for example as found in archeology and architecture. So, at the extreme end of "resistance" to systems and systems architects are theorists who reject a principled approach, simply in virtue of the fact that it is a principle-approach, that is, *anarchy*.

In sum, then, the history of the systems of Western psychology may be characterized as emphasizing structure, function (or both together in terms of "development"), or neither in terms of "eclecticism." A distinction exists between a moderate and a more extreme eclecticism, then, in that moderate eclecticism goes by the name "theoretical integration" and the name "unsystematic eclecticism" refers to extreme eclecticism, that is, "anarchy" (cf. Beutler 1983; cf. Feyerabend 1983, 1987; cf. Geelan 1997 cf. Hart 1986; cf. Prochaska and DiClementi 1986). Whereas eclecticism as "theoretical integration" falls within a kind of "pragmatism" invoking theory merely to secure the best fit available presently "between the intervention, the patient, the problem, and the setting" (Murray 1986: 414), "unsystematic eclecticism" often uses justifications from outside of the discipline in the attempt to alter theorizing internal to the discipline. For example, individuals without degrees in engineering are usually not chosen to engineer rollercoasters; however, if one were to see this as unfair or an example of the "tyranny of engineering," then one might advocate for non-engineers to engineer roller coasters. Of course, this book's emphasis on choices and commitment in the design of theories and systems for psychology stands by the suggestion that, though psychologists may be ignorant of the principles involved in their thinking and acting, it is not possible to avoid principles. For example, it is a principle of anarchy to not adhere to principles.

Thus, for the sake of organization across the chapters of this book we will adhere to the following general division regarding the principles of the history and systems of Western psychology: (a) principles related to the study of ψυχή in isolation; (b) principles related to the study of ψυχή not in isolation; (c) principles related to the appropriate way to study ψυχή. This general division may be characterized in terms of (a) the structure of ψυχή—which includes the tripartite "Orthodox" Western characterization and the various historically based shifts in emphases regarding structural-primacy, (b) the functions of ψυχή—which includes relations to environment (behavior) and relations within communities (social), action performance, and speech, and (c) methodological issues in psychology—which includes the various historically based concerns regarding causality and the conflict between psychology as a natural or a human science. Organizing the various historically based expressions and emphases of principles in terms of this general division should provide greater overall coherence for readers.

## 2.2 Hermeneutic Distinctions: On Naming and Reading

The purpose of this section is regulative. In other words, we will examine a number of distinctions here which will help readers navigate the remaining discussion in this book. Thus, this is not intended to be an exhaustive discussion of "hermeneutics." Moreover, this excursion into "hermeneutic distinctions," namely distinctions helpful for interpreting some of the worldview-shifts in the history of Western psychology, is not necessarily a pre-judgement in favor of understanding psychology as a "human science." Rather, these "hermeneutic distinctions" are directed at the philosophical and historical characterizations of the worldview-shifts.

Addressing the relation between word, thing, and concept, directly—though not exhaustively—this section will provide clarification relevant for understanding later discussions of the functions of ψυχή and the various historically based systems which rely upon hermeneutics-related distinctions for differentiation from other systems. The distinctions to be discussed include: (a) Aristotle on "naming," (b) definition, (c) truth, (d) the relation between science and methodology, and (e) styles of reading and historiography. Again, anticipating what will be considered more fully below, a brief explication of these distinctions here will be helpful; for example, much resistance—rooted primarily in Postmodernism—may be conjured up in Contemporary Period theorists upon reading the word "essential." In addition, then, to clarifying this book's use of the term "essential," this section will also provide the groundwork from which readers may appreciate multiple historically based conflicts across approaches, theories, and systems of Western psychology.

Aristotle began his work titled (*The*) *Categories* by noting: "When things have only a name in common and the definition of being which corresponds to the name is different, they are called *homonymous*. Thus, for example, both a man and a picture are animals." (1956: 1a1–3). He contrasts this term with *synonymous* and *paronymous*; however, before discussing their differences, consider the reference to "a picture." By recognizing that "a picture" is an image of the thing, we may see even more relevance here for psychology; that is, both the image of the sandwich "in" ψυχή and the edible thing composed of bread "outside" ψυχή may be signified by the term "sandwich." However, only one of those "sandwiches" has nutritional content. Therefore, for Aristotle, whereas the one is imaginary, the other is real. In this way it is clear that though someone may suggest that "meaning slides" as an articulation of the homonymous nature of terms, Aristotle would not accept such a characterization. Why? Because Aristotle may be called a kind of "essentialist."

In general, "essentialism" is simply the position that there are at least some things that have essential properties. The key to understanding essence, according to Aristotle, hinges on how "definition" functions. In a similar structure to the above quote, Aristotle explained, "When things have the name in common and the definition of being which corresponds to the name is the same, they are called *synonymous*." (1956: 1a5–7). Notice his phrase "definition of being." Volumes could be written on this topic; thus, we will just state the idea here as directly as possible. The Scholastic philosophers of the Middle Ages referred to Aristotle's characterization of naming in the following way: "equivocity" for *homonymous*; "univocity" for *synonymous*; "denominative" for *paronymous*. When different uses of the same term are said to be "equivocal" it means that, despite being the same word, the uses have different meanings: (dog) bark and (tree) bark; (financial) bank and (river) bank, and so on. In this way, the fact that the same terms, that is, arrangement of letters, appear in different uses is merely "accidental," and not "essential," to the different meanings. *Paronymous* terms—usually verbs—are called "denominative" because they are terms derived from nouns or adjectives. For example, "I see you eyeing my sandwich." "Eyeing" here (and its variant "eye ballin") is a verb derived from a noun (eye ball). However, it is univocity which interests us most here.

We need one more distinction, then, and by combining it with univocity, we can think through the way Aristotle envisioned "essence." The next distinction is between, on the one hand, that which is re-presented by being signified by a name and, on the other hand, the name in performing the signification. Aristotle cross-references two distinction, that is: the difference between "said of" and "not said of" and the difference between "present in" and "not present in." Thus, we arrive at a fourfold distinction: (1) "said of" and "not in"; (2) "in" and "not said of"; (3) "said of" and "in"; (4) "not said of" and "not in." (Aristotle 1956a: 1a20–1b5). In regard to the first, according to standard explications, we say "Socrates is a man." Whereas "man" is "said of" Socrates, "man" is not "in" Socrates. To believe that "man" were in Socrates would be to believe that every other "man" is—at least in part—Socrates. Of course, that is not the case. Aristotle's second example (2) is "knowledge." We say "knowledge is "in" Socrates, but we do not say that Socrates is knowledge.

Aristotle's third example may be a little tricky to understand, given the second example. (3) Aristotle's example is about the term "subject." Thus, in regard to "a subject," we say "knowledge is in a subject, the soul, and is also of a subject," for example "grammar." Notice—this is quite important—if it were not for Aristotle's "word-concept-thing" understanding of signification, then Aristotle would consider these two uses of "subject" to be homonymous; however, given his understanding of signification, the "subject" is always already, first and foremost, a subject of predication in the process of signification. Finally, (4) Aristotle's last example is about the indexical "this," that is, the "concrete particular" man or horse that we call "Socrates" or "Bucephalus," respectively. This last example led Scholastic philosophers to make a distinction between "the this" and "the what" or the "thisness" and the "whatness" of a being. Moreover, it is "the what" that indicates the essence of the being in question, and it is "the what" that is used in the being's definition.

Notice, then, in regard to Aristotle's first cross-reference of distinctions (1) that "man" is "said of" Socrates but not "in" Socrates reveals that the word "man" points to a universal *concept*. Further, this concept can function like a kind of category in regard to reality. For example, "man" may be "said of" Socrates, Plato, Aristotle, and Alexander "the Great" *univocally*. What is more, there seems to be—Aristotle apparently believed—a hierarchy among such *universals*, for example universal concepts. That is to say, notice that "animal" may also be said univocally in reference to Socrates, Plato, and so on; however, using the term "animal" also applies to cats and dogs. Hence, Aristotle reasoned that even though "animal" accurately and univocally refers to the beings called "Socrates" and "Plato," the term is not *specific* enough to indicate what the category to which Socrates and Plato belong *essentially* is. In this way, Aristotle deemed the universal concept "animal" to be the "genus" (i.e. in general, generic, genre) and the "specific difference" between Socrates and cats and dogs to be "rationality." As a result, "rational animal" characterizes a kind of natural category in terms of univocity and universality.

Finally, given all this terminology, we may say that "the whatness"— the category of what—to which Socrates and Plato belong indicates their essence. Of all that may be said of Socrates and Plato, for example that they enjoyed sandwiches or liked to dress in togas, they are essentially rational animals—*what* a human or "man" *is* is a rational animal. Recalling the previous paragraph; therefore, the definition of "man" is the logical (because we are still involved in Aristotle's "word-concept-thing" understanding of signification) genus combined with the specific difference. As a result, Aristotle uses definition to indicate a *thing's* essential nature (cf. Aristotle 1967: 141b24; cf. Aristotle 1964: 100a1–b3), and in this way, of course, definitions constitute the foundations of scientific knowledge for Aristotle (cf. Deslauriers 2007: 15). Aristotle contrasts "accidental" with "essential." It is merely accidental that Socrates wore one toga instead of another or had a certain length of beard. Hence, if we are to have *scientific* knowledge, it must be about what is essential not what is accidental (cf. Aristotle 1984: 1026b22–24).

In other words, suppose we want to have a science which studies plumbing. We might set out to study the kinds of actions that plumbers perform. However, we would not be interested in studying all of the actions that plumbers perform, lest we would need to consider such activities as: in what direction is a plumber's head pointed when the plumber sleeps at night; how much mayonnaise do plumbers put on sandwiches, and so on. Yet, notice, even though we may say that those activities are activities performed by plumbers, those activities are not *essential* to plumbing. Whereas we might attempt an objection here by suggesting psychology needs to study all aspects of an individual—including the accidental aspects of that individual, notice that, on the one hand, there can be no science of an individual, in that the individual is not a universal, and, on the other hand, psychology is the science or study of ψυχή, not some one particular person only. Thus, whatever will be the definition of ψυχή, it must be meant univocally and understood as applying universally to all instances of ψυχή. "For the definition of [ψυχή] ought to be true of every [ψυχή]." (Aristotle 1967: 139a26–27).

The above covers parts (a) and (b) of this section. What remains are: (c) truth, (d) the relation between science and methodology, and (e) styles of reading and historiography. Thus, the following distinctions regarding truth will be helpful for us, not only because they provide clarification regarding important vocabulary terms. The following distinctions may be considered "standard" in Western philosophy regarding how a claim may be understood as true (cf. Papineau 2012: 45–50; cf. Puntel 2001). The truth of claims may be divided into "semantic," "epistemological," and "ontological" truths. The distinction regarding "semantic" truths is "analytic" as opposed to "synthetic" truths. As a perennial example has it, we can know that the claim "All unmarried men are bachelors" is true, merely by knowing the meaning of all the words involved in the claim. That type of truth is "analytic" truth. In regard to the claim "The majority of the people in the building you are currently in are bachelors," it is not clear merely from the words used in the claim whether it is true or false; rather, we would need to check the facts of the situation.

The distinction operable in regard to "epistemological" truth is between *a priori* and *a posteriori*. Though at times this distinction may sound a good deal like the "semantic" distinction, this distinction is between kinds of knowledge; yet, at the same time, there may be some overlap, since we are talking about truth claims, that is, meaningful statements, one must be able to understand the meaning of the claim. A classic example, then, shows that so long as we understand the meaning of the term "triangle," then we can have *a priori* knowledge that the next triangle we encounter will have three sides. An example of an *a posteriori* claim would be "Cats like to eat mayonnaise." In order for us to know whether that claim is true, we would have to perform observations. Notice, then, the semantic distinction is analogous with the epistemological distinction; yet, at the same time, the former is about the meaning of words, and the latter is about having knowledge.

The distinction operable in regard to "ontological" truth claims is between "necessary" and "contingent" truth. Now, this distinction can be even trickier depending on how we conceive of "chance," or whether we believe in "free choice." Supposing we believe in chance and free choice, then we may say that necessary truths are truths that could not have been otherwise, and contingent truths are truths that could have been otherwise. We will think about these distinctions a good deal more; however, at this point, it will be enough to note that "ontological" truth claims refer to beings or the nature of events and things. Thus, there are what may seem trivially true examples, that is, "If an animal-body is not alive, then it is dead." The point is not so much about the meaning of the words or our knowledge as it is about the necessity of being. That is, necessarily, some natural thing is either alive or dead.

Combining the distinctions regarding naming and definition along with those regarding truth, we may now describe the distinctions regarding science and methodology. To begin, when we know that we are dealing with a system, we need to know how the system is to be understood. That is, are we dealing with an atomistic or holistic system? In regard to the former, all of the parts come together to form the whole. In regard to the latter, the whole is greater than the sum of its parts. Many philosophical puzzles emerge regarding the being of the whole—if in fact it is greater than the sum of its parts; however, for our purpose at this point, we merely want to notice how to think through such a characterization of a system. An example from Aristotle's *Metaphysics* should suffice.

According to Aristotle, imagine having all of the materials needed to construct a house. Suppose the material to be merely laying in a heap. We may even go so far as to think that every part of the house is already fashioned to specification, so long as we think of all the fashioned parts as merely being in a pile or heap. Now, Aristotle points out (1) those parts make up a whole heap; (2) the parts of the heap could be exhaustively fashioned, that is, without any parts left over to make something other than a house; (3) when the parts of the heap are re-organized such that those same parts go from *being* a heap to *being* a house, then at the moment the heap becomes a house, the house may be understood as more than the heap, that is, the sum of the parts (cf. Aristotle 1984: 1041b5). Just how relevant this distinction is for thinking through psychology may be surprising. Ultimately, it seems the principle of how to understand the constitution of the system under examination—whether it be atomistic or holistic—has a reciprocal relationship with the methodology one uses to examine the system. That is to say, one selects a method for examining organic wholes, when one believes there are organic wholes—greater than the sum of their parts—to be examined, and one selects a method for examining uni-dimensionally analyzable wholes, when one believes the system to be examined is exhaustively represented by its parts.

In regard to the history of Western psychology, as we shall see, to generalize approaches to the question of how to methodically study ψυχή, we need both the distinction between natural and human sciences and atomistic and holistic systems. If we are following Aristotle's essentialism, we may think that science investigates naturally occurring kinds, and therefore, if there is to be a science of ψυχή, then we will need to approach it in terms of it universal and univocally identifiable parts. Yet, we would need to further clarify how the parts should be understood as relating to the whole. For example, ψυχή itself may even be understood as a part of a greater whole. In contradistinction to the universality and univocal identifiability as criteria, a more "human science" approach may treat the categories to be examined as more of a "social construction" (cf. Daniel 1986). Such an approach would place more emphasis on the historicity of the parts of a system and the historicity of the principles involved in the organization of the parts of a system. Yet, again, further clarification would be needed regarding whether the system in question were understood as atomistic or holistic.

Given that some may understand Aristotle's essentialism as having a kind of *a priori* necessity, that is, epistemological and ontological truth to it, how may there even be room for a more "human science" reading of the relation between word, concept, and thing? The answer involves how concepts are understood to be "universal." On the one hand, the context of this question is called "the problem of universals," and, again, much could be said about the problem. On the other hand, a brief characterization of different readings of "universals" is sufficient for the purpose of this book. For we are not attempting to solve the problem in as much as we want to be acquainted with the different possible answers to use as so many different characterizations when thinking through the history and systems of Western psychology. In other words, we can understand the philosophical principles involved in the various ways the different understandings of universals are characterized without attempting to solve the philosophical problem which would eliminate all but one characterization.

The possible positions are: "Platonic Realism," "Moderate Realism," "Conceptualism," and "Nominalism." Basically, Platonic Realism takes universals to be things themselves. That is, a *category* of material things may be understood as a real non-material thing, or as an idea that does not depend on human minds for its reality. Moderate Realism takes universals to be real, but only in relation to the actual things which fit into the universal category. That is to say, there is no Platonic heaven in which we find the "universal triangle," but rather individual triangles whose presence makes the univocal name "triangle" refer to something real. Conceptualism holds that the universals are concepts in minds, and though we may be able to use these concepts to "pick out" things external to minds, such ability does not mean that the universals are real outside the mind. Nominalism takes universals to be merely names; that is, they only have a "vocal," so to speak, reality, and that "reality" may be merely conventional. Thus, notice Realism, Conceptualism, and Nominalism places emphasis on thing, concept, and word, respectively.

Finally, in regard to the relation between science and methodology, these possible positions function like principles. For example, the difference between "description" and "explanation" indicates a perennial distinction regarding science and methodology. Staying with our philosophical distinction between things, concepts, and words, a "description" refers to the use of words to describe some thing (or event), and an "explanation" refers to a special kind of description; that is, one that accounts for things or events in terms of essences or causes. This means an explanation is a description in univocal terms regarding the universal aspects of things involved in some event (or state of affairs). "Causation," then, is considered a part of an explanation because it refers to a characterization of *relations* between the universal aspects involved. Thus, we are said to "solve" a problem when we provide an "explanation" in regard to the descriptions found in a problem. Yet, as we will see below, the closing of the Early Modern Period involved David Hume's (1711–1776) infamous skepticism regarding causation, and in many ways, we still feel the ripples from Hume's skepticism in the Contemporary Period.

One way to paraphrase the results of Hume's skepticism regarding causation is in regard to the oft quoted: "Correlation does not imply causation," or even better, "Correlation does not necessarily mean causation." We may characterize the movement forward in history regarding this skepticism as a movement from "Correlation does not necessarily mean causation" to "There may be no such *thing* as causation" or "Causation is not *real*" (emphases for the sake of referring to previously discussed distinctions). The results may also be paraphrased in terms of "description" and "explanation"—basically (think Aristotle's Four Causes here) exchange "explanation" for "cause." That is, "There is no such *thing* as explanation," or "Explanation is not *real*." Notice, then, if explanation is a special kind of description, which turns out to be illusory, then we are—as one standard Contemporary narrative has it—left only with descriptions and descriptions of descriptions. Hence, these distinctions—between description and explanation—are essential for thinking through the history of psychology, and we will discuss them throughout the rest of the book. For now, a note regarding methodology is in order.

One standard Contemporary approach to the methodological dimension of psychology attempts to undermine explanation, and, thereby, a natural science methodology in the study of ψυχή—despite, or precisely because of, its association with the "scientific method." Thus, the distinction between description and explanation points directly to the distinction between psychology as a "human science" and psychology as a "natural science." Recall Dilthey's—in no uncertain terms—suggestion that:

> Psychology can be a foundational human science only if it stays within the limits of a descriptive discipline that establishes facts and uniformities among facts. It must clearly distinguish itself from explanative psychology, which strives to derive the whole human, cultural world by means of certain assumptions. (Dilthey 1989: 84)

Of course, these "certain assumptions" are those discussed above regarding universal specification of things. It is in this way that distinctions may be understood as "hermeneutic" in that they refer to different ways of describing or "interpreting," as opposed to a process of essential specification. In regard then to this essential tension between description and explanation, "interpretation" becomes a principle in the study of ψυχή. As we will see, this principle can be pushed to the extreme of questioning that there are any things at all or, at least, that there can be no real difference between the identity of a thing and the concepts and words used to describe it (cf. Berger and Luckmann 1966; cf. Fleck 1979; Gergen 1985).

The historical period associated with such an extreme understanding of the principle is, of course, called "Postmodernism." One way to *describe* "Postmodernism" would be to note the manner in which proponents of Postmodernism identify standard narratives—such as those found in the study of ψυχή—and call the formation of such narratives into question, often suggesting alternative narratives, since no narrative can be a "best explanation" of reality. One way this is accomplished is by highlighting various "styles" of interpreting or "reading" reality. This makes sense, of course, because—as the story goes—we do not have "reality" so much as we have words, such as the word "reality." Just as above we noted, then, that explanation leads to the "solution" of problems, description without explanation is said to lead to "dissolution." The idea being that the problem itself is merely present due to a nexus of description or interpretation—the "bewitchment of language." It is thought, then, that a re-description may result in the problem's being "dissolved" back into mere words. Thus, two more "hermeneutics-related" distinctions will suffice for now: the distinction between hermeneutics and deconstruction and distinctions regarding different styles of reading.

The distinction between hermeneutics and deconstruction may be understood by recalling that "hermeneutics" points to the study of different ways of describing or "interpreting" things, as opposed to a process of essential specification. "Deconstruction," then, points to the fact that whatever interpretation is presently accepted, it will eventually be re-described or "interpreted-away," so to speak. It is as if, were hermeneutics a snapshot of description change, deconstruction would be a—seemingly perpetual—time-lapse image of description change. In this way, both hermeneutics and deconstruction fall on the description over explanation side of the debate, and both participate in the "human science" reading of ψυχή. What is more, deconstruction—despite being associated with Postmodernism—is actually the way out of Postmodernism. That is to say, whereas Postmodernists may justify the re-structuring of knowledge and power systems based on the idea that the structure is not grounded in an essential explanation, deconstruction reveals that whatever new structure takes the place of the old structure, the new structure will itself not be grounded in an essential distinction. Thus, despite "being in the same camp," so to speak, regarding psychology as a science and description over explanation, Postmodernists tend to not like the deconstructionist "gadfly" who undermines what may be seen as a Postmodern political agenda. This distinction emerges as essential for contemporary psychology, as we will discuss below; however, it is beneficial to briefly explicate it here, so as to show an awareness of the distinction and related issues as we move through the historically based principles in subsequent chapters.

In conclusion, we will discuss "styles of reading." This discussion points back to the Introduction's discussion of historiography in that historiography may be understood as a "writing" that involves the interpretation and "reading" of the past. We may identify "three modes of reading" and "four styles of writing history." In regard to the former:

> there are three modes of reading: (1) reading aloud, (2) 'phonic' reading, where, as in thinking, the sounds of what is read remain in the mind, and (3) normal 'efficient' rapid reading, where the sense 'eliminates' the sound. Poetry (and usually drama) always requires phonic reading. The translator, at least, has to be ready to switch (switching the sound on) to phonic reading when faced with conversation in the texts and rhetorical writing such as poetry and drama. (Newmark 1998: 1; cf. Vlieghe 2016)

Notice that "switching the sound on" regarding words reveals a different way to "read" and interpret the meaning of the words. Further, whereas "reading aloud" invokes a performative "reading" of the words, "efficient" or "normal" reading performs a type of selection (i.e. "turning off the sound"). Highlighting the "selection" or "interpretation" taking place is important because the meaning of what is read is ultimately founded upon the groundwork laid by such interpretation. In this way, a Postmodern strategy for approaching natural science and essential specification is to emphasize the importance of what is "marginalized" or "excluded" before "natural science" even begins its interpretations.

On the one hand, the Postmodern strategy may be read as a critical description of the scientific hypothetico-deductive method itself. On the other hand, the method of natural science "makes things that work," and one engineer reading the instructions provided from another probably does not care to have illustrations and comments regarding the facial expressions or voice inflections from the engineer(s) producing the instructions. Yet, and this becomes an interesting peculiarity involved in the study of ψυχή, is it the case that "theatrics" and "performance" influence the results? To draw an analogy that might infuriate some "natural scientists" (cf. Sokal 1996; cf. Sokal and Bricmont 1998), is the principle of superposition or something like wave-particle duality (cf. Schrödinger 1926) operative in the study of ψυχή (cf. Chapman and Chapman 1982; cf. Schwartz et al. 2005; cf. Bruza et al. 2015)?

Finally, the history and systems of psychology is itself not immune to such criticism. Consider the following way to systematize (or "write") the history of psychology: (a) Canon-formation, (b) Doxography, (c) Rational Reconstruction, and (d) Historical Reconstruction. Whereas Doxography is thought to perform the most "interpretive violence" to the historicity of past thinkers, texts and systems, Historical Reconstruction is thought to perform the least "interpretive violence." However, recalling our discussion of Presentism and Historicism above, it will always be possible for someone to advance the critical claim that Historical Reconstruction is too interpretation-based and temporally displaced to be non-Presentist enough. Such a tension will always be a part of Canon-formation. "Canon-formation" refers not only to the practice of determining what readings are to be considered legitimate to study within a discipline, but it also involves determining which styles of interpretation are deemed appropriate to bring to the readings. For example, it is nearly impossible to find a textbook for the History and Systems of Psychology today which includes a chapter on "demonic possession." Thus, Canon-formation functions at the level of disciplines analogous to the way "natural science" selects what will count as an object to be studied.

"Doxography" refers to "awkward attempts to make a new question fit an old canon" (Rorty 1984: 62). This would be like using history to inquire into Aristotle's theory of "neural backpropagation." Doxography is, therefore, the style of interpreting the past which most often receives the criticism of "anachronism." In attempting to frame the history of psychology in terms of progress, some History and Systems textbooks, despite projecting a rational or historical reconstruction, lapse into Doxography (cf. Baydala and Smythe 2012). What seem to be among the greatest criticisms of Doxography are that, one, such textbooks include large amounts of information, and sometimes it seems as though the only relevance is that the information pertains to the historical period in question; two, by definition, Doxography does not attempt to articulate the historicity of the topics or artifacts under discussion. Rational reconstruction, in contrast, may or may not attempt to articulate the historicity involved. Rational reconstruction involves using history to help expand our own present viewpoint. This was praised above as a value of learning history.

Lastly, whereas rational reconstruction is "pragmatic" and possibly "philosophical," historical reconstruction may be "original," "pragmatic," or "philosophical." Historical reconstruction seeks to abide by the principle that, as "Intellectual Historian" Quentin Skinner states it: "No agent can eventually be said to have meant or done something which he could never be brought to accept as a correct *description* of what he had meant or done [emphasis added]." (Skinner 1969: 60; quoted in Rorty 1984: 50). In a self-critical note, then, we may say that in the writing of this book we are actively avoiding Doxography, and showing how to be critical of Canon-formation—while essentially following along the path of figures, texts, and topics considered Canonical in the West, as we oscillate between rational and historical reconstruction. This is, on the one hand, an admission of the inevitability of the Presentism of our viewpoint, while, on the other hand, an admission of a deep commitment to the affirmation of the historicity of psychology's subject matter, for example, even literally at the level of writing "ψυχή" as a reminder that those who study "neural backpropagation" are in solidarity with the concerns and commitments of Aristotle, among others.

## 2.3    Principles from the Philosophy of Psychology Necessary for Thinking Through the History & Systems of Psychology

The general principles under discussion in this section provide a philosophical vocabulary with which to think through the different worldview-shifts in the history of Western psychology. They may be divided into general principles of: (a) Ontology, (b) Ontological Priority, and (c) Agency, or the question of the "freedom of the will." Due to the historicity of the principles related to "Theory of Knowledge," or "Epistemology" and "Criteriology," their discussion, which continues here from Sects. 1.4 and 2.2 above is distributed across the historical periods as the third category of principles discussed in Chaps. 3, 4, and 5 below.

"Ontology" refers to the study of be-ing., or, more precisely, "ontology" refers to the study of the be-ing of beings. The convention of writing "being" with a hyphen emphasizes the term's use as the participle of the verb "to be," as opposed to a noun (cf. Wilhelmsen 1956: 59). Thus, if we were to count the beings in the room, each person in the room would count as a being; however, in order to signify the activity of being that person, so as to examine the activity, we emphasize the "ing" by writing "be-ing." In this way, we can think about the difference in be-ing of the different beings in the room, with less confusion.

So, on the one hand, when we ask: What *is* ψυχή? We are engaging in ontology. Volumes could be written on "ontology" and "The History of Ontology," so we will be purposefully succinct here, and in keeping with our discussion of "things, concepts, and words," notice how all three of them can be seen from the standpoint of ontology. Whereas philosophy of language or linguistics may be the proper domain for "words" and logic for "concepts," to ontology—it would seem at first—only the study of "things" belongs. However, ontology should be considered the most general and fundamental of all branches of philosophy in that if what we set out to study *is* at all, then ontology encompasses it. In other words, "concepts" have the kind of be-ing specific to them, for example we may say their be-ing is "mental" or that they are "mental" beings. Likewise, of words we may say their be-ing is "verbal" or "written," or, more generally, we could engage in an examination of the be-ing of signs, etc. Thus, the point emphasized here is that "ontology" should be considered the most general and fundamental of the branches of philosophy and that no(-) thing that we discuss in psychology can possibly escape its viewpoint. Of course, that is because if what we are talking about *is* any(-)thing at all, then, we can study its be-ing.

Since technically "ontology" names a genus and the "ontology of psychology" a species of general ontology, in order to be clear we will start with be-ing in general. As Paul J. Glenn (1893–1957) rightly noted, "Ontology is a *science*. That is to say, it is a body of doctrine, set forth in a manner that is systematic, logical, and complete, and it presents reasons to justify its data and to evidence its conclusions." (Glenn 1939: 3). One way to ask a first question, then, in regard to be-ing in general may be: How many different kinds of be-ing are there? For our purpose, the possible answers to this question are: One, Two, or Unknown. Further, the traditional possible characterizations of this enumeration are: Material, Non-Material (Mental or Spiritual), or Unknown. Thus, if someone takes a "monist" position, they believe there is only one kind of be-ing, and the next question we would ask is how they characterize that kind of be-ing. Of course, "materialism" tends to refer to a monist ontology in which all be-ing is characterized as material. When someone takes a "dualist" position, they believe there are two different kinds of be-ing, and the next question we would ask is how they characterize the relationship between these two different kinds of being—ultimately material and non-material.

Dualist ontology in regard to psychology is almost always depicted in terms of Descartes' infamous "mind-body" problem. Thus, the be-ing of the body is said to be material and the be-ing of the mind to be non-material. That some of the content of experience comes from the body and some from the mind characterizes a "problem of heterogeneity." That is to say, ultimately, how are we to account for the combination of two ontologically different be-ings? Dualists inevitably seem to privilege one of the kinds of be-ing over the other kind. In either case, we will examine the relationship between the different types of be-ing in terms of ontological priority. That is, the different ways to characterize the relationship between mind and matter or non-material and material give priority to one of the types of be-ing. What is more, the "problem of heterogeneity" persists for theorizing in psychology even if our dualism is only a "property dualism."

Recalling Aristotle's distinction between "essential" and "accidental," general ontology analogously differentiates between "substances" and "properties." In other words, just as we can make various changes to beings without changing the being essentially, so too we can understand non-essential property changes as changes to the properties of a thing, rather than changes to the thing's substance. For example, when a sitting Socrates stands up and dances or changes clothes, it is accurate to say that he has, in some way, changed; however, the change is not a "substantial change." A substantial change (think about "essence" and "species" from the discussion above) would be for him to change into a cat or, according to Aristotle, to die.

The distinction, then, between substance and property allows for different ways of relating, articulating, and responding to the "problem of heterogeneity." For example, it is possible for a theorist to recognize that there seem to be non-material be-ings, despite the theorist's commitment to only thinking of material as substantial. Thus, it is possible to be a "substance monist" and a "property dualist" simultaneously. In fact, this is one potential solution to the mind-body problem in that it denies heterogeneity. That is, the be-ing of the body has an experience and the properties of that experience which the body expresses are both material and non-material, for example sensations and thoughts. The important point here is that be-ing can be differentiated in terms of priority—substances are prior to their properties. Socrates must be before he can be dancing, and when he stops dancing he does not stop be-ing.

Now, because it is not always the case that substance is understood in terms of matter, Aristotle provided us with a standard vocabulary with which we can discuss substances, even if we cannot see or touch them. The term is "substratum" and its variant "substrate." Thus, we can speak of a substrate persisting "beneath" property changes. This is one of the ways philosophers argue that you are still the same person as you were when you were an infant—certainly you have changed since then; the idea is some substratum has persisted through all of the change between then and now. In order to avoid equivocation it is helpful to use "substrate" instead of "subject." The latter term refers to the subject in a predication. Again, ontological priority will help provide the principles with which to think through the special ontology of psychology. However, before proceeding to a discussion of ontological priority, we should discuss some standard ontological terms used to characterize dualistic relations in regard to properties and two principles of the special ontology of psychology: *qualia* and propositional attitudes.

We often find the following terms used to characterize dualistic relations: "Representation," "Reduction," "Elimination," "Supervenience," "Emergence," and "Epiphenomenal." The term "Representation" is used to characterize the sense in which one property is said to represent another. For example, the imagination is supposed to produce an image which represents some external body, for example a sandwich. In this way we could say imagination re-presents some(-)thing which is physical in a non-physical way. "Representation," then, is often used as the genus, or generic term, to cover all the ways in which ψυχή re-presents what it is originally external to it. In this way, a sensation, a perception, a fantasy image, a concept, and an idea, for example, may all be understood as different specifications, or types, of representation.

The term "Reduction" refers to reducing some theory to a different theory or the existence of some being to a different being. Thus, simply put, if there are two theories, say physics and psychology, and it turns out that all of the laws and theories of psychology can be explained by the laws and theories of physics, but not the other way around, then psychology could be "reduced" to physics. In terms of beings, perhaps the easiest example would be illusions. When we experience a "magic trick" for the first time we may not be able to adequately explain what happened, and when asked to do so we may produce all sorts of fantastic suppositions; however, when we hear an adequate explanation, for example, there were two ladies in the box and the magician cut the box between them, then those fantastic suppositions are reduced to the actuality of the situation. Similarly, in terms of mind-body dualism, some psychologists believe mental properties reduce to the physical properties of the body, and theories invoking mental beings ultimately reduce to theories involving non-mental beings.

Reduction plays an important role for thinking in psychology. As will be discussed below, physics and interaction between physical beings is often characterized as "mechanistic" and "deterministic." This means, of course, that given certain conditions, the behavior of physical systems seems to be quite predictable. Such is one of the benefits of understanding psychology as a natural science, that is the predictability and control associated with natural scientific experiments. In fact, this is so much so the case that some theorists—such as proponents of "Radical Empiricism" or "Positivism"—go so far as to suggest there may be little need to answer the ontological question, namely, what is ψυχή? However, when we ask the ontological question, as noted above, it can be answered in material or non-material, that is, physical or non-physical, terms. When emphasis is placed on physical description or explanation, then reduction may be the strategy used to limit the beings under discussion to those which can be accounted for mechanistically or deterministically.

The distinction at work here then is between "integrated" and "organismic" wholes. Whereas the natural science perspective tends to think of systems in atomistic terms, the human science perspective tends to think of ψυχή as a *gestalt*, that is, a whole that is greater than the sum of its parts. Thus, standardly, the parts may be "integrated" into a whole and the whole may be reduced to its parts from a natural scientific perspective. However, from a human science perspective, though integration is important, the essential feature of ψυχή and the beings studied by psychology may, in fact, be their ir-reducible nature. In fact, many theorists regarding ψυχή today seem to have accepted that there are some non-physical aspects or properties to the human psychological experience which cannot be reduced. Those aspects go under the name "*qualia*." After a brief word about them, we will conclude this discussion of reduction.

Though Charles S. Peirce (1839–1914) is often credited with first using the term in a way that points toward its present meaning (cf. Peirce 1982), C.I. (Clarence Irving) Lewis (1883–1964) is credited with solidifying the meaning of the term "*qualia*" to refer to the aspects of sensory experience which are non-material and purely subjective, such as each individual's experience of the color red or the scent of a rose.

There *are* recognizable qualitative characters of the given [in an experience], which may be repeated in different experiences, and are thus a sort of universals; I call these "qualia." But although such qualia are universals, in the sense of being recognized from one to another experience, they must be distinguished from the properties of objects. Confusion of these two is characteristic of many historical conceptions, as well as of current essence-theories. The quale is directly intuited, given, and is not the subject of any possible error because it is *purely subjective* [emphasis added]. The property of an object is objective. (1991: 121)

Lewis clarifies that by "universals" he does not mean the "'universals' of logic, which we discussed above." (Ibid: 61). Lewis was also concerned to note that *qualia* "have no names." (Ibid). That is to say, the particular visual sense-data of an individual's experience of the color red—the "what it is like" *for you* when you see the color red—is too subjective to be differentiated from others and thereby named; yet, so long as the color can be seen, then sensory experiences universally have such qualities, though the experience of the quality may be different for each individual (cf. Nagel 1974; cf. Levine 1983; cf. Jackson 1986; cf. Chalmers 1996).

Notice, that we do not need a special apparatus to be able to recognize the existence or presence of these aspects in our experiences. Thus, the standard way philosophers and psychologists began referring to our ability to pay attention to *qualia* is with the, perhaps historically unfortunate, term "introspection." The term may be unfortunate because it is so vague and general.[1] The "intro" prefix suggests one needs to look "in" or "inward." However, the *qualia* are an aspect of the representation itself, so there is no need to take the representation and then go searching for *qualia*. Lewis attempts to capture this relationship between *qualia* and representation by using the term "given." That is, the *qualia* are simply there in our experiences. *Qualia* are quite important then because they seem to represent a "line in the sand," so to speak, that even the most hard-nosed natural scientists cannot deny. In terms of reduction, since *qualia* seem to be irreducible to physical properties, the natural scientific strategy has been to deny the need to reduce them. In other words, natural science can get along fine by just ignoring them (cf. Kim 1998, 2005). Yet, the human science perspective points to the fact that *qualia*, in many ways, factor into the very things that make human life human and the value of "having" a ψυχή. For example, the smell of rose or a sandwich, the experience of humor, or the experience of love.

It is convenient, then, to speak of three different kinds of reduction; that is, to make a distinction between "explanation reduction," "ontological reduction," and "eliminative reduction" (cf. Fodor 1968). As a simple example, "explanation reduction" refer to the reduction of one explanation to another—this may or may not be considered a sign of "progress," that is, one theory replacing another. We have been discussing "ontological reduction," that is, a dualism regarding the properties of experience with the idea that the non-physical aspects reduce to—can be accounted for in terms of—the physical properties. However, "eliminative reduction," or simply "elimination" refers to the idea that the non-physical should and will be explained away; for example, whether in terms of a physical theory that shows psychological theory to be superfluous or in terms of the realization that non-physical beings are illusions. This latter characterization is the one more often claimed in the Contemporary Period, and is known as "Eliminative Materialism."

The position of Eliminative Materialism suggests mental properties do not actually exist, rather we tend to talk as though they exist because our language was merely a kind of "folk psychology" prior to advances made in technology and neuroscience (cf. Sellars 1956). Thus, the argument goes that talk of mental properties, for example belief, desire and love, should be "eliminated" in favor of talk regarding neurochemical activity. Moreover, notice, it is not that love *reduces* to sympathetic nervous system activity, which would suggest that love exists but depends on sympathetic nervous system activity for its be-ing; rather, love is supposed to be eliminated by sympathetic nervous system activity, such that were we always aware of the truth of nervous system activity, we would never have invented the word "love." Hence, it would follow for eliminative *materialists* that consciousness and mental properties are "illusions" (cf. Churchland 1981; cf. Dennett 1991; cf. Churchland 1992).

The term "supervenience" is often used to characterize the relation between a mental property and a property of the body when the mental property cannot be reduced to or eliminated in terms of the physical property of the body. Definitions of "supervenience" are usually highly technical sounding, and comment on it as a "relation of covariation." Simply put, we say M properties "supervene" on B properties only if variations in M properties will vary with respect to B properties. As one contemporary philosopher of mind noted,

> mental characteristics are in some sense dependent, or supervenient, on physical characteristics. Such supervenience might be taken to mean that there cannot be two events alike in all physical respects but differing in some mental respect, or that an object cannot alter in some mental respect without altering in some physical respect. (Davidson 1970: 88)

Thus, changes in the *qualia* of experience will have some co-varying changes to the body of the ψυχή in question, according to the principle of supervenience. As we will see later, supervenience plays a role in understanding how "causation" in psychology works. On the one hand, those who embrace the principle of supervenience accept the presence of non-physical properties or *qualia*. On the other hand, despite acknowledging the presence of ir-reducible non-physical properties, if causation can only occur in terms of physical interaction, then the natural science-based physicalists tend to think the non-physical properties are essentially undermined or irrelevant to the science of psychology—or, rather, biology.

Lastly, we will discuss "emergence," "epiphenomenalism," and "propositional attitudes" before discussing ontological priority. "Emergence" is another term used to characterize the ir-reducible relation between mental and physical properties. Thus, we often hear that "consciousness emerges, or is an emergent property, of the brain." The value of the characterization, ontologically, is thought to be the manner in which it uses physical be-ing to account for the origin of non-physical beings, despite the inability to reduce the non-physical beings to the physical. "Epiphenomenalism" is a term which extends the meaning of emergence with an explicit focus on causation. That is to say, when we say that two properties (one physical and one non-physical) are "epiphenomenal," then what we are saying is that the physical property accounts for the origin of (or causes) the non-physical property, and the non-physical property cannot be reduced to the physical; however, whereas the physical property has causal-power, the non-physical does not.

For example, *qualia* exist; however, it is not the smell of the rose that causes us to do anything subsequent to the experience. Rather, anything we do subsequent to the experience—despite our characterizing the cause of our subsequent action in terms of the *qualia*—is actually caused by the physical properties which were "epiphenomenal" with the *qualia*. It is important to notice that just as epiphenomenalism was originally discussed by William James (1842–1910) in the mechanistic terms of "automatism" (cf. James 1918), so too the principle of epiphenomenalism makes way for the determinism of the natural scientific perspective—relegating the non-physical properties to something like, Gilbert Ryle's (1990–1976) infamous characterization, a (causally inefficacious) "ghost in the machine" (1949).

Now, just as we can see a structural analogy between essence and accident and substance and property, so too there is a distinction to be made between "state" and "content." Thus, "property" and "state" are synonymous; however, we tend to use the term "state" when we want to focus on its content. Moreover, the initial importance of distinguishing between states and their content is to differentiate between, on the one hand, qualitative properties of experience regarding which we do not tend to distinguish between the property and its content (*qualia*), and, on the other hand, properties or states of experience regarding which we do tend to distinguish between the property and its content. Examples of the former type of property include sensations, tickles, and pains, and examples of the latter include beliefs, desires, and fears. Notice that the latter examples seem to have a "content" to them such that the property points beyond itself.

In other words, the latter examples involve what "phenomenologists" call "intentionality." Thus, it may be helpful to look at the meaning of "intentionality," and the classic statement of the meaning of "intentionality" comes from Franz Brentano (1838–1917).

Every mental phenomenon is characterized by what the Scholastics of the Middle Ages called the intentional (or mental) inexistence of an object, and what we might call, though not wholly unambiguously, reference to a *content* [emphasis added], direction toward an object (which is not to be understood here as meaning a thing) ... although they do not do so in the same way. In ... judgement something is affirmed or denied, in love loved, in hate hated, in desire desired and so on ... No physical phenomenon exhibits anything like it. (1973: 88–89)

Notice, then, for those who do follow the distinction, be-ing tickled may be understood as a property of the body; likewise, whereas pain would be a property of the body, worry would be a mental state, for example, about potential pain—in which case "pain" would be the "intentional" *content* of the mental state of worry.

Of course, the content of a state can be—and usually is—characterized in terms of a "proposition." Martin believes *it will rain*; Aristotle worries *the hemlock will be painful*. Thus, philosophers often refer to these states as "propositional attitudes." The term comes from Bertrand Russell (1872–1970).

What sort of name shall we give to verbs like "believe" and "wish" and so forth? I should be inclined to call them "propositional verbs." This is merely a suggested name for convenience, because they are verbs which have the form of relating an object to a proposition ... you might call them "attitudes," but I should not like that because it is a psychology term, and although all the instances in our experience are psychological, there is no reason to suppose that all the verbs I am talking of are psychological ... I can only say all I know are. (Russell 2010: 60)

Thus, in regard to the special ontology of psychology, in *describing* human experience in terms of the beings studied by psychology, we may say that ψυχή is said to have, or take, various "attitudes" toward "propositions." Because the content of propositional attitudes is usually expressed in the non-technical and non-jargon terms of "ordinary language," approaches in psychology that describe the activity of ψυχή in such a way are often labeled "folk psychology" or, the wider term, "commonsense psychology." However, as noted above, eliminative materialists believe we should eliminate such approaches to psychology completely.

In sum, so far in this section we have discussed the principles of general ontology, monism and dualism and substance and property, some standard ontological terms used to characterize dualistic relations in regard to properties, and two principles of the special ontology of psychology: *qualia* and propositional attitudes. We are now ready to discuss "ontological priority." Again, just as "priority" means to be deemed more important or to be dealt with first, the terms used to refer to types of "ontological priority" are often used to refer to entire systems of psychology. Thus, we have "Materialism," "Idealism," "Empiricism," "Nativism," "Vitalism," "Mechanism," "Behaviorism," "Structuralism," and "Functionalism."

In general, Materialism and Idealism are polar opposites. Put simply, "Materialism" (which at this point may be considered synonymous with "Physicalism") refers to a monistic ontological system in which everything, that is, all beings, are material. Thus, "Idealism" refers to a monistic ontological system in which everything, that is, all beings, are non-material. In this way, of course, "ontological priority" is given to material in the former system and the non-material in the latter. Moving on to dualisms, then, the relation between "Empiricism" and "Nativism" is analogous to that between "Materialism" and "Idealism." That is to say, in reference to ontology, "Empiricism" acknowledges a dualism of material and non-material beings; however, it gives priority to the material. "Nativism," then, in reference to ontology, refers to a dualism of material and non-material beings; however, it gives priority to the non-material. Here, of course, "priority" means a kind of "firstness" and position of importance over the other type of substance or property. Now, to be clear both of these terms—"Empiricism" and "Nativism"—have other meanings, and though these other meanings will appear below, some general remarks may benefit us here.

In regard to "theory of knowledge" or "criteriology" and "epistemology," "Empiricism" and "Nativism" refer to types of justification for our knowledge. Whereas "Empiricism" refers to our gaining knowledge through the material aspects of experience, "Nativism" refers to our gaining knowledge from the non-material "innate ideas" in regard to experience. What is more, the term "Empiricism" can be further clarified into "Classical Empiricism," "Sensationalism" or "Sensism," and "Radical

Empiricism" or "Positivism." The theory of knowledge characterization of "Empiricism" just given refers to "Classical Empiricism," that is, the source of our knowledge is the materially rooted bodily senses. Notice, that Classical Empiricism does not deny dualism. Sensationalism, then, is the position that does deny dualism, in favor of materialism. Why is this not simply materialism? Because "Materialism" refers to an ontological position, and "Sensationalism" refers to an epistemological position. Lastly, "Radical Empiricism" usually goes by the name "Positivism," which is a position identified by the "verification principle." This principle holds all knowledge—in order to count as knowledge—must receive verification through sensory-experience. What is the essential distinction between "Radical Empiricism" and "Sensationalism"? "Sensationalism" or "Sensism" is the epistemological position that denies the dualism, whereas "Radical Empiricism" does not deny the dualism, it only declares it unknowable.

The distinction between "Vitalism" and "Mechanism" invokes the distinction, regarding systems, between holism and atomism, respectively. The historical beacons regarding this distinction, and standardly invoked to explicate it, are Aristotle and post-Cartesian Early Modern philosophers. Basically, Aristotle took living biological things understood holistically to be the epitome of natural beings. Thus, natural beings are characterized, teleologically and holistically, by attributing a "vital force" to them. Since this "force" leaves the body when the body dies, the principle of "Vitalism" distinguishes ψυχή as *more than* a mere "meat machine." Of course, Descartes and the Early Modern conception of the body may be characterized in mechanical terms. That is, recalling the controllability and predictability of causation regarding physical systems, organic life has often been characterized in atomistic and mechanistic ways. For example, the body is mechanistically understood as a machine made out of meat, and the atomistic conception of such a machine suggest the whole is simply the integration of all its parts working together.

Similar to the tripartite characterization of "Empiricism," the Contemporary term "Behaviorism" may be characterized as threefold. It is important to keep in mind that "Behaviorism" is equally a technical term in both philosophy and psychology; this may be contrasted, for example, with the term "Psychoanalysis," which is not. We may distinguish between "Logical Behaviorism," "Methodological Behaviorism," and "Radical Behaviorism." Logical behaviorism "maintains that all mental predicates (or descriptive and explanatory terms) may be translated, paraphrased, defined, analyzed, reduced, eliminated, or replaced by behavioral and environmental terms." (Margolis 1984: 36). Methodological behaviorism is quite simply the idea that psychology should only study behavior; that is to say, psychology should not investigate "mental events," any kind of "internal experience," or relations between cognitions. In this way, methodological behaviorism is analogous to eliminative materialism's eliminative reduction of the mental, that is, non-material.

Lastly, "Radical Behaviorism" refers to B. F. Skinner's (1904–1990) position that mental states are only "collateral products of the contingencies which generate behavior" (1953: 75), and his outright denial—in his book titled *Beyond Freedom and Dignity*—of free will (1971). That is,

> mental or cognitive activities have been invented … What is involved in attention is not a change of stimulus or of receptors but the contingencies underlying the process of discrimination … Discrimination is a behavioral process: the contingencies, not the mind [nor the person], make the discriminations. (1953: 116–117)

In this way, radical behaviorism denies free will and also even the notion of a "self." For, "A self is a repertoire of behavior appropriate to a given set of contingencies." (1971: 194; cf. Wegner 2003). Thus, according to Skinner, logical, radical and methodological behaviorism amount to an understanding of the "contingencies" found within a "physical system," and "It is in the nature of an experimental analysis of human behavior that it should strip away the functions previously assigned to autonomous man and transfer them one by one to the controlling environment." (Ibid).

In regard to the philosophical principles of the systems of Western psychology, the terms "Structuralism" and "Functionalism" do not refer simply to "schools of thought," rather, they refer to explanatory choices and ontological characterizations. Given the goal of history of psychology textbooks to legitimate "movements" of psychology, there is a tendency to identify Wundt and Titchener with "Structuralism" and Dewey and the "American Pragmatists" with "Functionalism." This characterization is not wrong; however, the terms may also be understood as principles in regard to systems. In this way, "Structuralism" refers to the ontological parts and organization of ψυχή and the ontological structure of language, for example. Similarly, "Functionalism" as a philosophical principle refers to the study of, and explanatory use of, "function" in regard to ψυχή (cf. Angell 1907). As we will see, functionalism is historically characterized as the principle responsible for the movement away from behaviorism and toward the "Cognitive Revolution." Thus, in discussing functionalism we will also discuss the shift from what is called the "Identity Thesis" to "Multiple Realizability," and "Computationalism."

Recall above we noted the American Psychological Association's definition of structure: "a relatively stable arrangement of elements or components organized so as to form an integrated whole. Structure is often contrasted with function to emphasize how something is organized or patterned rather than what it does." (VandenBos 2007: 901). Further, we have invoked the term "structure" when speaking about parts of a system. Thus, "the concept of *structure* is of course intimately related to that of *analysis*—we reveal structures by analyzing wholes into parts." (Peregrin 2001: 1). Yet, when we shift from the term "structure" to "Structuralism," what new meaning does that latter term add?

In a chapter titled "How Do We Recognize Structuralism? (1967)," Gilles Deleuze (1925–1995) enumerates a number of criteria for recognizing "Structuralism." The most important for our purpose here are the first two, that is, a symbolic characterization and a relative positionality. Simply put, ontologically, the "structures" with which "Structuralism" is concerned are neither images, things, nor words, in as much as they are concepts (which do not refer to things or words). Second, there must be some originary point which determines the organization of the "structure," for example, an object of experience to which the organization of the structure then refers. Together, then, we may recognize that there is an object of experience and the concepts or words that refer to the object of experience may be understood as parts which relate to each other in a whole. This whole is understood as a "third realm." It is not itself a concept that refers to the object of experience, and it is not the object of experience; rather it is the "structure" in which the concepts or words relating to the object of experience have an organized location.

As we will see below, one of the important aspects of structuralism is the ability to theorize about "structure activation." This kind of theorizing can be found often throughout the history and systems of Western psychology. For example, it is a kind of structuralism to suppose ψυχή has a structure and to characterize experience in terms of its activation— sensation leads to perception, which leads to conceptualization and rational deliberation about the object experience. Thus, the notion of "spreading activation" across a connectionist network invokes a kind of structuralism (cf. Higgins 1991). Also, the idea that human motivation traverses an Id, Ego, Super-Ego invokes a kind of structuralism, and the idea that words are associated to one another invokes a kind of structuralism.

The idea that some individual thing performs a function naturally seems to suggest that other individual things could also perform the same function (cf. Dewey 1886, 1896; cf. Shoemaker 1981). This is the idea of "Multiple Realizability," which suggests that psychological *functions* could be accomplished by multiple different factors. Prior to "Functionalism," there was a tendency to adhere to the "Identity Thesis" when theorizing the relationship between physical and non-physical properties. In other words, there was an assumption that irreducibly mental aspects of human experience could be taken as tokens of a type or kind of mental activity and the type of activity or the individual tokens would have a one-to-one ratio with some physical activity. This kind of thinking comes up in "brain localization" projects and even may be seen in behavioral analysis. However, by shifting the ontological priority from the properties to the functions, functionalism provides a way to theorize non-physical properties—such as *qualia*—into causation relations of primarily physical systems. Simply put, whatever the *qualia* may be, it is the function it serves in a physical system that is important, that is to say, qualitative aspects—though not ontologically reducible—can be explanatorily reduced to otherwise physical theories.

Interestingly, then, though functionalism is "philosophically-responsible" for a move away from radical behaviorism (cf. Chomsky 1957, 1959) and to the inclusion of non-physical properties in theories regarding ψυχή (cf. Putnam 1975), it is also responsible for a move toward "Computationalism" (cf. Pylyshyn 1984; cf. Hurley 2005). This latter idea is often associated with the "Cognitive Revolution" or "Cognitive Turn," and connectionist ideas, such as those related to "Artificial Intelligence." Simply put, if, according to functionalism, the functions of ψυχή are multiply realizable, then they should be artificially realizable, since human and robot actions are "functionally equivalent" (cf. Heal 1986). If the connections and spreading-activations across neural networks of the brain could be modeled by computer programs, then perhaps a kind of artificial life, or at least, thinking could be spawned. It is as if, the activity of ψυχή is essentially a kind of "computation" taking place in the activity of the brain, and the result of this idea is twofold. First, the computational activity of ψυχή should be able to be simulated by a computer. Second, the functions of the activity of ψυχή should be multiply realizable, for example, by things other than human brains—this raises questions of robot pain, and so on.

Lastly, a less radical result of functionalism refers to the ideas of propositional attitudes and "Mindreading." We discussed the former idea above. In regard to the latter, we need to first distinguish between the terms "Mindreading" and "Mind Reading." Since the latter term is perhaps more familiar, we will start there. "Mind Reading," two separate words, refers to "extrasensory perception or ESP. This is often characterized as belonging to the genre of "psychic power" (cf. Rhine 1934, 1973). The former term, "Mindreading," one word, refers to the ability to represent, explain, predict, and respond to the "mental states" of others. The idea is often traced back to classical theories of empathy and sympathy; however, we can see it in action when, for example, we finish someone else's sentence before them. Notice, how, on the one hand, in regard to this example, explanations of how it is possible to finish someone else's sentence may invoke the *structure* of language or grammar. On the other hand, explanations of mindreading may invoke an awareness of the *function* the other person was attempting to perform, as evidenced by the person's actions and based on the situation, and so on.

Mindreading is often accounted for in terms of "simulation," and simulation may be understood in multiple ways. Systems which give ontological priority to physical be-ing may invoke the idea that watching someone perform certain functions produces neural activity in the observers brain which is similar to the neural activity in the brain of the person performing the function (cf. Mach 1897; cf. Place 1956; cf. Smart 1959), and, as a result, the observer is able to represent, explain, predict, and respond to the "mental states" of the performer. Simulation could also be understood in terms of behavioral mimesis or mirroring; that is, the repeated "rehearsal" of certain behaviors allows us to recognize the performance of the behavior patterns in others. Systems which give onto-logical priority to non-physical properties of socio-culturally based struc-tures may invoke the ability to recognize the propositional attitude being exhibited or the "language game" being played, and so on.

The final principle from the philosophy of psychology to discuss regards "the question of the freedom of the will" and of "Agency." As we acknowledged in regard to Radical Behaviorism, some systems of psy-chology do not believe humans have a free will. In order to better navi-gate thinking through this aspect of systems across the history of Western psychology, introducing philosophy's technical vocabulary on the issue of free will is beneficial. In order to compare systems across historical peri-ods, we should briefly characterize four (4) philosophical principles regarding freedom of the will, that is, Fatalism, Hard Determinism, Soft Determinism or Compatibilism, Incompatibilism, Libertarianism, and Indeterminism. For our purpose, the term "Fatalism" refers to events that cannot be changed, and this may include whatever it is that we do during those events. Thus, if they are in the future, then they are "on the way here," and nothing can be done to stop them from arriving. Of course, it is possible to take the position of Fatalism without thinking that *all* events are fated.

A distinction is standardly made between causal and logical determin-ism. The former holds that the laws of nature in combination with past states and events determine future states and events without any *chance* of a differently determined outcome. Logical determinism holds that every claim is either true or false, including claims made about the future (i.e. even though the future has not happened when the claim is made). Thus, logical determinism includes the "problem of foreknowledge," which in its deterministic characterization holds that if some being were able to have true foreknowledge of someone's action in the future, then that person's future action would be determined—they would not be free to act differently. In this way, the characterization of a system as closed in such a way that all events are caused by prior events in a chain of conditions is called "Hard Determinism" (cf. Zagzebski 1991, 2002).

The problems with Hard Determinism are often characterized in three ways. First, people may want to believe they could have acted differently than they did, perhaps even if only just changing something at the moment of the event itself. Second, people may want to understand action in terms of "agent causation," meaning that the agent of the action is in control over, or at least has, freedom of will. Third, people may want to believe the future is open, that is, it is contingent and not necessarily determined. Thus, the terms "Soft Determinism" and "Compatibilism" are synonymous. They refer to the idea that a deterministic system and free will are compatible. "Incompatibilism," then, refers to the idea that a deterministic system and free will are *not* compatible. "Libertarianism" (not the political term) refers to the idea that freedom of the will exists (it is not an illusion) and that determinism is a false characterization of reality. At the extreme opposite end of the spectrum, so to speak, is "Indeterminism," which holds that determinism is false because all events are the outcome of chance.

Given the amount of vocabulary terms introduced in this section, it may be beneficial to list them here. We discussed ontology and ontological principles such as: "Substance Monism," "Substance Dualism," and "Property Dualism." We discussed principles characterizing dualistic relations such as: "Representation," "Reduction," "Elimination," "Supervenience," "Emergence," and "Epiphenomenal." In this context we also discussed "*qualia*," "intentionality," and "propositional attitudes." In regard to ontological priority, we discussed principles and distinctions such as those regarding: "Materialism," "Idealism," "Empiricism," "Nativism," "Vitalism," "Mechanism," "Behaviorism," "Structuralism," and "Functionalism." This included a discussion of logical, methodological and radical Behaviorism. We also discussed the principles of "Multiple Realizability," "Mindreading," "Simulation," and "Computationalism." Finally, we discussed principles regarding "Agency," specifically in regard to the possibility of "freedom of the will."

In conclusion, the above distinctions should inform our discussion of the following historically based systems of psychology. What makes this activity an activity of "thinking through" the systems is that priority shifts from historical period to period is constituted by shifts in the priority of the principles operative to think in regard to ψυχή from the different historical points of view regarding systems. Perhaps the most striking example—which is why it appears in the chapter titles—occurs when the principles and distinctions regarding "methodology" shift in priority over those regarding ontology. Of course, ontology has such an essential role in the constitution of systems that theorists attempting to avoid it need to stipulate as much. Which is to say that the principles and distinctions of ontology will continue to be operable as we think through the history and systems of Western psychology, even when considering the point of view of "systems" which attempt to ignore ontology by emphasizing method and even those which are avowedly anarchist.

## Notes

1. The method of "introspection" refers to the observation and examination of one's own mental states, and is often contrasted with "external observation." However, the Leibnizian term "apperceive" or "apperception" would have been much better.

## Bibliography

Angell, James Rowland. 1907. The Province of Functional Psychology. *Psychological Review* 14 (2): 61–91.
Aristotle. 1964. *Prior Analytics*. Trans. A.J. Jenkinson. In *The Complete Works of Aristotle: The Revised Oxford Translation* (1995), ed. J. Barnes, vol. I, 39–113. Princeton, NJ: Princeton University Press.
———. 1967. *Topics*. Trans. J. Brunschwig. In *The Complete Works of Aristotle: The Revised Oxford Translation* (1995), ed. J. Barnes, vol. I, 167–277. Princeton, NJ: Princeton University Press.

————. 1984. *Metaphysics.* Trans. W.D. Ross. In *The Complete Works of Aristotle: The Revised Oxford Translation* (1995), ed. J. Barnes, vol. II, 1552–1728. Princeton, NJ: Princeton University Press.

Baydala, Angelina, and William E. Smythe. 2012. Hermeneutics of Continuity: Theorizing Psychological Understanding of Ancient Literature. *Theory & Psychology* 22 (6): 842–859.

Berger, Peter L., and Thomas Luckmann. 1966. *The Social Construction of Reality: A Treatise in the Sociology of Knowledge.* New York: Anchor Books.

Beutler, Larry E. 1983. *Eclectic Psychotherapy: A Systematic Approach.* New York: Pergamon.

Brentano, Franz. 1973. *Psychology from an Empirical Standpoint.* London: Routledge.

Bruza, Peter D., Zheng Wang, and Jerome R. Busemeyer. 2015. Quantum Cognition: A New Theoretical Approach to Psychology. *Trends in Cognitive Science* 19 (7): 383–393.

Chalmers, David. 1996. *The Conscious Mind.* Oxford: Oxford University Press.

Chapman, Loren J., and Jean Chapman. 1982. Test Results Are What You Think They Are. In *Judgment Under Uncertainty: Heuristics and Biases,* ed. D. Kahneman, P. Slovic, and A. Tversky, 239–248. Cambridge: Cambridge University Press.

Chomsky, Noam. 1957. *Syntactic Structures.* The Hague: Mouton de Gruyter.

————. 1959. A Review of B.F. Skinner's *Verbal Behavior. Language* 35 (1): 26–58.

Churchland, Paul M. 1981. Eliminative Materialism and the Propositional Attitudes. *The Journal of Philosophy* 78 (2): 67–90.

————. 1992. Activation Vectors Versus Propositional Attitudes: How the Brain Represents Reality. *Philosophy and Phenomenological Research* 52 (2): 419–424.

Daniel, Stephen L. 1986. The Patient as Text: A Model of Clinical Hermeneutics. *Theoretical Medicine* 7 (2): 195–210.

Davidson, Donald. 1970. Mental Events. In *Experience and Theory,* ed. L. Foster and J.W. Swanson, 79–101. Amherst, MA: University of Massachusetts Press.

Dennett, Daniel C. 1991. *Consciousness Explained.* Boston: Little Brown.

Deslauriers, Marguerite. 2007. *Aristotle on Definition.* Leiden: Brill.

Dewey, John. 1886. Psychology as Philosophic Method. *Mind* 2 (42): 153–173.

————. 1896. The Reflex Arc Concept in Psychology. *The Psychological Review* 33 (4): 357–370.

Dilthey, Wilhelm. 1989. *Introduction to the Human Sciences*. Eds. and Trans. R.A. Makkreel and R. Rodi, *Wilhelm Dilthey: Selected Works*, vol. I. Princeton, NJ: Princeton University Press.

————. 2010. *Ideas for a Descriptive and Analytic Psychology (1894)*. Trans. R.A. Makkreel and D. Moore. In *Understanding the Human World*, eds. R.A. Makkreel and R. Rodi, *Wilhelm Dilthey: Selected Works*, vol. II, 115–210 Princeton, NJ: Princeton University Press.

Feigl, Herbert. 1959. Philosophical Embarrassments of Psychology. *American Psychologist* 14 (3): 115–128.

Feyerabend, Paul. 1983. *Against Method*. New York: Verso.

————. 1987. *Farewell to Reason*. New York: Verso.

Fleck, Ludwik. 1979. *Genesis and Development of a Scientific Fact*. Eds. T.J. Trenn and R.K. Merton and Trans. F. Bradley and T.J. Trenn. Chicago: University of Chicago Press.

Fodor, Jerry. 1968. *Psychological Explanation: An Introduction to the Philosophy of Psychology*. New York: Random House.

Gazzaniga, Michael S. 2006. My Brain Made Me Do It. In *Ethical Brain*, ed. M.S. Gazzaniga The, 87–104. New York: Harper Collins.

Geelan, David R. 1997. Epistemological Anarchy and the Many Forms of Constructivism. *Science & Education* 6 (1–2): 15–28.

Gergen, Kenneth J. 1985. The Social Constructionist Movement in Modern Psychology. *American Psychologist* 40 (3): 266–275.

Glenn, Paul J. 1939. *Ontology: A Class Manual in Fundamental Metaphysics*. St. Louis, MO: B. Herder Book Co.

Hart, J.T. 1986. Functional Eclectic Therapy. In *Handbook of Eclectic Psychotherapy*, ed. J.C. Norcross, 201–225. New York: Brunner-Mazel.

Heal, Jane. 1986. Replication and Functionalism. In *Language, Mind, and Logic*, ed. J. Butterfield, 45–59. Cambridge: Cambridge University Press.

Henriques, Gregg R. 2004. Psychology Defined. *Journal of Clinical Psychology* 60 (12): 1207–1221.

Higgins, E. Tory. 1991. Expanding the Law of Cognitive Structure Actication: The Role of Knowledge Applicability. *Psychological Inquiry* 2 (2): 192–193.

Hurley, Susan. 2005. The Shared Circuits Hypothesis: A Unified Functional Architecture for Control, Imitation, and Simulation. In *Perspectives on Imitation: From Neuroscience to Social Science, Vol. I: Mechanisms of Imitation and Imitation in Animals*, ed. S. Hurley and N. Chater, 177–193. Cambridge, MA: MIT Press.

Jackson, Frank. 1986. What Mary Didn't Know. *Journal of Philosophy* 83 (5): 291–295.

James, William. 1918. *The Principles of Psychology*. Vol. 1. New York: Dover Publications.

Kagan, Jerome. 2013. Equal Time for Psychological and Biological Contributions to Human Variation. *Review of General Psychology* 17 (4): 351–357.

Kim, Jaegwon. 1998. *Mind in a Physical World*. Cambridge: Cambridge University Press.

———. 2005. *Physicalism, Or Something Near Enough*. Princeton, NJ: Princeton University Press.

Klein, D.B. 1970. *A History of Scientific Psychology*. New York: Basic Books.

Krstic, Kruno. 1964. Marko Marulic—The Author of the Term 'Psychology'. *Acta Instituti Psychologici Universitatis Zagrabiensis* 36: 7–13.

Ladd, George Trumbull. 1892. Psychology as So-Called 'Natural Science. *The Philosophical Review* 1 (1): 24–53.

Lamanna, Marco. 2010. On the Early History of Psychology. *Revista Filosófica de Coimbra* 19 (38): 291–314.

Lapointe, François H. 1973. The Origin and Evolution of the Term "Psychology". *Rivista Critica di Storia della Filosofia* 28 (2): 138–160.

Leonelli, Sabina. 2016. *Data-Centric Biology: A Philosophical Study*. Chicago: University of Chicago.

Levine, Joseph. 1983. Materialism and Qualia: The Explanatory Gap. *Pacific Philosophical Quarterly* 64 (4): 354–361.

Lewis, C.I. 1991. *Mind and the World Order: Outline of a Theory of Knowledge*. Boston: Dover Publications.

Lilienfeld, Scott O. 2012. Public Skepticism of Psychology: Why Many People Perceive the Study of Human Behavior as Unscientific. *American Psychologist* 67 (2): 111–129.

Margolis, Joseph. 1984. *Philosophy of Psychology*. Upper Saddle River, NJ: Prentice Hall.

Mach, Ernst. 1897. *Contributions to the Analysis of the Sensations*, Trans. C.M. Williams. Chicago: The Open Court Publishing Co.

Merz, John T. 1965. *A History of European Thought in the Nineteenth Century*. New York: Dover.

Miller, Gregory A. 2010. Mistreating Psychology in the Decades of the Brain. *Perspectives on Psychological Science* 5 (6): 716–743.

Murray, E.J. 1986. Possibilities and Promises of Eclecticism. In *Handbook of Eclectic Psychotherapy*, ed. J.C. Norcross, 398–415. New York: Brunner-Mazel.

Nagel, Thomas. 1974. What Is It Like To Be a Bat? *Philosophical Review* 83: 435–450.

Newmark, Peter. 1998. *More Paragraphs on Translation.* Toronto, Canada: Multilingual Matters.

Papineau, David. 2012. *Philosophical Devices: Proofs, Probabilities, Possibilities, and Sets.* Oxford: Oxford University Press.

Peirce, Charles Sanders. 1982. *Writings of Charles S. Peirce: 1857–1866.* Bloomington, IN: Indiana University Press.

Peregrin, Jaroslav. 2001. *Meaning and Structure: Structuralism of (Post)Analytic Philosophers.* Burlington, VT: Ashgate.

Peters, F.E. 1967. *Greek Philosophical Terms.* New York: New York University Press.

Place, U.T. 1956. Is Consciousness a Brain Process? *British Journal of Psychology* 47: 44–50.

Prochaska, James O., and Carlo C. DiClementi. 1986. The Transtheoretical Approach. In *Handbook of Eclectic Psychotherapy*, ed. J.C. Norcross, 163–200. New York: Brunner-Mazel.

Puntel, Lorenz B. 2001. Truth: A Prolegomenon to a General Theory. In *What Is Truth?* ed. R. Schantz. Berlin: Walter de Gruyter.

Putnam, H. 1975. The Nature of Mental States. In *Mind, Language and Reality: Philosophical Papers*, vol. 2, 429–440. Cambridge: Cambridge University Press.

Pylyshyn, Zenon. 1984. *Computation and Cognition.* Cambridge, MA: MIT Press.

Raue, Charles G. 1889. *Psychology as a Natural Science Applied to the Solution of Occult Psychic Phenomena.* Philadelphia, PA: Porter & Coates.

Rhine, Joseph B. 1973. *Exta-Sensory Perception.* Wellesley, MA: Branden Press.

Rorty, Richard. 1984. The Historiography of Philosophy: Four Genres. In *Philosophy in History: Essays on the Historiography of Philosophy*, ed. R. Rorty, J.B. Schneewind, and Q. Skinner, 49–76. Cambridge: Cambridge University Press.

Russell, Bertrand. 2010. *The Philosophy of Logical Atomism.* London: Routledge.

Rust, John. 1987. Is Psychology a Cognitive Science? *Journal of Applied Philosophy* 4 (1): 49–55.

Ryle, Gilbert. 1949. *The Concept of Mind.* Chicago: University of Chicago Press.

Scalambrino, Frank. 2017. *Living in the Light of Death: Existential Philosophy in the Eastern Tradition, Zen, Samurai & Haiku.* Castalia, OH: Magister Ludi Press.

Schrödinger, Erwin. 1926. An Undulatory Theory of the Mechanics of Atoms and Molecules. *Physical Review* 28 (6): 1049–1070.

Schwartz, Jeffrey. M. Henry, P. Stapp, and Mario Beauregard. 2005. Quantum Physics in Neuroscience and Psychology: A Neurophysical Model of Mind-Brain Interaction. *Philosophical Transactions of the Royal Society of London. Series B* 360 (1458): 1309–1327.

Sellars, Wilfrid. 1956. Empiricism and the Philosophy of Mind. In *Minnesota Studies in the Philosophy of Science*, ed. H. Feigl and M. Scriven, vol. I, 253–329. Minneapolis, MN: University of Minnesota Press.

Shoemaker, Sydney. 1981. Some Varieties of Functionalism. *Philosophical Topics* 12: 93–119.

Skinner, B.F. 1953. *Science and Human Behavior*. New York: Macmillan.

———. 1971. *Beyond Freedom and Dignity*. Indianapolis, IN: Hackett Publishing.

Skinner, Quentin. 1969. Meaning and Understanding in the History of Ideas. *History and Theory* 8: 3–53.

Smart, J.J.C. 1959. Sensations and Brain Processes. *The Philosophical Review* 68 (2): 141–156.

Sokal, Alan D. 1996. Transgressing the Boundaries: Towards a Transformative Hermeneutics of Quantum Gravity. *Social Text* (46/47): 217–252.

Sokal, Alan D., and Jean Bricmont. 1998. *Fashionable Nonsense: Postmodern Intellectuals' Abuse of Science*. New York: Picador.

Titchener, Edward B. 1914. On 'Psychology as the Behaviorist Views It. *American Philosophical Society* 53 (213): 1–17.

VandenBos, Gary R. 2007. *APA Dictionary of Psychology*. Washington, DC: American Psychological Association.

Vidal, Fernando. 2011. *The Sciences of the Soul: The Early Modern Origins of Psychology*. Trans. S. Brown. Chicago: University of Chicago Press.

Vlieghe, Joris. 2016. How Learning to Read and Write Shapes Humanity: A Technosomatic Perspective on Digitization. In *Social Epistemology and Technology: Toward Public Self-Awareness Regarding Technological Mediation*, ed. F. Scalambrino, 127–136. London: Rowman & Littlefield International.

Wegner, Daniel M. 2003. *The Illusion of Conscious Will*. Cambridge, MA: MIT Press.

Wilhelmsen, Frederick D. 1956. *Man's Knowledge of Reality: An Introduction to Thomistic Epistemology*. Upper Saddle River, NJ: Prentice Hall.

Wundt, Wilhelm. 2014. *Lectures on Human and Animal Psychology*. Trans. J.E. Creighton and E.G. Titchener. New York: Routledge.

Zagzebski, Linda T. 1991. *The Dilemma of Freedom and Foreknowledge*. Oxford: Oxford University Press.

————. 2002. Recent Work on Divine Foreknowledge and Free Will. In *The Oxford Handbook of Free Will*, ed. R. Kane, 45–64. Oxford: Oxford University Press.

# 3

# Pre-Modern to Early Modern: From Mirror of God to Mirror of Nature

## 3.1 Principles of Psychology from Socrates and Plato

There are two issues which anyone discussing Socrates (470–399 BC) and Plato (c. 428–347 BC) should mention as disclaimers. First, if Socrates wrote any philosophical dialogs or produced any philosophical works in writing, none of them have survived. Therefore, it is usual and customary to mention the scholarly disclaimer that "We don't really know exactly what Socrates thought." This is standardly referred to as "The Socratic Problem" (cf. de Vogel 1955; cf. Boys-Stones and Rowe 2013; cf. Cain 2007). At the same time, this does not stop us from discussing the "philosophical thoughts of Socrates" as mentioned by his contemporaries and students—especially Aristophanes (c. 450–c. 386 BC) and his students Xenophon (c. 430-c. 350 BC) and Plato. Second, though Plato's writings were not lost, there is still the problem of the relation between the dialog form in which he wrote and interpreting it toward knowing "this is what Plato thought." This is standardly referred to as "The Problem of Interpreting Plato's Dialogs." At the same time, despite these disclaimers, scholars, of course, continue to talk about "Plato's philosophy" based on what he wrote in his *Dialogs* (cf. Corlett 2005; cf.

© The Author(s) 2018
F. Scalambrino, *Philosophical Principles of the History and Systems of Psychology*,
https://doi.org/10.1007/978-3-319-74733-0_3

Coulter 1976; cf. Blondell 2002; cf. Klagge and Smith 1992; cf. Gadamer 1980; cf. Heidegger 2003; cf. Kahn 1996; cf. Zuckert 2009).

What this means for the principles of psychology emerging from ancient Greek philosophers can be safely summed in the following way. It certainly seems to be the case that Socrates was interested in wisdom for the sake of ψυχή. For example, Plato famously attributed to Socrates the claim, "The unexamined life is not worth living." (Plato 1997a: 38a5–6). Moreover, this activity of "examining life," that is, one's own life and the lives of others, was characterized in a twofold way. On the one hand, this activity is "philosophy," and, on the other hand, to perform this activity is to "care for ψυχή." The passage is worth quoting at length:

> As long as I draw breath and am able, I shall not cease to practice philoso-
> phy, to exhort you and in my usual way to point out to any one of you
> whom I happen to meet: "… are you not ashamed of your eagerness to
> possess as much wealth, reputation, and honors as possible, while you do
> not care for nor give thought to wisdom or truth, or the best possible state
> of your soul [ψυχή]?". (Plato 1997a: 29d4–e2; cf. Plato 1997c: 107c)

This idea, then, of the "best possible state of ψυχή" points to an original association between psychology and ethics and morality. That is to say, the discussion of ψυχή by Socrates and Plato is, ultimately, in the service of soteriology. We want to live the best life we can, and so we need wisdom (i.e. philosophy) to do so. Moreover, with what should this wisdom be concerned so that we may live the best possible life? The answer, according to Socrates and Plato: ψυχή. Hence, we find the principles of psychology emerging from ancient Greek philosophers contextualized in terms of ethics, morality, teleology, and, especially, soteriology.

Given the difficulties with attributing philosophical principles to Socrates, beyond the principle that the very goal of philosophy is to care for ψυχή, we may also, at least, attribute the principle of "freedom" to Socrates. That is, Socrates believed in the principle of freedom to such an extent that he, ultimately, became a martyr for it—when he was told he could no longer philosophize he accepted "execution." Thus, to Socrates we attribute the principles of psychology that ψυχή is a non-determined be-ing, that is, "free," and the principle that some ways of thinking are better than others insofar as these ways of thinking lead to a better state of be-ing for ψυχή. Presumably, then, Plato's philosophy may be read as an explication of the theory of be-ing and the theory of knowledge which account for the best possible state of be-ing for ψυχή. As a result, Socrates and, especially, Plato have a psychology, that is, an account of ψυχή, articulated for the sake of "saving" ψυχή from a worse state of be-ing. This will, of course, continue to be the context and purpose of psychology through the Middle Ages.

If we were to try to identify one principle in Plato's psychology which we may use to organize the remaining principles of his psychology, it would be: the principle of the immortality of ψυχή (esp. Plato 1997c: 78b–80b, 1997e: 608d). This is the case for a number of reasons; however, the most important two are the following. First, all theories of ψυχή (viz. theories which take ψυχή to be non-illusory) may be divided into those which believe ψυχή to be immortal and those which believe ψυχή is not immortal. Second, when you think of ψυχή as immortal, it immediately casts a light on ψυχή from which other principles follow. Thus, from the principle of the immortality of ψυχή we arrive at the principle of re-incarnation. This contextualizes the discussion of the structure of ψυχή in that the various functions of ψυχή may be organized according to a structure the appropriate activation of which leads to salvation, and that is precisely the kind of psychology we find in the writings of Plato.

According to Plato, the ψυχή (e.g. the "soul") is immortal, despite the obvious fact that bodies die (cf. Plato 1997c: 105c). Without going too deeply into Plato's philosophy here, we may simply say that Plato understood ψυχή as a non-material be-ing, similar to a geometric *form*. Though you may flatten any number of rubber tires, doing so does not destroy the form of circle. That is, appropriately placing the *material* of rubber into the *form* of a circle constitutes a "tire." However, when that tire is destroyed the form in which the material formerly was is not destroyed. As the "form of the body," ψυχή is not destroyed when the body dies (cf. Plato 1997b, c, e). Though this does point to a kind of dualism, there are two primary reasons why Plato does not have a "Mind-Body Problem" such as that which will later be found in Descartes' philosophy (cf. Ostenfeld 1987). First, the dualism between ψυχή and body found in Plato is not a substance dualism since the body cannot exist without ψυχή. Second, the principle of re-incarnation makes it such that not only may more than one body be attributed to one ψυχή (across multiple embodied-lives or incarnations), but also from the point of view of the one ψυχή in regard to the multiple embodiments, each body is like a kind of "shadow" of ψυχή, that is, a "surface effect" in regard to the material dimension.

In his famous "Cave Allegory," (Plato 1997e: 514a–520a) which may be found at the beginning of Book VII in Plato's *Republic*, the allegorical theme of "shadows" and the play of shadows is polysemic. That is, Plato uses the theme to characterize multiple aspects of ψυχή. At the existential-level, found in the *Republic*'s culmination, that is, Book X, the play of shadows characterizes the multiple re-incarnations of ψυχή until it is able to fully liberate itself from the process of re-incarnation. Again, without explicating it here, we may say that Plato's psychology affirms the principles of Fatalism in that Plato seemed to believe certain events (but not all events) which occur in each embodiment of ψυχή are "fated" in that they could not be avoided based on the particularities of each existence and embodiment. One way to quickly visualize this is in terms of dropping a floating device into a flowing stream. Depending upon where in the stream the device is dropped subsequent stages of the stream will be encountered. Though, of course, there may be ways to trivialize this example, it still works to help those not trained in philosophy gain some type of visualization of the relationship between the conditions of one's coming-into-be-ing and the subsequent events experienced during that embodiment.

Next, at the structural-level, the shadows refer to the power of imagination to perceive materially instantiated beings. Just as at the existential-level the body, that is, ψυχή's material-instantiation, is like a shadow in relation to ψυχή, so too other beings are primarily non-material. Further, because the power of imagination is associated with the body (a theme the principles of which will receive an explicit articulation later from Aristotle), the products of the power of imagination may be understood as shadows of "true reality," according to Plato. That is to say, the *form* is more important than its many *material* instances. Learning, then, according to Plato is a kind of "remembering." The Greek term is *anamnēsis*, and it is usually translated as "recollection." This is because when ψυχή understands what a *thing* is, it does so by recognizing the form of which the thing is a material instance, and since, ultimately, the forms and ψυχή are timeless in their original natural state, for Plato, ψυχή is recollecting its original state in which it related to the forms without a physical body. In doing so, notice, ψυχή is reminded of itself as it truly is.

Thus, ideas are most important among the structures we experience, and ideals are most important in determining ψυχή's activity. Notice, even when that means one is faced with martyrdom for ideals. As a result, Plato's soteriology may be explicated in terms of the reciprocal relation between ethical ideals and the structure of ψυχή. For, in structural terms, it is a certain activation of ψυχή which will lead to its ultimate liberation from the process of re-incarnation. As a result, ultimately, we will clarify the structural-, functional-, and existential-levels as they relate to the theological-level for Plato. For example, in his dialog titled *Phaedo*, aka "On ψυχή" or "About ψυχή" by ancient commentators and echoing a principle of the ancient Eleusinian Mysteries, Plato described embodiment as a kind of "prison" for ψυχή (cf. 1997c: 62b; cf. Plato 1997d: 249e4–250b1; cf. Burkert 1989; cf. Ruck 1986; cf. Scalambrino 2016a; Wasson et al. 2008). Liberation from the prison of physical-embodiment turns out to be the context—as a kind of goal and purpose for physically embodied ψυχή—with which to ultimately organize the principles of, and clarify, Plato's psychology.

According to Plato, the structure of ψυχή is tripartite, and this division coincides with the Western "Orthodox" view of the structure of ψυχή. Namely, ψυχή is divided into "affection," "cognition," and "conation," a term more commonly expressed by "volition." We should note that these three parts of ψυχή coincide with the organizing principles of "*pathos*," "*logos*," and "*ethos*," respectively (cf. Burnyeat 1976). This helps clarify Plato's psychology; he characterized the function of ψυχή in terms of desire or love, which structurally may be understood as the use of volition in an ethical way—a way which refers to the use of cognition (*logos*) to guide volition (*ethos*) in controlling how ψυχή is affected (*pathos*), through the body. This is the famous "*Scala Amoris*" or "Ladder of Love" (cf. Plato 1997f: 209e–212a; cf. Frede 1993; cf. Iglesias 2016: 91; cf. Reeve 2006: xxxii; cf. Scalambrino 2016b), which will be contrasted later with Aristotle's "*Scala Natura*" or "Ladder of Nature."

The function of ψυχή is soteriological, then, insofar as its appropriate functioning "in a body" will eventually accomplish a restoration to its natural state; yet, we must keep in mind that as a non-material be-ing, the natural state of ψυχή for Plato is actually a super-natural state—a state in which ψυχή does not have a physical body. This will also be contrasted later with Aristotle's understanding of ψυχή's natural state in terms of physical and ethical harmony. Thus, Plato's characterization of ψυχή's natural state is in terms of ethical and theological harmony. It will be helpful to briefly discuss two stories found in Plato's dialogs. The first is known as "The Charioteer Allegory" (1997d: 246a–254e) and the second as the "*Scala Amoris*" (1997f: 209e–212a).

In his "Charioteer Allegory," Plato speaks of "a pair of winged horses and a charioteer" (1997d: 246a). The chariot may be understood as referring to the body, the charioteer the intellect, and the horses as the forces of impulsion. The horse "on the right" Plato calls "noble" and a "lover of honor." The horse "on the left" Plato calls "ignoble" and a "lover of pleasure" (1997d: 253a–254e). The story allegorizes physically embodied ψυχή. In other words, the horses represent the forces of desire which *affect* ψυχή through its be-ing physically embodied. The charioteer's gaining control of the horses represents the ability of ψυχή to use its intelligence to function in a way that returns it to its original non-physically embodied state. The example Plato uses is love, specifically when a person is in the presence of someone they love, that is, the "beloved."

It is as if the body relates to love through the impulsions of the horses, and the intellect relates to love more form(al)ly. It is "as if by a bolt of lightning," according to Plato, "When the charioteer sees that face [of the beloved], his memory is carried back to the real nature of Beauty." (Plato 1997d: 254b4). On the one hand, notice the reference to *anamnēsis*. That is, the charioteer, which represents the intellect of ψυχή, recollects the "Platonic heaven" or realm of the forms through its encounter with the beloved. However, the "ignoble horse" on the left (i.e. "sinister horse"), relates to the beloved in terms of the beloved's present material instance. Thus, in order for the charioteer to go toward the realm in which the beloved truly *is*, the charioteer must contend with the material-loving sinister horse. On the other hand, because ψυχή is presently physically embodied the charioteer, the chariot, and the horses must be understood as representing a whole. Thus, we are back to the ethical component of Plato's psychology, because the actions performed by the individual in the presence of the beloved are either directed by the horses or the charioteer, and it is, according to Plato, only when the actions are directed by the charioteer that ψυχή gains ground toward liberation from physical-embodiment.

Now, of all the ancient Greek terms for "love," in Plato's dialogs two different terms are featured. They are "*erôs*" and "*philia*" (cf. Santas 1979). On the one hand, of course, these two different terms—representing erotic love and platonic love, respectively—coincide with the love of the horses and the love of the charioteer, respectively. On the other hand, these two different terms characterize the change which occurs regarding ψυχή's desire and volition as it turns ("Cave Allegory" reference intended) away from the material dimension and is restored to its natural original state. Because this is understood as a kind of "ascension" for ψυχή away from its present physical-embodiment, the accomplishment of this change is characterized as a kind of climbing a "ladder" or "stairway." Thus, the movement refers to the "*Scala Amoris*," that is, the ladder of love, and the story in which the *Scala Amoris* is invoked describes a person becoming a *philo*sopher. In other words, *philia* is the word for love in the etymological definition of "philosophy" as the love of wisdom (*sophia*). In this way, just as the Cave Allegory describes a prisoner ascending from a cave and being free as a philosopher, so too the *Scala Amoris* refers to the change in direction for ψυχή such that ψυχή may be freed from the process of be-ing physically embodied.

Finally, in regard to function, because the theological-level unifies the structural-, functional-, and existential-levels for Plato, we will briefly discuss Plato's theological principles here insofar as they provide clarification for his psychology. For, as the Italian Renaissance Neo-Platonic philosopher and Catholic priest Marsilio Ficino (1433–1499) noted regarding the Charioteer, "before Socrates can affirm that love restores us to heaven, he has to examine a number of things concerning the condition of the soul, both divine and human." (Ficino 1981: 86). The three theological principles we will discuss, then, are the principle of the

"Transcendentals," the principle of the "daimon," and the principle of *"henosis."* Whereas the Transcendentals give us some idea of what is beyond the cycle of re-incarnation for ψυχή, the latter two principles further explicate Plato's soteriology regarding ψυχή from a theological point of view.

The ontological distinction between the "categorical" and the "transcendental" is essential for clarifying and organizing Plato's principles. Simply put, if we were to categorize every *thing* that *is*, then we would discover some properties cannot be contained by the categories of be-ing. What that means is that though things themselves belong in one category or another (the cat is not a tree), some properties of things "transcend" or "climb across" the different categories of be-ing. These properties are called the "Transcendentals." Just as both a cat and a tree can *be* good and beautiful, so too Goodness, Beauty, Truth, Unity (Oneness), and Be-ing, are the universal properties of Be-ing itself, that is, the Transcendentals. There is, of course, much more that can be said here; however, we will continue to explicate Plato's principles of psychology, rather than launch into a fuller discussion of the Transcendentals. What is important for us to recognize is that for Plato were we to "purify" the be-ing of each thing, then that thing would reduce down to its properties of pure be-ing until the material properties by way of which it may be physically categorized are eliminated. Hence, from a theological perspective, then, it is as if divine be-ing (as pure be-ing) is all Good, all Beautiful, True, Unified (or One) and it Is (cf. Plato 1997c: 70d).

Now, combine the insight regarding pure be-ing from the theological perspective with the structural, functional, and existential principles of psychology noted above. The idea is that when ψυχή recollects the realm of the forms, it is recollecting pure be-ing, which includes the "higher" more pure aspects of its own structure, and, recalling the Charioteer Allegory, the extent to which ψυχή is able to navigate toward the realm of pure be-ing is the extent to which ψυχή is able to purify itself in relation to the material-based properties which constitute the categorical existence of its present embodiment. Moreover, from the perspective of be-ing physically embodied ψυχή is "uniting" with pure be-ing when it purifies itself. Thus, in regard to what we called the existential-level discussed by Plato in Book X of his *Republic*, with each physical-embodiment endured by ψυχή in the process of re-incarnation, the extent to which ψυχή is able to purify itself during each incarnation is the extent to which it is able to unite and "grasp onto," so to speak, pure be-ing—as if grasping something so that it may pull itself from the material-quicksand of physical-embodiment. This union with the divine is called "*henosis.*"

Anticipating what will be considered more fully below, the principle of *henosis* seems to endure throughout the history of Western psychology as a structural and functional principle of ψυχή. However, the Modern Period may be seen as an attempt to strip the principle of its theological context. In order to understand the principle of *henosis* and its role in organizing Plato's principles of psychology we need to briefly discuss one more perennial principle—the principle of the "daimon." As Plato describes the process of re-incarnation at the moment in which ψυχή receives a new physical-embodiment, in addition to the fated events, ψυχή chooses a "daimon" (Plato 1997e: 617e). For our purpose here, we will simply say the term "daimon" refers to a non-physically instantiated voice that is "heard in the mind." Thus, the daimon was understood as a be-ing somehow mid-way between the divine realm of pure be-ing and humans (cf. Diamond 1996; cf. Greenbaum 2016; cf. Scalambrino 2016a, for a deeper discussion of the daimon). Moreover, regarding the structure of ψυχή, in the *Timaeus* Plato refers to the *daimon* as "the most sovereign part of our soul [ψυχή] as god's gift to us, given to be our guiding spirit." (Plato 1997g: 90a).

Though it may seem strange upon first hearing it: the daimon is another perennial principle in the history of Western psychology. For our purpose, notice the following. The ancient Greek prefix "*eu*" means "good" or "well," and, interestingly, when combined with the word "*daimon*" it creates the ancient Greek term translated as "happiness," that is, *Eudaimonia.* Thus, it is as if when a person has a good relationship with the voice in their mind, then they are capable of flourishing and experience a state of be-ing we call "happiness." Notice, because the Greeks seemed to believe these be-ings may be good or bad, *daimons* are often compared to guardian angels *or* tempting *demons*, respectively; thus, in the Middle Ages the daimon was contextualized in terms of "*Psychomachia*" or "Soul War." This is the idea often invoked in popular culture as an angel on one shoulder and a devil on the other shoulder as they both attempt to persuade you—it may also be seen as a variant of Plato's Charioteer Allegory. Further, in the Modern Period, stripped of theological connotation, the principle of the daimon is understood as the principle of conscience. However, as we will see in our discussion of principles from the Middle Ages, a distinction can be made between the daimon and conscience insofar as "the concerns of the *daimon* seem to be confined to future contingencies (as opposed to pangs of conscience after the act) and does not always have to do with judgments of moral value." (Beckman 1979: 76).

In sum, we may now see how the structural-, functional-, existential-, and theological-levels combine to organize and clarify Plato's principles regarding ψυχή. In order for ψυχή to liberate itself from the process of re-incarnation, it must purify itself during its present physical-embodiment—this is why Plato's psychology is ultimately in the service of soteriology and the origin of Western psychology is characterized in terms of ethics, morality, and theology. Thus, the extent to which ψυχή is able to purify itself during its present physical-embodiment determines the extent to which ψυχή is united with divine pure be-ing upon disembodiment. If that union (*henosis*) is not sufficient, then ψυχή receives another physical-embodied with its accompanying fated events and daimon. Plato is clear that ψυχή chooses these accoutrements, so to speak, of its next embodiment; however, it is also clear that there are constraints on ψυχή's choices which involve ψυχή's development along the *Scala Amoris*. For example, if you are so *affected* by the power of money to acquire material-gain that you love money in this physical-embodiment, then when faced with choices from your perspective you will be choosing what you love, but from the perspective of pure be-ing you will be misunderstanding the true value of be-ing physically embodied in those types of lives. The same goes for the daimon; you select the "co-pilot," so to speak, whom you think will help you accomplish whatever it is you love.[1]

In this way, Plato's psychology is soteriological and teleological, since ψυχή's self-knowledge is always already in the service of the purification of its be-ing. Moreover, knowledge of the structure and function of ψυχή characterizes ψυχή's development toward restoration to its original state of be-ing—making the actualization or accomplishment of that state of be-ing its purpose or *telos*. The principles of Plato's psychology, then, provide a narrative description of ψυχή's categorical existence in the physical with which ψυχή may recollect its transcendental existence toward liberation from the cycle of re-incarnation. Thus, from the perspective of purified ψυχή, it is as if the shadowy state of physical-embodiment were a mere epiphenomenon. Moreover, to the extent that the experience of time depends on a continuum of physical change for ψυχή to "count," then purified ψυχή in the "Platonic Heaven" is timeless. So, again, if we were to turn the point of view, from the perspective of purified ψυχή it is as if the process of be-ing embodied may be characterized as a kind of "pulsing" in and out, as it were, of the physical realm (cf. Scalambrino 2011; cf. Scalambrino 2017). The term for this is "palingenesis," which comes from the ancient Greek *palin* (again) and *genesis* (to begin).

Now that we have discussed the principles and distinctions associated with (a) the structure of ψυχή and (b) the functions of ψυχή in Plato's psychology, we will conclude this section with a discussion of (c) the methodological issues in Plato's psychology. Just as Alfred North Whitehead famously noted that the "safest general characterization of the European philosophical tradition is that it consists of a series of footnotes to Plato" (Whitehead 1985: 39), having covered this much ground in Plato will help make discussion below more concise. As we will see when we begin discussing principles of Western psychology from the Modern Period, Pre-Modern thinkers were more ontology-centric than methodology-centric; however, it will be helpful for us to discuss methodology—as Presentist as such an endeavor may be—for at least the sake of recognizing the continual presence of principles differently contextualized and emphasized across the history and systems of Western psychology.

We often hear of something called the "Socratic Method," whether it be in regard to Plato, classroom exercises, or Law School. In perhaps its most basic description, the "Socratic Method" refers to a question and answer process. This may be between multiple individuals or a person thinking-through some topic. The technical term for this type of back-and-forth is called "dialectic," and we may distinguish between "constructive" and "destructive" dialectic. Whereas the former refers to the type of back-and-forth for the purpose of leading toward some novel—at least for one of the interlocutors—conclusion, the latter refers to a process in which one of the interlocutors is asking questions for the sake of criticizing some initial opinion(s) or claim(s). For, understanding

> that the essence of things is the ultimate goal in science, as in the rational world in general, Plato formulated his dialectics as a method, or operational principle. It may be described as a procedure to carry one from the superficial material of things to the underlying forms... Dialectic is a process of thinking or reasoning which contrasts with observation or immediate contact. (Kantor 1963: 102)

This can be seen repeatedly in Plato's dialogs, especially the ones in which Socrates is featured as a character. For our purpose, we need only mention two more methodological principles regarding Plato's psychology. They are "myth-making" and "theurgy" (cf. Uždavinys 2010: 65–70; cf. Jung and Kerényi 1969).

Though both of these principles characterize Plato's methodology, as we will quickly notice, they flow directly from his ontology. That is, just as the power of imagination is associated with the physical body, the "higher" and more "pure" structures of ψυχή are beyond the power of imagination. Yet, in order to discuss these higher aspects of be-ing it is often valuable to invoke metaphors and allegories, that is, images. Thus, the process of constructing images for the sake of describing that which is beyond the power of imagination is called "myth-making," and the narrative products of the process are called "myths." On the one hand, myths are non-falsifiable, for example ψυχή is not actually in a "cave" or driving a chariot, so it would do little good to try to prove that ψυχή is not in a cave or driving a chariot. Yet, on the other hand, the historicity of these "myths" is different from the connotation given to the term in the Contemporary Period—where "myth" means "fallacy" or "necessarily false." Therefore, myth-making may be understood as an essential principle of Plato's methodology.

Lastly, the purification and *henosis* process noted above may also be characterized in terms of a methodology for Plato. In other words, recall the process of purification and recollection for ψυχή results in the revelation of truth. Thus, one may purposefully embark on the process of purification and recollection for the sake of discovering the truth of be-ing. Interestingly because accomplishing such purification is tantamount to be-ing like, if not fully assimilating oneself to, the pure be-ing of divine beings, this process as a purposeful method may be called "theurgy." If *henosis* is the union brought about by our purification from the perspective of physically embodied ψυχή recollecting in regard to its present incarnation, then theurgy is action in the other direction, so to speak, from the realm of divine pure be-ing on physically embodied ψυχή. In this way, referencing the Neoplatonist Iamblichus' (c. 245–c. 325) *On the Mysteries*,

> the *theurgical*, as universal and divine, is the opposite of anything particular and individualistic, anything based on one's subjective whims and egocentric drives. Without the fundamental realization of our own nothingness … no one can be saved, because in theurgical union gods are united only with gods, or rather "the divine is literally united with itself" (Iamblichus 2003: 47.4–47.8). This should in no way be conceived as communication between the mortal man and the immortal divinity (as one person addressing another), but rather communication of the divine in us with the divine in the universe. (Uždavinys 2010: 83)

It is as if "theurgy" refers to a method by way of which the mind of ψυχή purifies to a mirror of the divine, that is, pure be-ing, or stated in a more contemporary way, it is as if Plato has a theurgical method through which ψυχή's mind may become a mirror of God. It is in this way that one may say of dialectic that it is "the method of attaining assimilation to God through consciousness of the ultimate One-in-the-many, prior to the return to the One itself." (Anton 1992: 15–16). The "One-in-the-many" is the pure be-ing which is in every being, the transcendental dimension of every *thing*. It is as if we re-collect the transcendental from within the categorical experiences of be-ing.

## 3.2    Principles of Psychology from Aristotle

Given the ground already covered in the Plato section above, this section begins with a discussion of Aristotle in regard to Plato's principle of the immortality of ψυχή, it then moves directly to Aristotle's (c) methodology culminating in a discussion of the principles from Aristotle regarding the (a) structure and (b) function of ψυχή. As we will see, these latter two aspects of Aristotle's psychology together constitute a veritable developmental psychology and the beginnings of a naturalistic learning theory in terms of "associationism." One perennial exegetical issue regarding "Aristotle's philosophy," in general, is the question of its relation to "Plato's philosophy," in general. Keeping in mind "The Problem of Interpreting Plato's Dialogs," the standard response to this question involves mentioning that Aristotle was Plato's student for twenty (20) years. It also involves noting that despite their differences—and there are some quite significant differences—Aristotle may be understood as "systematizing" Plato toward a kind of "science" of philosophy. This is an important description of the relation between Plato and Aristotle, since later we will learn that Immanuel Kant's relation to Aristotle is much like Aristotle's relation to Plato; that is, Kant may be understood as "systematizing" or "re-organizing" Aristotle.

Recalling how, above, we identified "the principle of the immortality of ψυχή" as essential for organizing the principles of Plato's psychology, Aristotle disagreed with Plato regarding this principle. Thus, the relation between Plato's psychology and Aristotle's psychology is analogous—though not identical—with the contemporary distinction between the human science and the natural science approaches to the study of ψυχή. One of the primary reasons that the relation is not identical is that Aristotle's approach is holistic, and he believes in the non-material substantial be-ing of God. So, though he does not have a Cartesian mind-body problem, he also does not see non-physical be-ing as mere epiphenomenon. However, having said all that, Aristotle held that when the individual body dies, then the ψυχή associated with that body also ceases to be.

In order to understand Aristotle regarding the principle of the immortality of ψυχή it is helpful to examine how Aristotle famously described ψυχή. In his treatise, which is standardly considered the first scientific treatment of, and textbook on, ψυχή, titled "On ψυχή" (which we often refer to in one of its Latin or English translations as *De Anima* or *On the Soul*), he gives three different analogies, or metaphors, in terms of: an ax (1956: 412b13–14), an eye (Ibid: 412b20–22), and a ship's captain (Ibid: 413a8–9). Anticipating what will be considered more fully below, it is important to consider the suggestion by Aristotle scholar's that in discussing his third analogy for ψυχή it seems to raise "the possibility of some enduring aspect of soul essentially uninvolved with body yet still functional." (Polansky 2010: 168; cf. Tracy 1982). However, despite this possibility, we will stand by his more straightforward statements which clearly deny the principle of the immortality of ψυχή.

Aristotle's analogies for ψυχή immediately illuminate his psychology for us. First, "Suppose that a tool, for example an ax, were a *natural* [not artificial] body, then being an ax would have been its essence, and so its ψυχή; if this disappeared from it, it would have ceased to be an ax" (Aristotle 1956: 412b13–14). Second, he went on to apply the analogy to "the parts of a living body," as opposed to the non-living, artificial, ax. "Suppose that the eye were an animal—sight would have been its soul [ψυχή] ... the eye being merely the matter of seeing; when seeing is removed the eye is no longer an eye, except in name—no more than the eye of a statue or of a painted figure." (Ibid: 412b20–22). Lastly, he notes that it is not clear whether ψυχή may be "the actuality of its body in the sense in which the sailor is the actuality of the ship." (Ibid: 413a8–9).

Before delving into Aristotle's formal definition of ψυχή, notice what the analogies in combination suggest. Aristotle seems to understand ψυχή as the power or principle the presence of which constitutes a natural body's be-ing alive and what it is. That is, the ψυχή of a body determines—like a form to its matter—what the body is, that is, its essence. Further, to say that ψυχή is the power of sight is to say that its presence in relation to its body is the performing of the very function which makes the body what it is. The ψυχή of the eye is its actual vision, that is, no vision no eye-ψυχή. Finally, the sailor analogy points to the more Modern and Contemporary problem of "mental causation." Can the ψυχή direct and control its body or cause change to physical bodies? Of course, it certainly seems as though seeing something influences the directions in which the eye moves.

In order to understand Aristotle's formal definition of ψυχή, we need to understand how he intends the meaning of the term "actuality." Not surprisingly, the principles of actuality and potentiality are a hallmark of Aristotle's philosophy. To begin, "actuality" translates two different terms in Aristotle—*energeia* and *entelecheia*, and "potentiality" translates "*dynamis*," which means "power" or "potency" and resembles the term "dynamic." Noticing that Aristotle's second term translated as "actuality" includes the Greek term "*telos*," the actuality of *entelecheia* connotes the contemporary understanding of "self-actualization," as if there is a structure with parts originally non-actualized but with the *potential* to-be actualized; thus, *entelecheia*—indicating the actualization of what the thing essentially had the potential to be—connotes completion or maturation. In a similar, but different way, *energeia*—looking a good deal like the contemporary term "energy"—means something like "being-at-work being-what-it-is." (cf. Sachs 2001; cf. Polansky 1983). Thus, the actual eyesight of the eye may be understood as the actualization of the properly organized parts of the eyeball that is seeing (*entelecheia*), and as the eye continues to actually see, it continues to be what it is (*energeia*) an actual eye, that is, not merely a potential eye.

Lastly, when Aristotle discusses the relation between potentiality and actuality there is another distinction which is essential for us, if we are to think through Aristotle's psychology. The distinction is between "first potentiality," "second potentiality," and "actuality," and the classic example is the potential to learn French. We may say that two different individuals are both born with the potential to speak the French language. In this way they are "equal." However, when one of them learns how to speak French, then they are in a different relation to the activity of speaking French than they were originally. Thus, for Aristotle, they have moved from "first potentiality" to "second potentiality," and when they activate that "second potentiality," then *"voilà"* they are *actually* speaking French. Notice that moving from first potentiality to second potentiality is a "first actuality."

We are now ready for Aristotle's formal definition of ψυχή. Recalling Aristotle's Four Causes from above, Aristotle's holism is implied in his "hylomorphism," which refers to physical bodies as matter (*hylē*) and form (*morphē*) composites. Keep in mind these composites are *gestalts*, that is, the *actual* whole is greater than the sum of its parts (cf. Aristotle 1984: 1050b1). According to Aristotle, then,

> given that there are bodies of such and such a kind, namely, having life, the soul [ψυχή] cannot be a body; for the body is the subject or matter, not what is attributed to it. Hence the soul [ψυχή] must be a substance in the sense of the form of a natural body having life potentially within it. But substance is actuality, and thus soul [ψυχή] *is the actuality of a body* ... the soul [ψυχή] is *the first actuality of a natural body having life potentially* [emphasis added]. (1956: 412a17–27)

Aristotle's naturalistic perspective shines through here: just as the parts of a house may be organized in such a way (or not) so that they become a house and a house comes into be-ing, so too when a natural body is orga-nized in a way proper to its essential functions—like seeing for the eye –, then the actualization that constitutes the be-ing alive of the natural body is its ψυχή. The sailor analogy interestingly comes into play here, then, in that ψυχή emerges from the vitality of the properly formed physical being, and afterward is capable of directing that physical body.

Fascinatingly, this emergence is from universal be-ing, not from matter (i.e. not as contemporary physicalists often articulate a naturalistic posi-tion); however, it is still the case for Aristotle that when the organization and vitality of the body cease to be, then ψυχή also ceases to be: "the soul [ψυχή] cannot be without a body." (Aristotle 1956: 414a20). This may require some clarification; according to Aristotle:

> *the study of the soul* [ψυχή] ... *must fall within the science of nature.* Hence a physicist would define an affection of soul [ψυχή] differently from a dialectician; the latter would define, e.g. anger as the appetite for returning pain for pain, or something like that, while the former would define it as a

boiling of the blood or warm substance surrounding the heart. The one assigns the material conditions, the other the form or account; for what he states is the account of the fact, though for its actual existence there must be embodiment of it in a material such as is described by the other [emphasis added]. (Ibid: 403a27–403b4)

First off, notice in this quote Aristotle associates *explanation* with the science of nature and *description* with dialectic. Contemporary psychologists seem to have a tendency to interpret statements from Aristotle such as this block quote in too Modern of a context, rather than in terms of the historicity of "Aristotle's divisions of science." For example, Aristotle divides the different branches of knowledge and learning into (1) "theoretical," (2) "practical," and (3) "productive" sciences. Moreover, he frequently reaffirms the principles of this division; that is, the theoretical sciences seek knowledge for its own sake, the practical sciences for the sake of improving behaviors and excellence in action, and the productive sciences for the sake of producing useful or beautiful creations (cf. Aristotle 1950: 192b8–12; cf. 1984: 1025b25; cf. 1967: 145a15–16).

In this way, when Aristotle deemed psychology a natural science he still understood it as a theoretical science. This means his naturalistic perspective is still different from the eliminative position which he, in the above block quote, associates with approaching ψυχή from the perspective of physics. Physics, of course, was also a theoretical science; however, as Aristotle noted above, physics is concerned with matter and Aristotelian psychology with form. Moreover, Aristotle considered medicine a productive science. Therefore, in addition to the fact that Aristotle sees the difference between the methods of natural science and medicine as that between the theoretical sciences and the productive sciences, Aristotle's relation to Hippocrates (460–370 BC) regarding psychology is analogous only in regard to the extent their subject matters coincide in biology (cf. Hergenhahn 2009: 51). Thus, in regard to the methodology for Aristotle's psychology, it is involved in the principle of "knowledge for its own sake," as a theoretical science. For this reason, on the one hand, we find a distinction between dialectic and demonstration, reflecting a similar emphasis found in Plato's dialogs. On the other hand, though Aristotle may technically be called an "empiricist," and he does engage in "inductive" reasoning regarding ψυχή; anticipating a later discussion of "Modern empiricism," we will need to clarify the place of Aristotle's induction in his methodology of psychology *as a theoretical science.*

That is, with this in mind, Aristotle's methodology may be characterized as a clarifying and streamlining of the "Socratic Method." Thus, as it was with Plato, "dialectic" may be understood as a three-step process, whether this be in terms of the resolution of two contradictory terms, for example thesis, antithesis, and synthesis, or whether it be in terms of a development of a (1) first idea into (2) something different with a (3) return to supplement the first idea. Hence, the previous technical characterization also still holds: we may distinguish between "constructive" and "destructive" dialectic. Here is a helpful analogy regarding these vocabulary terms: "Dialectic: Discovery:: Demonstration: Justification." That is to say, dialectic has an interesting twofold function which may be characterized in terms of "discovery." Whereas destructive dialectic discovers ways to criticize arguments and discern their truth by having the parts of arguments placed into its three-step process, constructive dialectic discovers truth by developing meaning. In this way, dialectic begins with phenomena, in that "phenomena" may refer to opinions or products of perception (cf. Owen 1986). Because we have already discussed the destruction and construction of opinions regarding the "Socratic Method" above, here we want to focus on dialectic in regard to products of perception, especially in relation to demonstration. This points to the heart of Aristotle's methodology. Moreover, though we may attribute "induction" and "inductive reasoning" to Aristotle, we must keep his "word-concept-thing" understanding of signification in mind—his induction is dealing primarily with "concepts" and secondarily with "things," even in the case of perceptual experience.

Notice that if you cannot justify your position or claim, then you seek to *discover* support—whether in the form of evidence or other opinions—with the idea that once you acquire the needed justification, you will be able to *demonstrate* the validity of your position or the truth of your claim. It is worth quoting Aristotle at length here.

The premise of demonstration differs from the premise of dialectic in that the former is the assumption of one member of a pair of contradictory statements (since the demonstrator does not ask a question but makes an assumption), whereas the latter is an answer to the question which of two contradictory statements is to be accepted. This difference, however, will not affect the fact that in either case a syllogism results; for both the demonstrator and the interrogator draw a syllogistic conclusion by first assuming that some predicate applies or does not apply to some subject. (Aristotle 1964b: 23b24–24a34)

Focusing on the "syllogistic conclusion," Aristotle will require that the results of both dialectic and demonstration must be stated in terms of a rational deductive argument such that the conclusion logically follows from the combination of premises. In regard to demonstration, then, on the one hand, "hypotheses are the origins of demonstrations." (Aristotle 1984: 1013a16). On the other hand, "By the starting points of demonstration I mean the common beliefs, on which all men base their proofs." (Aristotle 1984: 996b26–30; cf. Barnes 1969).

This points to the heart of Aristotle's methodology and what is standardly understood to be the first systematization in regard to scientific inquiry with the essential distinction that Aristotle's empiricism was a more passive observation than Modern controlled experiment (cf. Dickinson 1986: 49). For what Aristotle was discussing here is the formulation and logical examination of hypotheses, and, in general, "scientific knowledge" involves knowing the principles, causes, and elements from which knowledge may be *demonstrated* and *justified* (cf. Ziman 1978). Initially these must be *discovered*.

When the objects of an inquiry, in any department, have principles, causes, or elements, it is through acquaintance with these that knowledge and understanding is attained. ... therefore, in the science of nature too our first task will be to try to determine what relates to its principles. (Aristotle 1950: 184a10–17)

In this way, ψυχή functions as a kind of principle itself to explain "the functioning of all mortal living things" (cf. Polansky 2010: 163), ψυχή functions as a principle in works by Aristotle such as *Parts of Animals* (1937) and the *Generation of Animals* (1965). Thus, with Aristotle we already have a "developmental psychology," however, it is articulated in terms of his methodology and natural science. We will discuss this next; to conclude this discussion of Aristotle's methodology, notice that by isolating the structure of the "Socratic Method" Aristotle articulated a kind of "scientific method" in that dialectic may be used regarding phenomena (accepted opinions of others or phenomena of perceptual experience) and through such discovery demonstrations may be logically formulated to justify initial hypotheses.

What remains to be said about Aristotle's psychology, then, is a discussion of his developmental psychology and learning theory. As we noticed from the American Psychological Association's definition of "development," it derives from taking a synchronic understanding of structure and making it diachronic by combining function with structure. Whereas the structure and function of ψυχή for Aristotle are ontological principles of organic (i.e. holistic) natural beings, considering the structure of ψυχή over time regarding the natural functions of the composite being—the ensouled natural body or the embodied ψυχή—both a natural teleology and a natural soteriology emerge. That is to say, the natural development of a being in regard to its natural functions constitutes the actualization of the parts of its structure which were previously in potentiality. Of course, Aristotle takes this to be the purpose of the natural beings ψυχή. As a simple example, if the natural-physical body does not receive nutrition, then it will not survive; therefore, the presence of a principle of growth and nutrition (ψυχή) "in" the body serves the purpose of sustaining the life of the body. Similarly, it is by actualizing the potentiality to consume nutrition that an ensouled body "saves" itself, that is, soteriology. Thus, the natural functions of the structure of ψυχή actualized over time constitute Aristotle's developmental psychology; however, the historicity of his theory is such that he characterized ψυχή's actualization over time in terms of teleology and soteriology.

The principle of "associationism" is essentially the naturalistic reading with which to oppose Plato's theory of recollection, that is, *anamnēsis*. In its basic form, then, the principle of association provides a way to account for co-occurrence, for example of sensations, feelings, perceptions, or concepts. Because we are able to associate images, words, concepts, and things with one another, we are able to learn. Recall, Plato's theory of *anamnēsis* was presented in the context of the question: Is *learning* more like putting sight into the blind or more like remembering? The naturalistic reading, then, provides an account of learning that is more like putting sight into the blind. As will be emphasized in discussion of the Modern Period, where theories of knowledge showcase rationalism—knowing by rational inference and intuition—in contrast to empiricism—knowing in terms of evidence from the embodied senses. Though it may technically be anachronistic to attempt to characterize Aristotle's philosophy in terms of the epistemological positon of "empiricism," we can still see the principle of association and the empirical principle of learning through the senses at work in Aristotle's philosophy of psychology.

As if distinguishing a theory of learning from the naturalistic standpoint and in direct contradistinction from Plato's theory of recollection, we can find passages such as the following in Aristotle's writings.

> When we recollect, then, we undergo one of the earlier changes, until we undergo the one after which the change in question habitually occurs. And this is exactly why we hunt for the successor, starting in our thoughts from the present or from something else, and from something similar, or opposite, or neighboring [contiguous]. By this means recollection occurs. (Aristotle 2006: 451b16–20)

It is standardly noted, then, that with the above declaration Aristotle provided the first "scientific," or, at least, systematic, statement of the "laws of association," that is, the laws of similarity, contrast, and contiguity. Further, in Aristotle's philosophy "habit" often functions as a principle of explanation, so much so that he may be seen as, at least, sketching out the parameters for Modern theories of behavioral conditioning, cognitive accounts of memory function such as "priming," and even neuroscientific eliminativist accounts of learning.

> It can happen that by undergoing certain changes once, a person is more habituated than he is by undergoing other changes many times. And this is why after seeing some things once, we remember better than we do after seeing other things many times. (Ibid: 451b10)

Of course, the principle of habit is showcased most prominently in Aristotle's ethics. Moreover, it is Aristotle's ethical theory which may be seen as providing a kind of culmination to the structural and natural-functional accounts of ψυχή found in his *De Anima*. In fact, it is in terms of Aristotle's ethical theory that we will find his remaining principles regarding the structure and function of ψυχή.

Recalling Plato's *Scala Amoris*, Aristotle's naturalistic perspective provides us with what is standardly called a *Scala Natura* in contrast. That is to say, whereas it was an "ascension" in regard to desire and love which differentiates ψυχή in terms of teleology and soteriology, for Aristotle it is natural, that is, biologically based, function which differentiates ψυχή in regard to development and thriving or terrestrial happiness. Aristotle famously differentiated types of ψυχή based on natural functions into: (1) "vegetable" or "plant" ψυχή with the natural functions of "nutrition, growth, and reproduction," (2) "animal" ψυχή with the natural functions of "sense perception and appetite or desire," and (3) "human" ψυχή with the use of reason and rationality as a differentiating natural function (cf. Aristotle 1956). On the one hand, we want to recognize the *Scala Natura* here. That is, there is a "natural hierarchy" which may be seen across the natural functions. In this way, natural function may be seen as a principle of explanation for Aristotle as well. As we move "up" from the plant to human ψυχή, notice each subsequent level retains the potential to perform the functions found at the "lower" level of ψυχή, while at the same time gaining more power, that is, the potency to perform even more ψυχή-based functions. Thus, the *Scala Natura* describes the natural hierarchy of beings in nature in terms of the type of ψυχή which constitutes their be-ing (cf. Benjafield 2012: 12–13).

On the other hand, the principle of natural function also differentiates the plant ψυχή from the animal ψυχή, and so on. This differentiation also characterizes the limits to the structures of the different types of ψυχή in terms of teleology and soteriology—the azalea has no desire to paint a sunset. In this way, just as ψυχή is the actualization of a living body, the teleological structure of ψυχή will be—for Aristotle—functionally constrained by the natural capacities of the body. It is worth noting that this is one of the reason's Aristotle does not have a mind-body problem; that is, just as for him there is no ψυχή without a living body, so too:

> we can dismiss as unnecessary the question whether the soul [ψυχή] and the body are one: it is as though we were to ask whether the wax and its shape are one, or generally the matter of a thing and that of which it is the matter. (Aristotle 1984: 412b5–9)

To more fully explicate Aristotle's teleology and soteriology regarding human psychology—not his plant or animal psychology—we must look at his account of human excellence. The account is exclusively human in that it takes into account physical-embodiment and the use of rationality; moreover, it provides a further level of distinction specifically in regard to Aristotle's human psychology. That is to say, the above noted capacities indicating steps along the *Scala Natura* are all contained within the human ψυχή, that is, humans are capable of nutrition, reproduction, sense perception, and so on. However, there is more to the structure of the human ψυχή than what was necessary to state in order to merely differentiate it from the plant and animal.

Aristotle also used the principle of natural function to enumerate the various human excellences. Though it is of course possible to ask of all natural functions whether they are being completed well—for example is this being perceiving its environment accurately or receiving sufficient nutrition?—these natural functions of physical-embodiment involve the specifically human ψυχή function of the use of reason.

> Now each function is completed well by being completed properly in accordance with its virtue. And so the human good proves to be activity of the soul in accord with virtue, and indeed with the best and most complete virtue, if there are more virtues than one. (Aristotle 2009: 1098a17)

Further, whereas above we characterized Plato's theurgy as if it were a supernatural capacity for "action in the other direction," that is, *from beyond* physical-embodiment *to* physical-embodiment. Aristotle's virtue theory may be characterized in terms of a naturalization of this action in the other direction by way of the power of "habit." For, "It should be said, then, that every virtue causes its possessors to be in a good state and to perform their functions well." (Ibid: 1106b17). Now, though it would be beyond the scope of this book to launch into a discussion of Aristotle's accounting for different human virtues, his discussion of different "character types" is precisely a discussion of the higher structure of the human ψυχή noted above.

According to Aristotle there are technically six (6) "character types" in regard to his virtue ethics; however, we will only examine the four (4) human character types. These are: (1) Virtuous, (2) Continent, (3) Incontinent, and (4) Vicious character types. Recalling what we referred to above as the Western "Orthodox" view of the structure of ψυχή and its characteristic divisions into "affection," "cognition," and "conation," we noted three organizing principles: "*pathos*," "*logos*," and "*ethos*." These principles may be used to illustrate distinctions across the character types. The Continent character type is one in which the individual feels the temptation to act in accordance with *pathos*, rather than *logos*; however, they tend to overcome the *pathos*, thereby establishing an *ethos* that tends to "hold in" the temptations of *pathos*, that is, to choose in accordance with *logos*. The Incontinent character type is the exact opposite; having a tendency not to "hold in" the temptations of *pathos*, this character type establishes an *ethos* that tends to choose not in accordance with *logos*. The Virtuous character type chooses in accordance with *logos* and has established such a strong *ethos* tendency that this character type does not experience the temptations of *pathos*. The Vicious character type is the exact opposite; having a tendency to not concern itself with *logos*, it merely looks for opportunities to "discharge" its vices, that is, act in accordance with *pathos*. (cf. Aristotle 2009: 1102a–1114b).

Though there is, of course, much more that could be said about Aristotle's character types, this explication should be sufficient to illustrate three points. First, the character types coincide with the ship captain analogy of ψυχή. That is to say, it is in terms of the organizing principles of *pathos*, *logos*, and *ethos* that we may articulate how ψυχή is able to exert influence over an otherwise deterministic physical embodiment, that is, primarily in terms of habit (*ethos*). As Aristotle explained, "Someone may say that all people aim at the apparent good, but have no control over the appearance, but *the end appears to each person in a form answering to that person's character* [emphasis added]." (Ibid: 1114b1). Second, the teleological and soteriological aspects regarding the structure and function of ψυχή are shown here in that becoming Virtuous "saves" ψυχή from the deterministic "animal" *pathos* of its physical embodiment. Only as Virtuous, Aristotle suggested for us, can ψυχή actualize its freedom.

Notice, it is in terms of be-ing Virtuous, then, that Aristotle explains *Eudaimonia*, that is, human thriving and happiness, and in this way completes the naturalistic account of that which received a supernatural account in Plato. For it is through the actualization of natural function that ψυχή achieves the highest excellence possible, given the conditions of human physical-embodiment. Lastly, we should inquire why it is that action in accordance with *logos* can lead to happiness. The answer may be seen in looking at the wider context of ψυχή's natural functions. That is to say, for Aristotle it is as if the principles of structure and function constitute all of nature; ψυχή is constituted by natural functions and relates to its environment in terms of the natural functions which are operable for both it and the environment in its present situation. Put simply, this amounts to saying that there is a "Natural Law" governing situations, and acting in accordance with it may be the best for which we can hope, that is, such accord with nature is excellence for ψυχή. This will be thematized further in the next section.

## 3.3    Principles from the Philosophy of Epicurus, Epictetus, and the Catholic Church

Given the content of this section we begin with two disclaimers. First, on the one hand, the influence of Christianity—especially through the philosophical principles established in the Middle Ages by Catholic philosopher-priests—on subsequent psychology is undeniable; however, our interest here is to explicate philosophical principles, not to provide an interpretation of Christianity. Second, we are not considering Eastern or Middle Eastern principles of psychology, and for that reason Buddhist, Hindu, Jewish, or Islamic principles of psychology, for example, will not be discussed here. Of course, the shift in worldview from Aristotle to Christianity may be characterized as a move toward the supernaturalism of Plato; yet, it is in a way that affirms, rather than denies, many of Aristotle's principles regarding ψυχή. This is perhaps most easily noticed by discussing some principles from Epicurus (341–270 BC) and Epictetus (55–135) as to "bridge" into this section from the notion of Natural Law with which we concluded the Aristotle section. Specifically we will discuss principles of desire from Epicurus, principles of freedom from Epictetus, and both as they relate to Natural Law. In regard to the Catholic philosopher-priests of the Middle Ages, then, we will discuss the following principles: (1) the structural principles of intentionality and conscience, (2) the functional principles of the "interior life," personhood, and confession and prayer, and (3) Ockham's methodological principle, aka "Ockham's razor," which, inadvertently perhaps, allowed for the principles of Modern science to "revolutionize" the history of Western psychology (cf. Swindal 2017).

The principle of free will is essential for psychology. Just like the principle of the immortality of ψυχή, the position one takes in regard to these principles immediately makes the resulting system incommensurable with other systems. Arguing for the value of some types of choice over others is fruitless if your audience believes "choice" is an illusion. The "free will problem," is standardly thought to have originated with the Hedonist Epicurus (cf. Huby 1967; cf. Schneewind 1998); however, the idea of a "free will" is standardly thought to have originated with the Stoic Epictetus (cf. Frede 2011; cf. O'Keefe 2005). Whereas Epicurus and Epictetus share the naturalistic perspective with Aristotle, Epicurus and Epictetus were materialists. Further, though the cosmologies of these three philosophers may be characterized in significant contrast, their psychologies agree in terms of holism (cf. Gill 2006b); moreover, this is thought to be the case, despite the fact that Epicurus is famously an atomist in terms of his cosmology. Thus, he believed the material universe is not fully deterministic since there is an element of chance involved; he called this "the swerve"— atoms sometimes "swerve," thereby, adding an element of chance such that one could have acted differently than one did.

In fact what some have called the "substantial holism" common to these three philosophers regarding ψυχή seems to have been the model for the subsequent distinct notion among Catholic philosophers of ψυχή as a "substantial form." Their substantial holism in regard to ψυχή amounts to an understanding of the structure of ψυχή according to the following three principles: (1) all ψυχή is body, but not all body is ψυχή, (2) only what is extended in space and capable of action exists—therefore ψυχή is extended in space, and (3) ψυχή cannot exist without the body—therefore ψυχή is not immortal (cf. Gill 2006a: 209). Though it is considered presentistic and anachronistic to place Plato and Aristotle on the spectrum of positions regarding "free will," whereas Epicurus was an Incompatibilist and not a Determinist, Epictetus advocated for a Fatalistic worldview and yet was a Compatibilist. However, despite these differences, there are multiple similarities, such as: Aristotle's divisions of ψυχή, what may be called the Hedonist principle of pursuing pleasure and avoiding pain, and a principle of rational agency. This latter principle may be seen in terms of the Hedonist Epicurus' principles regarding desire and the Stoic Epictetus' principles of comprehension or under-standing. Further, insofar as these principles illuminate Hedonist and Stoic articulations of teleology and soteriology, then they also illuminate structural and functional interpretations of ψυχή toward an articulation of Hedonist and Stoic psychologies.

There is a distinction between three types of desire for Epicurus: (1) "natural and necessary" desires, (2) "natural and non-necessary" desires, and (3) "vain and empty" desires. The classic examples include: (1) desires for food and shelter, (2) desires for luxurious food or luxurious shelter, and (3) desires for power, wealth, fame, and the like (cf. Epicurus 1994). Epicurus pointed out that whereas the first of the types of desire are easy to satisfy, they are necessary for life, difficult to eliminate, and they are naturally limited, that is, if you are hungry, your desire can be satisfied by a limited amount of food, the second and third types of desire are not necessary for an individual to survive. Moreover, desires of the third type have no natural limit. It is for these reasons, then, that the desires can be associated with the natural functions of embodied ψυχή, on the one hand, and a "Natural Law" may be developed, on the other. That is to say, it seems to be a Natural Law that there is a natural limit to certain types of desire and not to others. Those who go against the Natural Law will suffer unnatural experiences, or, at least, so goes the Natural Law theorizing of these ancient Greek ethicists.

In order to understand the Stoic principles of comprehension and understanding—and their relation to the Natural Law—it is helpful to initially think about their cosmology. Stoic cosmology is cyclical, and the individual is subordinate to universal nature, which has a teleology and progresses circuitously, as if in terms of an endless Big Bang and Big Crunch cycle. At the moment before the Big Bang, there is only God, and through the Big Bang the universe is produced out of God; however, God is not thereby separate from the universe. Moreover, as a fiery kind of *material,* God was characterized by the Stoics as a kind of "craftsman-like fire." This is the context, then, for a Stoic psychology (cf. Epictetus 1998), and in order to understand Stoic Compatibilism, we should keep in mind how individual embodied ψυχή's are always already subordinate to the endless cycling of God as nature.

Whereas Stoic Fatalism follows directly from Stoic cosmology, Stoic Compatibilism may be seen by examining the process by which a Stoic relates to fate. For example, according to Epictetus,

> Remember that you are an actor in a drama such as the playwright wishes it to be. If he wants it short, it will be short; if long, long. If he wants you to play a beggar, play even that capably; or a lame man, or a ruler, or a private person. For this is yours, to play the assigned role well. Casting is the business of another. (Epictetus 1998: §17)

Further, "Don't seek for things to happen as you wish, but wish for things to happen as they do, and you will be free from disturbance." (Ibid: §8). Notice, then, that Epictetus is not suggesting that ψυχή's body will never experience pain or discomfort; rather, he is suggesting that ψυχή will not be as disturbed by the pain and discomfort as it could be. Moreover, notice that the mechanism that is supposed to free ψυχή from disturbance is characterized in terms of thinking and understanding. How is this supposed to work? Precisely by understanding that whatever it is you are experiencing you could not have avoided experiencing it. Now, on the one hand, this sounds exactly like Determinism and a lack of freedom, because you could not have avoided the experience. However, ψυχή is free to understand the experience in different ways. Thus, the Stoics see Determinism (as Fatalism) and free will as Compatible.

On the other hand, what are the different ways in which ψυχή can relate to its fated experiences? Recalling Aristotle, ψυχή can relate in terms of *pathos* or *logos*. The Stoics are sometimes criticized as "lethally high-minded" because they see relating to fated events emotionally as "*pathetic*." In order to cultivate Stoic "*a-pathy*" one needs to be more *logical* and accept that the experience was fated, that is, determined. For instance, consider this bit of Stoic wisdom:

> As for everything that delights your mind or is useful or beloved, remember to describe it as it really is, starting with the smallest thing. If you are fond of a pot, say "it is a pot that I am fond of." For then, if it breaks, you will not be upset. If you kiss your child or your wife, say that you are kissing a human being. Then if they die you will not be upset. (Epictetus 1998: §3)

For the Stoic, precisely because they are fatalistic, the best we can hope for is to get a grip on what it is that we have been fated to endure. The classic statement of the prescribed use of rational agency called "katalepsis," that is, to get a conceptual grip or logical comprehension, comes from Cicero's discussion of Zeno of Citium (c. 334-c. 262 BC), the founder of the Stoicism:

> he would display his hand in front of one with the fingers stretched out and say 'A visual appearance is like this'; next he closed his fingers a little and said, 'An act of assent is like this'; then he pressed his fingers closely together and made a fist, and said that that was comprehension (and from this illustration he gave to that process the actual name of *katalepsis*, which it had not had before) … (Cicero 1967: 2.145)

To sum, it is as if though ψυχή can neither escape the experience of the natural laws nor of the sequence of the events in the flow of God's cosmic unfolding, ψυχή does have rational control over the part of its structure with which it relates to its fate. This fate includes not just the external natural functions of the environment but also the natural functions of one's fated embodiment. Stoic Compatibilism and the Stoic understanding of Natural Law have been referred to as the system "into which the Church

Fathers were able to pour the first conceptions of Christian natural law and to impart them to the world of their time." (Rommen 1998: 10).

One of the ways, then, to philosophically characterize the context of Catholic psychology is in terms of the movement of a kind of return to the supernaturalism of Plato informed by the alterations and "progress" exemplified by naturalistic thinkers such as Aristotle, Epicurus, and Epictetus. Recall from the above discussion of theurgy and Plato's philosophy, we referenced "action in the other direction" to characterize the capacity for a supernatural power to intervene or interact with physically embodied ψυχή. This, of course, becomes an essential point of departure for Catholic psychology. Beyond Aristotle's discussion of natural function and the excellences or virtues regarding natural function, Catholic philosophers enumerated the supernatural, or theological, virtues of "Faith, Hope, and Love (e.g. Charity)." The perennial definition comes from Aquinas:

> additional principles must be given by God to man by which he can thus be ordered to supernatural happiness. ... These additional principles are called theological virtues: first, because they have God as their object, inasmuch as by them we are rightly ordered to God; secondly, because they are infused in us by God alone; and finally, because these virtues are made known to us only by divine revelation in Sacred Scripture. (Aquinas 1920: I–II, q. 62, a. 1)

Notice, then, that through Catholic psychology the structure of ψυχή is again considered necessarily in relation to the divine. That is to say, just as we saw in Plato and Stoicism, ψυχή functions appropriately when in the proper relation to embodied experience. Thus, even "mental health," for example the possibility of happiness, becomes subsumed under morality.

Thus, these principles of psychology developed from the previous philosophers; yet originating from the Catholic point of view, regarding the structure of ψυχή are "intentionality" and "conscience," and regarding the function of ψυχή are the principle of "interior life" and the principle of "personhood." In his commentary on 1 Corinthians 15—which it is quite interesting to read with the above comments about Stoicism in mind—Aquinas emphasizes, against Plato, that the person is not identical with the soul, that is, ψυχή:

> the Platonists positing immortality, posited re-incorporation, although this is heretical. … it is clear that man naturally desires his own salvation; but the soul, since it is part of man's body, is not an entire man, and my soul is not I. (Aquinas 2012: §924)

Put simply, the idea is that the *person* is greater than the sum of its parts, and just as the composite of ψυχή and physical-body may be understood in the Aristotelian terminology of form and matter, respectively, so too through resurrection from the dead the material part of the composite— it is believed—will be replaced by a celestial or non-physical body; therefore, as fully spiritual the *person* will live forever.

As an integral and spiritual component of the physically embodied and living person, there are principles regarding ψυχή which contribute to the trajectory of the person into its non-physically embodied life. These principles are "intentionality" and "conscience." The former principle characterizes the person's free will in regard to sin and may be retrospectively thought operable in differentiating Aristotle's character types; further, re-asserting the *Scala Amoris*—though re-contextualized now in terms of free will and Christian Love—"holiness is in the will and we are saved by what we love" (Sheed 1946: 10 & cf. Ibid: 61). The latter principle characterizes the internal dialog indicative of an *ethos*, and may be understood as relating to the notion of the *daimon* from Plato. Aristotelian character-building now is directed at a super-natural afterlife with the potential for the super-natural happiness of beatitude, beyond any temporary happiness for which the naturalistic philosophers advocated.

In terms of function, then, intentionality and conscience as structural aspects of ψυχή in relation to one another constitute ψυχή's "inward-facing," so to speak, functional principle of the "interior life" of the person (cf. Garrigou-Lagrange 2015: 4–17). Personhood, as Aquinas indicated above, has become an important principle in that it is not knowledge "in" ψυχή that unites it with the transcendental dimension, it is the willing "of" ψυχή that unites its holistically understood person with God. "Outward-facing," then, would be the soteriological-theurgical component from Plato after progressing through dialectical exchange with the philosophies of Aristotle, Epicurus, and Epictetus, among others. This component may be characterized in a number of ways; however, for our purpose, we will point to "confession" and "prayer" in that these principles have, throughout the history of Western psychology, been considered psychotherapeutic (cf. Jung 2001, 2014; cf. Worthen 1974). Thus, with Catholic philosophy Western psychology reached the pinnacle of its identification with morality.

It is now standard to locate the groundwork for the Modern Period's movement away from the Medieval-Scholastic system of the Middle Ages in the principles of the excommunicated Catholic monk William of Ockham (1285–1347), especially his nominalism and what is referred to as "Ockham's Razor" (cf. Swindal 2017; cf. Kugelmann 2011). In regard to the "problem of universals" discussed above and in opposition to the "realist" philosophers we have been discussing thus far, Ockham was a "nominalist." In order to get clear on Ockham's position, recall from the discussion of Aristotle's methodology, dialectic was understood in the context of his "word-concept-thing" understanding of signification. Ockham basically emphasizes that it is a mistake to treat a word as a thing. Words are just names, and as such may not refer to any *thing* in *reality* at all. On the one hand, Ockham's nominalism, then, has a lasting effect on Aristotle's dialectic—despite its naturalistic perspective (cf. Ockham 1990; cf. Maurer 1978; cf. Panaccio 2004). Basically, Ockham separates induction from dialectic, leaving a kind of empiricism without realism in its place. We can still investigate the things of reality; however, Ockham was against considering their *description* to be real. Ockham himself continued to use dialectal arguments; however, history attests that he successfully re-framed the use of dialectic as a means of persuasion, rather than a scientific method for discovering truth (cf. Maurer 1999: 113–125; cf. Stump 1989: 253).

On the other hand, Ockham's razor may be seen as an articulation of a principle stated in Aristotle's discussion of demonstration. According to Aristotle, "Let that demonstration be better which, other things being equal, depends on fewer postulates or suppositions or propositions. For if they are equally familiar, knowing will come about more quickly in this way; and that is preferable." (Aristotle 1964a: 86a34–36). However,

Ockham's combination of this principle with nominalism may be seen as a shift toward a different methodology (cf. Brampton 1964). Both Galileo (1564–1642) and Newton (1643–1727) emphasize Ockham's razor as a "principle of parsimony," Ernst Mach (1838–1916) emphasized it as a "principle of economy," and Stephen Hawking, while celebrating it, indicates "Heisenberg's uncertainty Principle" as an evolved version:

> We could still imagine that there is a set of laws that determine events completely for some supernatural being who, unlike us, could observe the present state of the universe without disturbing it. However, such models of the universe are not of much interest to us ordinary mortals. It seems better to employ the principle of economy known as Ockham's razor and cut out all the features of the theory that cannot be observed. (Hawking and Mlodinow 2007: 91)

The effect of Ockham's razor as a scientific principle has been championed, then—especially as a principle of progress—against Pre-Modern "scientific" uses of dialectical reasoning. Simply put, basing a transcendental theory on reality is problematic, since there is disagreement regarding the words used to *describe* that reality (cf. Wood 1990: 194; cf. Wood 2015: 170). What this means is that it may be difficult—despite coherent uses of the term "be-ing"—to explain the relation between the be-ing of ψυχή and the be-ing of all beings (even when the Being of that be-ing is understood as a Person theurgically, so to speak, interacting with ψυχή).

Moreover, it may be consider *explanatorily* unnecessary for many thinkers. On the one hand, given an understanding of ψυχή as a physical being, discussion of the transcendental dimension in relation to ψυχή may be eliminated from the naturalistic perspective. On the other hand, as the Contemporary Period can attest, it is not clear if living by Ockham's razor means for psychologists that they must eventually also cut out the very of idea of ψυχή itself—in the service of ultimately becoming biologists. In this way, the approach of natural science to ψυχή has been to eliminate the previously supposed entities which have come to be considered explanatorily unnecessary, while at the same time avoiding positing any new beings if not necessary for explanation. This, as we have already seen has led to some systems of Western psychology in which personhood, freedom of the will and ψυχή itself have been considered explanatorily unnecessary (cf. Frankfurt 2009: 197). Notice, the idea that such aspects are humane or belong in descriptions of ψυχή in that psychology is a human science, have met with opposition from the natural science perspective which suggests that those are aspects of morality, theology, or politics and, ultimately, may not need to be included in a science of psychology.

## Notes

1. For many readers it may be helpful to think of this discussion as Plato's Western explication of the Eastern notion of "karma" (cf. Scalambrino 2017: 30–35).

## Bibliography

Anton, John P. 1992. Plotinus and the Neoplatonic Conception of Dialectic. *The Journal of Neoplatonic Studies* 1 (1): 3–30.

Aquinas, Thomas. 1920. *The "Summa Theologica" of St. Thomas Aquinas*. Trans. Fathers of the English Dominican Province. London: Burns Oates & Washbourne.

———. 2012. *Commentary on the Letters of Saint Paul to the Corinthians*. Ed. The Aquinas Institute and Trans. F.R. Larcher. Lander, WY: The Aquinas Institute for the Study of Sacred Doctrine.

Aristotle. 1937. *Parts of Animals*. Trans. W. Ogle. In *The Complete Works of Aristotle: The Revised Oxford Translation* (1995), ed. J. Barnes, vol. I, 994–1086. Princeton, NJ: Princeton University Press.

———. 1950. *Physics*. Trans. W.D. Ross. R.P. Hardie and Revised by R.K. Gaye (Rev.). In *The Complete Works of Aristotle: The Revised Oxford Translation* (1995), ed. J. Barnes, vol. I, 315–446. Princeton, NJ: Princeton University Press.

———. 1956. *On the Soul*. Trans. J.A. Smith. In *The Complete Works of Aristotle: The Revised Oxford Translation* (1995), ed. J. Barnes, vol. I, 641–692. Princeton, NJ: Princeton University Press.

———. 1964a. *Posterior Analytics*. Trans. W.D. Ross. In *The Complete Works of Aristotle: The Revised Oxford Translation* (1995), ed. J. Barnes, vol. I, 114–166. Princeton, NJ: Princeton University Press.

———. 1964b. *Prior Analytics*. Trans. A.J. Jenkinson. In *The Complete Works of Aristotle: The Revised Oxford Translation* (1995), ed. J. Barnes, vol. I, 39–113. Princeton, NJ: Princeton University Press.

———. 1965. *Generation of Animals*. Trans. A. Platt. In *The Complete Works of Aristotle: The Revised Oxford Translation* (1995), ed. J. Barnes, vol. I, 1111–1218. Princeton, NJ: Princeton University Press.

———. 1967. *Topics*. Trans. J. Brunschwig. In *The Complete Works of Aristotle: The Revised Oxford Translation* (1995), ed. J. Barnes, vol. I, 167–277. Princeton, NJ: Princeton University Press.

———. 1984. *Metaphysics*. Trans. W.D. Ross. In *The Complete Works of Aristotle: The Revised Oxford Translation* (1995), ed. J. Barnes, vol. II, 1552–1728. Princeton, NJ: Princeton University Press.

———. 2006. *On Memory & Recollection*. Trans. R. Sorabji. In *Aristotle on Memory*, ed. R. Sorabji, 47–60. Chicago, IL: University of Chicago Press.

———. 2009. *Nicomachean Ethics*. Trans. R. Crisp. Cambridge: Cambridge University Press.

Barnes, Jonathan. 1969. Aristotle's Theory of Demonstration. *Phronesis* 14 (2): 123–152.

Beckman, James. 1979. *The Religious Dimension of Socrates' Thought*. Waterloo, ON: Wilfrid Laurier University Press.

Benjafield, John G. 2012. *Psychology: A Concise History*. Oxford: Oxford University Press.

Blondell, Ruby. 2002. *The Play of Character in Plato's Dialogues*. Cambridge: Cambridge University Press.

Boys-Stones, George, and Christopher Rowe. 2013. *The Circle of Socrates: Reading in the First-Generation Socratics*. Indianapolis, IN: Hackett Publishing.

Brampton, C.K. 1964. Nominalism and the Law of Parsimony. *The Modern Schoolman* 41 (3): 273–281.

Burkert, Walter. 1989. *Ancient Mystery Cults*. Cambridge, MA: Harvard University Press.

Burnyeat, Myles F. 1976. Plato on the Grammar of Perceiving. *The Classical Quarterly* 26 (1): 29–51.

Cain, Rebecca Bensen. 2007. *The Socratic Method: Plato's Use of Philosophical Drama*. New York: Continuum International Publishing Group.

Cicero. 1967. *On the Nature of the Gods*. Trans. H. Rackham. Cambridge, MA: Harvard University Press.

Corlett, J. Angelo. 2005. *Interpreting Plato's Dialogues*. Las Vegas, NV: Parmenides Publishing.

Coulter, James A. 1976. *The Literary Microcosm: Theories of Interpretation of the Later Neoplatonists*. Leiden: Brill.

Diamond, Stephen. 1996. *Anger, Madness, and the Daimonic*. New York: SUNY Press.

Dickinson, John Peter. 1986. *Science and Scientific Researchers in Modern Society*. Lanham, MD: Bernan Press.

Epicurus. 1994. *The Epicurus Reader: Selected Writings and Testimonia*. Trans. L.P. Gerson and B. Inwood. Indianapolis, IN: Hackett Publishing.

Epictetus. 1998. *Encheiridion*. Trans. W.I. Matson. In *Classics of Philosophy*, L.P. Pojman, vol. I, 358–368. Oxford: Oxford University Press.

Ficino, Marsilio. 1981. *Marsilio Ficino and the Phaedran Charioteer*. Trans. M.J.B. Allen. Berkeley, CA: University of California Press.

Frankfurt, Harry. 2009. Freedom of the Will and the Concept of a Person. In *Free Will*, ed. D. Pereboom, 196–212. Indianapolis, IN: Hackett Publishing.

Frede, Dorothea. 1993. Out of the Cave: What Socrates Learned from Diotima. In *Nomodeiktes: Greek Studies in Honor of Martin Ostwald*, ed. R. Rosen and R. Farrell, 397–422. Ann Arbor, MI: University of Michigan Press.

Frede, Michael. 2011. *A Free Will: Origins of the Notion in Ancient Thought*, ed. A.A. Long. Berkeley, CA: University of California Press.

Gadamer, Hans-Georg. 1980. *Dialogue and Dialectic: Eight Hermeneutical Studies on Plato*. Trans. P. Christopher Smith. New Haven, CT: Yale University Press.

Garrigou-Lagrange. 2015. *The Three Conversions in the Spiritual Life*. Charlottesville, NC: TAN Books.

Gill, Christopher. 2006a. Psychophysical Holism in Stoicism and Epicureanism. In *Common to Body and Soul*, ed. R.A.H. King, 209–231. Berlin: Walter de Gruyter.

———. 2006b. *The Structured Self in Hellenistic and Roman Thought*. Oxford: Oxford University Press.

Greenbaum, Dorian G. 2016. *The Daimon in Hellenistic Astrology: Origins and Influence*. Leiden: Brill.

Hawking, Stephen, and Leonard Mlodinow. 2007. *A Briefer History of Time*. New York: Bantam Dell.

Heidegger, Martin. 2003. *Plato's Sophist*. Trans. R. Rojcewicz and A. Schuwer. Bloomington, IN: Indiana University Press.

Hergenhahn, B.R. 2009. *An Introduction to the History of Psychology*. Belmont, CA: Cengage.

Huby, Pamela. 1967. The First Discovery of the Freewill Problem. *Philosophy* 42 (162): 353–362.

Iamblichus. 2003. *On the Mysteries*. Trans. E.C. Clarke, J.M. Dillon, and J.P. Hershbell. Atlanta, GA: Society of Biblical Literature.

Iglesias, Maria R. Gómez. 2016. The Echoes of Eleusis: Love and Initiation in the Platonic Philosophy. In *Greek Philosophy and Mystery Cults*, eds. M.J. Martin-Velasco and M.J.G. Blanco. [Papers from the 2012 bimonthly meeting of the Iberian Society of Greek Philosophy.], 61–102. Newcastle upon Tyne: Cambridge Scholars Publishing.

Jung, C.G. 2001. *Modern Man in Search of a Soul*. Trans. W.S. Dell and C.F. Baynes. New York: Routledge.

———. 2014. *Psychology and Religion: West and East*. Trans. R.F.C. Hull. In *The Collected Works of C.G. Jung*, series eds. H. Read et al., vol. 11. Princeton, NJ: Princeton University Press.

Jung, C.G., and Carl Kerényi. 1969. *Essays on a Science of Mythology: The Myth of the Divine Child and The Mysteries of Eleusis*. Princeton, NJ: Princeton University Press.

Kahn, Charles. 1996. *Plato and the Socratic Dialogue: The Philosophical Use of a Literary Form*. Cambridge: Cambridge University Press.

Kantor, J.R. 1963. *The Scientific Evolution of Psychology*. Vol. I. Granville, OH: The Principia Press.

Klagge, James C., and Nicholas D. Smith, eds. 1992. *Methods of Interprting Plato and His Dialogues*. Oxford: Clarendon Press.

Kugelmann, Robert. 2011. *Psychology and Catholicism: Contested Boundaries*. Cambridge: Cambridge University Press.

Maurer, Armand. 1978. Method in Ockham's Nominalism. *The Monist* 61 (3): 426–443.

———. 1999. *The Philosophy of William of Ockham: In the Light of its Principles*. Irving, TX: Pontifical Institute of Mediaeval Studies (PIMS).

Ockham, William. 1990. *Philosophical Writings: A Selection*. Ed. S.F. Brown and Trans. P. Boehner. Indianapolis, IN: Hackett Publishing.

O'Keefe, Tim. 2005. *Epicurus on Freedom*. Cambridge: Cambridge University Press.

Ostenfeld, Erik. 1987. *Ancient Greek Psychology and the Modern Mind-Body Debate*. Aarhus: Aarhus University Press.

Owen, G.E.L. 1986. *'Tithenai ta Phainomena'. Logic, Science and Dialectic*, 239–251. London: Duckworth Publishing.

Panaccio, Claude. 2004. *Ockham on Concepts*. Aldershot: Ashgate.

Plato. 1997a. *Apology*. Trans. G.M.A. Grube. In John M. Cooper (Ed.), *Plato: Complete Works*. Indianapolis, IN: Hackett Publishing.

———. 1997b. *Meno*. Trans. G.M.A. Grube. In John M. Cooper (Ed.), *Plato: Complete Works*. Indianapolis, IN: Hackett Publishing.

————. 1997c. *Phaedo*. Trans. G.M.A. Grube. In *Plato: Complete Works*, ed. John M. Cooper. Indianapolis, IN: Hackett Publishing.

————. 1997d. *Phaedrus*. Trans. A. Nehamas and P. Woodruff. In *Plato: Complete Works*, ed. John M. Cooper. Indianapolis, IN: Hackett Publishing.

————. 1997e. *Republic*. Trans. G. M. A. Grube and Rev. C. D. C. Reeve. In *Plato: Complete Works*, ed. John M. Cooper. Indianapolis, IN: Hackett Publishing.

————. 1997f. *Symposium*. Trans. A. Nehamas and P. Woodruff. In *Plato: Complete Works*, ed. John M. Cooper. Indianapolis, IN: Hackett Publishing.

————. 1997g. *Timaeus*. Trans. D. J. Zeyl. In *Plato: Complete Works*, ed. John M. Cooper. Indianapolis, IN: Hackett Publishing.

Polansky, Ronald. 1983. *Energeia* in Aristotle's *Metaphysics* IX. *Ancient Philosophy* 3: 160–170.

————. 2010. *Aristotle's De Anima: A Critical Commentary*. Cambridge: Cambridge University Press.

Reeve, C.D.C. 2006. *Plato on Love*. Indianapolis, IN: Hackett Publishing.

Rommen, Heinrich A. 1998. *The Natural Law: A Study in Legal and Social History and Philosophy*. Trans. T.R. Hanley. Indianapolis, IN: Liberty Fund.

Ruck, Carl A.P. 1986. Mushrooms and Mysteries: On Aristophanes and the Necromancy of Socrates. *Helios* 8 (2): 1–28.

Sachs, Joe. 2001. *Aristotle's On the Soul and On Memory and Recollection*. St. Paul, MN: Green Lion Press.

Santas, Gerasimos. 1979. Plato's Theory of Eros in the *Symposium*: Abstract. *Noûs* 13 (1): 67–75.

Scalambrino, Frank. 2011. *Non-Being & Memory*. Doctoral Dissertation. Retrieved from ProQuest. (UMI: 3466382).

————. 2016a. *Meditations on Orpheus: Love, Death, and Transformation*. Pittsburgh, PA: Black Water Phoenix Press.

————. 2016b. Review of Jacques Lacan's *Seminar VIII* (On Transference). *Philosophy in Review* 36 (5): 211–214.

————. 2017. *Living in the Light of Death: Existential Philosophy in the Eastern Tradition, Zen, Samurai & Haiku*. Castalia, OH: Magister Ludi Press.

Schneewind, J.B. 1998. *The Invention of Autonomy*. Cambridge: Cambridge University Press.

Sheed, Frank J. 1946. *Theology and Sanity*. New York: Sheed & Ward.

Stump, Eleonore. 1989. *Dialectic and Its Place in the Development of Medieval Logic*. Ithaca, NY: Cornell University Press.

Swindal, James. 2017. Faith and Reason. *Internet Encyclopedia of Philosophy*. http://www.iep.utm.edu/faith-re/. Accessed 7 Apr 2017.

Tracy, Theodore. 1982. Soul/Boatman Analogy in Aristotle's *De Anima*. *Classical Philology* 77 (2): 97–112.

Uždavinys, Algis. 2010. *Philosophy & Theurgy*. Kettering, OH: Angelico Press.

de Vogel, Cornelia J. 1955. The Present State of the Socratic Problem. *Phronesis* 1 (1): 26–35.

Wasson, R. Gordon, Albert Hofmann, and Carl A.P. Ruck. 2008. *The Road to Eleusis: Unveiling the Secret of the Mysteries*. Berkeley, CA: North Atlantic Books.

Whitehead, Alfred North. 1985. *Process and Reality*. New York: Free Press.

Wood, Robert E. 1990. *A Path into Metaphysics: Phenomenological, Hermeneutical, and Dialogical Studies*. Albany, NY: SUNY Press.

———. 2015. *The Beautiful, the True, and the Good: Studies in the History of Thought*. Washington, DC: The Catholic University of America.

Worthen, Valerie. 1974. Psychotherapy and Catholic Confession. *Journal of Religion and Health* 13 (4): 275–284.

Ziman, John. 1978. *Reliable Knowledge: An Exploration of the Grounds for Belief in Science*. Cambridge: Cambridge University Press.

Zuckert, Catherine H. 2009. *Plato's Philosophers: The Coherence of the Dialogues*. Chicago, IL: Chicago University Press.

# 4

# The Early Modern Battle for the Archimedean Point

## 4.1 Principles from the Renaissance and the Modern Scientific Revolution

The purpose of this section is to introduce the Renaissance principles which influenced the "Modern Scientific Revolution" and Early Modern psychology. The discussion of René Descartes' (1596–1650) influence on Early Modern psychology, then, will be presented in terms of his innovations regarding the structural, functional and methodological principles in the study of ψυχή. Though names such as Copernicus, Galileo, and Francis Bacon are always associated with the Modern Scientific Revolution, we will invoke them here only insofar as is needed to indicate the principles of this historical period regarding Western psychology.

The following five (5) principles are standardly associated with the Renaissance: Classicalism, Secularism, Humanism, Perspectivism, and Individualism. The two historical events most often referenced as influencing the shift in worldview accomplished by the Renaissance are the "Western Schism" and the "Protestant Reformation." During the Western Schism (1378–1417) the corruption associated with the Catholic Church—such as concubinage and the sale of indulgences and religious

© The Author(s) 2018
F. Scalambrino, *Philosophical Principles of the History and Systems of Psychology*,
https://doi.org/10.1007/978-3-319-74733-0_4

offices—led to three different men all claiming to be the Pope. Ultimately, in regard to the principles operable in regard to the study of ψυχή, the Western Schism and the Protestant Reformation significantly called the authority of the Catholic Church into question. In fact, were we to characterize the conditions which led to the emphasis of these principles in Kuhnian terms, we could say that it was a "crisis of authority." Thus, where it was actually sacrilege to not adhere to the principles of the Catholic Church regarding the supernatural, due to the authority of the Church, the same held with regard to Aristotle's philosophical understanding of nature. Yet, just like the Schism and the Reformation regarding the Church, technological advances at the time made Aristotle's physics—especially his characterization of motion—increasingly difficult to accept.

The principle of Classicalism refers to the return to Classical sources in search of alternative methods, descriptions, and explanations from those offered by the Church and Aristotle or their combination as "Scholastic-Aristotelianism." Thus, the study of Plato—recall Aquinas' denouncing his ontological and soteriological views of ψυχή above as "heretical"—experienced a significant upsurge. The principle of Secularism may be characterized in multiple ways; however, for our purpose it represents the formulation into a principle of the separation of morality and theology from science. The principle of Humanism, then, takes human concerns and concerns for humanity—as opposed to concerns for the divine—as its point of departure. Whereas principles pertaining to the supernatural and the divine were Absolute and totalizing in character, the principles of the Renaissance were more Relativistic.

Such was especially the case regarding Renaissance aesthetics, for example manifesting in painting and sculpture, from where the principle of Perspectivism derived (cf. Edgerton 2009). In mereological terms we may say that Perspectivism represents a shift in emphasis from the whole to its parts—each part has a different perspective on the whole; moreover, this relegation of the whole can be radically conceived to the point of its vanishing, that is, the perspective of parts without a perspective from the point of view of a whole. Not only was such thinking important for a movement toward atomism away from Aristotle's holism but also toward Individualism. For all that may be said of the principle of Individualism, it is perhaps enough for us to note here the famous quote from Coluccio Salutati (1331–1406) "heaven belongs *by right* to those energetic men who have sustained great struggles and achieved fine works on earth" (Baudrillart 1907: 15; cf. Cassirer 1963: 73–74; cf. Burckhardt 1995; cf. Foucault 1988). In this way, a person is understood as able to actualize its unique individual potential to make a contribution to community and history.

As the historicity of Renaissance self-commentary shows, there was a distinction operable at the time between "old" and "new philosophy." There was a call for a "new philosophy" to replace the old authorities given the Renaissance "expectation of what a philosophy should do, and a sentiment that the old philosophy was not doing it properly." (Menn 1998: 34; cf. Edwards 2013; cf. Knight 1982). The call for a "new philosophy" was first and foremost understood as a call for a new method. The basic idea here is that now that the authority of Aristotle and the Church had been called into question what is needed is a method to replace such "appeal to authority." Essentially there were two types of methodology which were contenders: induction and deduction. In terms of the early distinction between dialectic and demonstration, induction and deduction function as types of demonstration. Whereas the conclusions from inductive methodology claim probability, those from deductive methodology claim certainty. When these methods are taken to be the centerpieces of respective theories of knowledge in the Early Modern Period, the theories of knowledge are Empiricism and Rationalism.

Though in hindsight it is standard to refer to the Rationalist Descartes as the "Father of Modern Philosophy," in terms of the "new philosophy" he is rather at its conclusion than its origination. At the origin of the "new philosophy" was the beginning of Empiricism. Bernadino Telesio (1509–1588) advocated for Radical Empiricism in the form of Sensationalism (cf. Kristeller 1964; cf. Leijenhorst 2010). His methodology was followed by the less radical Empiricism of Francis Bacon (1561–1626). With Classicalism's revival of interest in Plato's philosophy came both Nicholas of Cusa (1401–1464) and Marsilio Ficino (1433–1499) and the development of a principle of "dynamic intermediation," using Plato's idea of the *Scala Amoris*, between God and the Cosmos (cf. Cassirer 1963). Just as in Plato, Recollection changes ones relation to embodiment, so too ψυχή's ability to witness the Transcendental dimension allows for humans to witness holiness, despite the carnality of physical-animal-embodiment. Telesio may be seen as attacking this idea covertly by criticizing the idea of conceptual-mediation of reality in general—think Occam's razor here. In other words, his Radical Empiricism was supposed to end the process of using, especially Aristotle's, ideas to mediate the experience of nature. The hope was that somehow nature might "speak for herself." The "new philosophy" was in search of a "non-discursive" relation to nature out of which its truth may be revealed, and it would find such a relation in terms of mathematics.

In this way, the importance of art in the Renaissance for science cannot be overstated insofar as the innovations taking place in terms of Perspectivism and the deciphering of mathematical relations found in nature could be understood as the discovery of the human ability to "read" the "book of nature." On the one hand, this may be articulated in terms of methodology. On the other hand, this relation between art, mathematics, and nature originated with Leonardo da Vinci (1452–1519) and was carried forward in principle by Galileo. In his *Republic* Plato famously characterized the difference between dialectic and mathematics in terms of "upward" and "downward" movement, respectively (Plato 1997: 511d–523a; cf. Cornford 2013: 67; cf. Cassirer 1963: 171–172). Leonardo and Galileo both conceived of their methodologies as attempts to combine these two movements, and, when seen in terms of the combination of induction and deduction, this are often characterized as the birth of the "scientific method" (cf. Crombie 1996; cf. Drake and Levere 1999). Given this groundwork, we can now understand Descartes' place in relation to the Renaissance and the "new philosophy."

There is an issue which anyone discussing Descartes may mention as disclaimer. During Descartes' lifetime people were still being killed for making "heretical" claims; Giordano Bruno (1548–1600) was burned at the stake for, among other beliefs, his affirmation of the Copernican system (cf. Isaiah 40:22) and belief in re-incarnation (cf. Bruno 2004; cf. Bruno 1998; cf. Yates 1964), and Galileo was convicted of heresy as recently as 1633. Thus, disclaimer is often made that Descartes' concern to remain alive may have influenced the manner in which he presented his thoughts (cf. Gibson 2017). Be that as it may, Descartes, of course, famously wrote a *Discourse on Method* (1637) in addition to works titled "Rules for the Direction of the Mind" (1628), and *Principles of Philosophy* (1644), all of which deal explicitly with methodology.

Descartes' methodology may be seen as the perfect combination of dialectic and demonstration toward a non-heretical justification of the mathematization of nature by using the "upward" movement of critical dialectic to arrive at a certainty from which to begin the "downward" movement of demonstration. Plato emphasized that mathematics begins with hypothetical first principles and dialectic with non-hypothetical first principles, and whereas the "scientific method" of Leonardo and Galileo must still begin with hypothetical principles in observing nature, Descartes pointed to a non-hypothetical certainty by observing ψυχή. Further, given the importance of the principle of interiority or "the interior life" for the Christian understanding of salvation, Descartes' Subjectivism and principle of self-consciousness fit nicely into a Christian worldview. Moreover, Descartes' method affirmed the relativistic needs of the "new philosophy" in that it grounded subject-object binary opposition in terms measurement dependent on the point of view of the observer. His method seemed to allow for the co-ordination of objective certainty with the subjective certainty he had established through his infamous principle of the *Cogito*.

In brief, Descartes' *Meditations on First Philosophy* (1641) may be read as a way of meeting the methodological criteria for the "new philosophy." The first two meditations represent his critical-dialectic in which he engages in hyperbolic doubt until he arrives at a certainty; that is, he cannot doubt that he is doubting, and as a kind of thinking, this thinking means that some thinking thing exists (or in the language of the *Discourse on Method*: "I think, therefore I am" *Cogito Ergo Sum*). After arriving at this certainty of the subject, he then proceeds to demonstrate how it is possible to be certain of objects. Thus, Descartes understood the *Cogito* as the Archimedean point needed to lift science out of the jurisdiction of the Church. There are a number of principles which move to the foreground through Descartes, then, which are different from the principles emphasized in Pre-Modern thinking.

The overarching way to refer to what Descartes accomplished is that he shifted philosophy from a "Theo-centric" model to an "Ego-centric" model. Moving philosophy from dialog to soliloquy, Descartes anchored the different "worlds" of spirit and nature in mind and body by affirming a substance dualism based on the *Cogito*. From there Descartes was able to characterize mind in terms of rationality and body in terms of mathematics. He affirmed the principles of Nativism in that "the natural light" of rationality contains Innate Ideas with which we identify the various qualities of nature which may then quantified. On the one hand, his methodology ushers in the principle of mechanism by regarding the physical interactions between bodies in nature to be understood as mathematically determinable and, thereby, deterministic. On the other hand, his methodology infamously left us with the "Mind-Body Problem," in that subsequent thinkers note the inadequacy of his theorizing to account for interaction between two heterogeneous substances, that is, mind and body; or—put another way—how can there be freedom within, or in relation to, mechanistic and deterministic nature?

In sum, we have seen the impetus for Descartes' methodology in regard to the Renaissance call for a "new philosophy," and we have seen it characterized in terms of its emphasis regarding principles upon which Modern thinking is founded, for example Ego-centric justification. Just as the Modern Period is often characterized as a reduction or elimination of Aristotle's Four Causes to the Material and Efficient causes in an affirmation of Ockham's razor, the "Modern Scientific Revolution" affirmed the principle of atomism over holism and mechanism over teleology. In regard to the structure of ψυχή, then, for Descartes animal ψυχή is mechanistic—so much so that animals are essentially machines—and the rational ψυχή (as it was called above by Aristotle) for Descartes is the mind with its mechanical operations of volitions, affections, and judgments (cf. Meditation III). In regard to function, the will affirms or denies, that is, pursues or avoids, just like a machine. In Meditation VI, Descartes criticizes Aristotle's metaphor of the ship captain for ψυχή, suggesting that the "thinking thing" that is, the mind is one with the body. Anticipating what will be considered more fully below, Descartes' methodology with its rational, mechanical, and atomistic systematization of substance dualism will be debated primarily regarding its Mind-Body problem—at times in terms of freedom and nature.

## 4.2 Principles from the Age of Enlightenment: Early Modern Subjectivity and Personality

As could be expected by considering his moniker, the "Father of Modern Philosophy," Descartes' accomplishment of the "new philosophy" established the context regarding how to understand ψυχή for the Modern Period. Most importantly for psychology is the general problem of ψυχή's identity, or, more specifically, the problem of subjectivity and the problem of personality in the wake of the "new philosophy." This section will state these problems as they emerged from Descartes' work before addressing the responses which constitute Early Modern philosophical psychology. In general there are four (4) types of response, and these responses cover a number of philosophers from Locke to Kant. It is this period of time (from Descartes to Kant) that History and Systems of Psychology textbooks usually address as a "direct" influence on Contemporary psychology; moreover, there is a clear line of development across this period of time. Just as Descartes' psychology has been labeled the "way of ideas" and Locke's the "new way of ideas," so too we have Locke's *Essays on Human Understanding* and Leibniz's *New Essays on Human Understanding*. Further, whereas Berkeley's contribution is a more extreme version of Locke's, Hume's is even more extreme.

Thus, moving into Late Modernism and more contemporary theories of psychology, there are six (6) endpoints to the four (4) types of response to Descartes' "new philosophy" to be taken up out of Early Modern philosophy: (1) the Radical Empiricism of Positivism, (2) Locke's Newtonian Empiricism (with or without its extreme articulation by Berkeley), (3) the "Associationism" of Hume's Nominalistic Empiricism, or the reactions to Hume: (4) Wolff's development of Leibniz's philosophical psychology, (5) Thomas Reid's "Folk Psychology," and (6) Kant's Transcendental Psychology. It is especially valuable for a psychologist to understand the incommensurabilities present between these various systems as responses to the Modern problematic set in motion by Descartes, since the principles and the relations between the principles of these incommensurable systems may be used to clarify the identities and incommensurabilities of Contemporary systems of psychology.

According to Kant, in regard to the Age of Enlightenment there is a "motto of enlightenment," and it exhorts: "Have courage to use your own understanding!" (Kant 1983: 41). Though we are, of course, only concerned to discuss psychology here, the Age of Enlightenment may be understood as a period of time—prompted by the principles of the Renaissance—in which thinkers were doing just that in regard to all the aspects of human existence, especially the natural and the human sciences. However, despite its spirit, the Age may still be seen in terms of its collective activity and development of solutions to perennial philosophical problems characterized in terms of the principles emphasized by the Modern Period. Thus Descartes bequeathed the Age with the problem of subjectivity and, as if it were the price to be paid for acquiring the "new philosophy," Early Modern subjectivity was haunted by "Solipsism."

Recall that Descartes' method found certainty by following ideas to the point of being certain that the presence of ideas cannot be doubted. As a result this is often called "the way of ideas." Anticipating what becomes of this way of ideas in Modern philosophy, it is interesting to note its relation to what above we called Aristotle's "word-concept-thing" understanding of signification. As we will discuss in a moment, in combination with the shift from a Theo-centric to an Ego-centric worldview the "word-concept-thing" understanding of signification leads to Solipsism, that is, the idea that there is no way to know how our ideas and concepts relate to things. In regard to the problem of subjectivity, recall Descartes' characterization of essentially everything that is mental. In Meditation III Descartes makes the following two seminal claims: On the one hand, "I first group all my thoughts into certain classes … Some of these thoughts are like images of things … Some of these thoughts are called volitions or affects, while others are called judgments." (Descartes 2006: 20). On the other hand, "here I must inquire particularly into those ideas that I believe to be derived from things existing outside me. Just what reason do I have for believing that these ideas resemble those things?" (Ibid: 21).

For Descartes, it is as if combining the principles of secularism and individualism accomplished a separation, so to speak, from the "Unity" of the Transcendental dimension, leaving Early Modern philosophy with a Mind-Body problem, the problem of subjectivity, and Solipsism. For example, what is the Cartesian subject? As Franz Brentano once characterized explicitly in regard to the first quote above from Meditation III: "it is one thing to *produce* the judgment and quite another thing to *be* that judgment." (Brentano 1966: 29). Recall from Descartes' statement of the *Cogito* in Meditation II: "I am therefore precisely nothing but a thinking thing." (Descartes 2006: 15). In this quite literal way, then, the Cartesian subject is the subject of judgement. Now, if the Theo-centric system were still operable, this subject could be characterized—as Berkeley essentially would come to characterize it in his 1710 *A Treatise Concerning the Principles of Human Knowledge*—as a *thought* in the mind of God. However, in light of the principle of Secularism and the project of the "new philosophy," Descartes' subject is—again—quite literally the *thoughts* present—like a ghost—in a machine made of meat, and to quote Descartes: "nothing but."

On the one hand, notice that in conjunction with Descartes' substance dualism this characterization of subjectivity should seem highly problematic. That is, because of the Mind-Body problem we cannot even say—as Locke would come to characterize it in his 1689 *An Essay Concerning Human Understanding*—that the body "has" these ideas. It is for this reason that the Cartesian subject has invoked—in fact, by Descartes himself—the imagery of a *camera obscura* (cf. Olson 2014). On the other hand, in regard to the historicity of Descartes' articulation of such a subject, it may not have seemed as problematic to Descartes as it may from a more panoramic view of the history Western philosophy. The basic idea comes down to the distinction between "conscience" and "conscious" in what may be called the Early Modern principle of self-consciousness. Notwithstanding the daimon of ancient Greek philosophy, recalling that reflection on one's actions would have had a moral context in the Middle Ages, it has been suggested that with the advent of Secularism such refection, by taking on a non-moral context, produced the division between *conscience* and being self-*conscious* (cf. Balibar 1992; cf. Lewis 1960). In this way, what Descartes may have simply meant was that the very awareness of the ideas as ideas was a kind of self-conscious *idea*, and from the point of departure of self-consciousness, one recognizes the subject in the subject-object binary opposition to be the ideas (cf. Thiel 2011: 43–45; cf. Angell 1904: 376–390).

Taken in combination, then, that is, the Cartesian subject and the principle of the *camera obscura*, or in other terms the "way of ideas" and a secular "word-concept-thing" understanding of signification, we arrive at Solipsism. Just as the principle of the *camera obscura* refers to the way the image inside of its dark space is an inversion of the thing outside it, so too we arrive at the second quote noted above from Descartes' Meditation III: "here I must inquire particularly into those ideas that I believe to be derived from things existing outside me. Just what reason do I have for believing that these ideas resemble those things?" (Descartes 2006: 21). Thus, the problem of Solipsism is that one may not be able to know whether any *thing* outside one's own mind truly exists (cf. Johnstone 1991). Given these problems in Descartes' characterization of ψυχή, we are now in a better position to understand the four (4) types of response to Descartes' "new philosophy"—covering a number of philosophers from Locke to Kant—and to provide context for understanding the various philosophical principles which emerge regarding psychology in the Modern Period (cf. Brennan 2003: 89–117).

First, there was the "positivist" response. In regard to this period in Western history we may characterize the two different types of positivistic response as "sensorium-positivism" and "contractual-positivism." Basically, positivism takes sensory experience to be the exclusive source of knowledge; if some *thing* cannot be confirmed through sensory experience, then it does not exist. For this reason, positivism is associated with materialism and the idea that if whatever it is that is under discussion cannot be found in space, then it does not exist. Thus, the principle of the spiritual, or non-material, characterization of ψυχή as not in space (and thereby not confirmable through sensory experience) amounts to revealing "ψυχή" as a fiction (cf. Riskin 2002: 19–68). The Early Modern philosophers associated with sensorium-positivism are Étienne Bonnot de Condillac (1714–1780) and Julien Offray de La Mettrie (1709–1751). Condillac not only denied Descartes' principle of nativism, he denied the presence of non-material "mind" at all. In this way, of course, Condillac was a material monist (cf. de Condillac 2001). La Mettrie, emphasizing the principle of mechanism, understood psychology as essentially a physiology of meat machines governed by the hedonistic principle (cf. de

La Mettrie 2003). Hence, Solipsism is thought to be avoided because we are all material things, the self-animating of which may recognize other things through sensory experience.

Though similar to the above French "sensorium-positivism," an English "contract-positivism" may be attributed to Thomas Hobbes (1588–1679). Though Hobbes too affirmed the principle of material monism, the essential distinction between the two types of positivistic ways to avoid the problem of Solipsism is that subjectivity for Hobbes requires a contract (cf. Frost 2005). In this way, the Hobbesian subject differs from the Cartesian subject in that it is not the subject of judgment, that is, words or ideas; rather, it is the subject of contractual agreement (cf. Byron 2015; cf. Deleuze 2005). Moreover, though Hobbes also understood humans as meat machines operating in accordance with the hedonistic principle, he revered the creative-power which comes from mathematical ability such that he thought that through such a capacity humans might be thought of as "mortal gods" (cf. Miller 2011). Thus, it is as if for both of these types of positivism the structure of ψυχή is understood as material, and the function of ψυχή is understood in mechanistic terms governed by the hedonistic principle; the subject is the material body, and the person is (emphasizing the legal nature of the term) the capacity to enter into a contractual agreement.

Second, there was the "Mental Passivity" response. This response was born out of the empiricism of John Locke (1632–1704), and we should keep in mind that Locke characterized himself as an "under-laborer" for Newton. Some of the key principles associated with Locke are his re-emphasis of Aristotle's idea of *tabula rasa* to use against Descartes' principle of nativism and his use of Aristotle's principle of association to breathe Protestant Christianity into Hobbes' characterization of personhood. Locke was—like Descartes—a substance dualist; however, Locke characterized the relation between body and mind—matter and spirit—in terms of Aristotle's Efficient Causation. In other words, the mind is a "blank slate" and ideas are "written" on it through the sensory experiences of the body. Moreover, Locke characterizes this relation in terms of the *camera obscura*, and, anticipating what will be considered more fully below, it is worth quoting at length:

this is the only way that I can discover; whereby the ideas of things are brought into the understanding ... external and internal sensation are the only passages that I can find of knowledge to the understanding. These alone, as far as I can discover, are the *windows* [emphasis added] by which light is let into this dark room: for methinks, the understanding is not much unlike a closet wholly shut from light, with only some little opening left, to let in external visible resemblances, or ideas of things without; would the pictures coming into such a dark room but stay there, and lie so orderly as to be found upon occasion, it would very much resemble the understanding of man, in reference to all objects of sight, and of the ideas of them. (Locke 1841: 93–94)

As noted above, the problem of Solipsism haunts Early Modern philosophy to such an extent that—as can be seen in the above quote—Locke's philosophy of experience has been characterized as a "veil of ideas" or a "veil of perception," such that the things on one side of the veil are different from the way they appear on the other side. Locke's "windows" allow for the external things and their internal re-presentations to correspond in terms of "primary qualities," with "secondary qualities" pertaining only to their re-presentation.

Now, technically Gottfried Wilhelm Leibniz (1646–1716) should be discussed next; however, since he initiates the "Mental Activity" response, he is discussed below; yet, it should be noted that his response to the *camera obscura* imagery is to suggest that ψυχή (what he calls "monad") has "no windows" (Leibniz 1989: 214 [*Monadology* §7]). Thus, though both of the next two representatives of the "Mental Passivity" response may be understood as taking this position, technically Leibniz took it first. The first of the next two representatives, then, Bishop George Berkeley (1685–1753) was, of course, interested in a non-secular reading of Locke's "new way of ideas" and "veil of perception." In this way, Berkeley advocates for three principles: first, the principle of spiritual monism—he claims that the be-ing of every thing that is either mental or depends on a mind; second, the principle of "dogmatic idealism"—he claims that there is no such thing as "matter." Lastly, both of these are captured in what is sometimes called "Berkeley's principle," that is, "to be is to be perceived." (Berkeley 1910: 32). In regard to the "veil of perception" or "ideas" he argued: "Properly and immediately nothing can be perceived but ideas. All material things therefore are in themselves insensible, and to be perceived only by their ideas." (Berkeley 1979: 41). He then asked the rhetorical questions:

> But how can that which is sensible be like that which is insensible? Can a real thing in itself *invisible* be like a *color*; or a real thing which is not *audible*, be like a *sound*? In a word, can anything be like a sensation or idea, but another sensation or idea? (Ibid)

Thus, in regard to the relations among words-ideas-things, he concluded: "I am not for changing things into ideas, but rather ideas into things; since those immediate objects of perception, which according to you, are only appearances of things, I take to be the real things themselves." (Ibid: 77), and as a result, "all those bodies ... of the world, have not any subsistence without a mind ... their being is to be perceived ... From what has been said it follows there is not any other Substance than Spirit, or that which perceives." (Berkeley 1910: 32–33).

Finally, David Hume (1711–1776) took a similar position; however, as an atheist he eliminated any principle which might contribute to a revival of a Theo-centric system. Since the time of at least Aristotle, there has been a principle of empiricism, which was considered axiomatic in Scholasticism—call it the Peripatetic principle—that: "Nothing is in the intellect that was not first in the senses." Whereas every empiricist affirms this principle, Hume points out that there is no sensory verification for a number of ideas in the intellect; he showed that such ideas are rather grounded in the "association" of other ideas. Though the principle of the association of ideas had been around since Aristotle, Hume was the first Modern thinker to employ it in an atheistic context. In doing so, he suggested ideas such as "causation" and "the self" are based on "relations of ideas." (cf. Hume 1993: 15; cf. Waxman 1994; cf. Bricke 1980). Hume infamously argued:

> Philosophers begin to be reconciled to the principle, *that we have no idea of external substance, distinct from the ideas of particular qualities.* This must pave the way for a like principle with regard to mind, that *we have no notion of it, distinct from the particular perceptions.* (Hume 1985: 677)

The main thrust of Hume's argument is threefold. First, this complete denial of a "mind," just like his denial of a "self" or "person," can be seen as an Early Modern affirmation of the principle of elimination. Next, on the one hand, the ideas we have which are based on "relations of ideas" are not reality-based. They are "constructs." The study of the principles which influence or determine the construction of these ideas has become a major concern in Contemporary psychology. On the other hand, "Hume's problem" may be characterized in terms of *a priori* propositions.

That is, if *either* ideas like "causation" are not reality-based, since we have no sensory verification for them *or* such ideas have pragmatic value (however we can never know how they relate to mind-external reality), then—in either case—how are *a priori* judgments possible? In other words, how can humans make accurate predictions about causation—for example how motion in one billiard ball will *cause* motion in another billiard ball—before ever having a similar experience on which to base the prediction? Hume's problem—as we will discuss further in other sections—has had a significant impact on subsequent thinking, especially in regard to the philosophy of science. In sum, then, it is as if across these three representatives of the empirical "Mental Passivity" response to Solipsism, the "new way of ideas" leads to the extreme position requiring either God to secure the subject and remove the problem of Solipsism or the complete removal of the subject and, thereby, the problem of Solipsism, in favor of *social* (i.e. non-Solipsistic) justifications for constructs such as the "self" or the "subject" (cf. Yolton 1984). Moreover, for Locke and Hume, the structure of ψυχή is understood as material, and the function of ψυχή is understood in mechanistic terms with "will" governed by the hedonistic principle and "understanding" governed by the principle of association.

Third, there was the "Mental Activity" response. This response was born out of the rationalism of Leibniz (1646–1716). On the one hand, the guiding principle here, in general, follows the way of ideas by suggesting "mind" is known through ideas, and—emphasizing activity—that body is known through action. On the other hand, Leibniz's influence is often underestimated by Contemporary psychologists. Yet, we should be able to recognize among the following principles from Leibniz just how far-reaching—beyond even Modern psychology—his thinking continues to be. Leibniz's psychological principles include (1) unconscious influences on the mind, which were identified with activity of the body (cf. Leibniz 1997: 54–59; cf. Leibniz 1989: 214–216), (2) innate potencies and dispositions as intense folds within ψυχή (cf. Deleuze 1993), (3) he combined the idea of innate potencies with an inside out, so to speak, version of Plato's theory of Recollection—the beginnings of a psychodynamic archetype theory (cf. Leibniz 1997: 52), and (4) by conceiving of "resistance" to unconscious influences as an activity, Leibniz was able to reconfigure the idea of passivity into activity: passive reception is actually an active release of the resistance (Ibid: 171–176).

Leibniz invented the term "apperception"—the capacity to perceive oneself perceiving—in his discussion of Locke's discussion of human understanding. Critically invoking the Peripatetic principle, he noted, against Locke's *tabula rasa*, "Someone will confront me with this accepted philosophical axiom, that there is nothing in the soul [ψυχή] which does not come from the senses. But an exception must be made of the soul [ψυχή] itself." (Leibniz 1997: 111). Leibniz's nativism, then, is far more radical than Descartes' in that what would be consider "the body" previously is now considered the activity of innate potentialities—the development of ψυχή's intense folds (cf. Parkinson 1982). Self-consciousness takes on the metaphor of a "mirror" (again) with Leibniz, and Leibniz attempts to return to the mind as mirror of God metaphor by claiming the *interiority* of ψυχή (recall it is conceived by Leibniz as a monad—*camera obscura*—without windows) mirrors the Cosmos or Nature; however, through appropriate activity (morality) ψυχή can be clarified so as to realize that the Cosmos it is reflecting is God (cf. Scalambrino 2015).[1]

Before Kant's philosophy took its rightful place, towering over the previous Early Modern philosophers, there was an attempt to systematize Leibniz's philosophy particularly worth mentioning for psychology. That attempt was made by Christian von Wolff (1679–1754). The "Mental Activity" response was essentially a German endeavor, and before Kant Wolff's philosophy was famously celebrated in Germany. As can be seen by the titles of his major works in psychology, Wolff attempted to re-interpret Early Modern philosophy taking Leibniz as a point of departure—*Empirical Psychology* (1732) and *Rational Psychology* (1734).

Though this would basically be the same strategy Kant would later employ, Wolff's interpretation remained within the scope of the position of Rationalism, like Leibniz.

The Leibnizian roots of the major and lasting principles with which Wolff is credited may be clearly seen. On the one hand, Wolff's focus on the potentialities located in ψυχή by Leibniz became "faculty psychology," that is, the association of the study of psychology with mental faculties. On the other hand, the previous Cartesian distinction understood as the Mind-Body Problem was now understood—through Leibniz back to Aristotle's divisions between animal and human—in terms of ψυχή as sensation and imagination (Body) and understanding and reasoning (Mind). Thus, according to the "Mental Activity" response: methodologically it pushes even further—as with the strategy found in Berkeley and Hume—into the *camera obscura* model; the structure of ψυχή is understood as spiritual, and the function of ψυχή is understood in terms of activity—including what was previously understood as "passive" bodily functions as they relate to mind.

Fourth, there was the "Folk Psychology" response. In addition to being identified as a critic of both Berkeley and Hume specifically and the "way of ideas" generally, Thomas Reid (1710–1796) also founded the "Scottish School of Common Sense." It is founded on an appeal to a "common sense," which is thought to be composed of intuitive judgments, which Reid called "first principles" "principles of common sense" or "self-evident truths." (Reid 1853: 230). Of course, the suggestion is that some philosophical problems are mere extravagances, founded on decadent-thought, or simply unnecessary concerns is often followed by the suggestion that there is a kind of knowledge "common" to humans which allows them to understand situations as they really are and without any further or unnecessary explication. This has been associated with the "folk" (from the German "Volk") as the way in which "the people" commonly understand—in our case—mental operations and psychology (cf. Gallie 2010: 42; cf. Bering 2006; cf. Nichols 2004).

Thus, Reid's criticism of the "way of ideas" suggests that it leads to skepticism regarding aspects of reality that common sense knows better than to doubt: especially "causation" and having a "self." For example, Reid claimed "I am not thought, I am not action, I am not feeling; I am something that thinks and acts and suffers" (Reid 1853: 345). Anticipating what will be considered more fully below, "Folk Psychology" and "Common Sense" are often (necessarily) the target of some of the more reductive and eliminative explanations regarding the structure and functions ψυχή. Moreover, another question which will be of interest in the final sections of the book: supposing "Folk Psychology" to be an accurate characterization of ψυχή: to what extent is that characterization a cultural and historical construction?

## 4.3    Principles from Kant's Copernican Revolution: The Transcendental Dimension Regained

Despite all that could be said about the contributions made to Western thought and psychology by Immanuel Kant (1724–1804), the following section is designed for the purpose of helping those studying the history and systems of Western psychology to understand Kant's pivotal place and critical difference from the thinkers discussed thus far. Hence, this section is composed of a brief disclaimer and characterization followed by a series of seven (7) questions and brief answers aiming at Kant's accomplishments as contributions to the history of Western psychology. It is not uncommon for History and Systems of Psychology textbooks to make comments like: "The importance of Kant for the psychological tradition cannot be overestimated." (Kantor 1969: 211). However, the amount of training required to be able to truly work with Kant's thoughts is usually too much to expect of anyone who is not a "philosopher," so a resource of perhaps inestimable value to psychologists goes untapped.

Just as we noted above that Whitehead suggested all of Western philosophy may be a "footnote to Plato," Lewis White Beck (1913–1997) famously pointed out: "There is a saying among philosophers, 'You can philosophize with Kant or against Kant, but you cannot philosophize without him'" (Beck 1950: 1). Similarly, Richard Rorty said of Kant, "He simultaneously gave us a history of our subject, fixed its problematic, and professionalized it (if only by making it impossible to be taken seriously as a 'philosopher' without having mastered the first *Critique*)" (Rorty 1979: 149). Moreover, Kant's philosophy has been—as we will see— rightly called "revolutionary." In fact, Kant's "Critical Philosophy" is essentially constituted by three different books, the *Critique of Pure Reason*, the *Critique of Practical Reason*, and the *Critique of the Power of Judgment*. Though all of these books contain valuable and original insight into ψυχή, given the depth and complexity of Kant's thought we will barely be scratching the surface here of the first of those books.

 *Question 1: What is Kant's "Copernican Revolution"?* Kant's revolution may be stated in terms of a response to Hume or in terms of Aristotle's "word-concept-thing" understanding of signification. We will briefly state all both. According to Kant,

> Up to now it has been assumed that all our cognition must conform to the objects; but all attempts to find out something about them *a priori* though concepts that would extend our cognition have, on this pre-supposition, come to nothing. Hence, let us once try whether we do not get farther … by assuming that the objects must conform to our cognition. (Kant 1998: B xvi)

The above quote is considered the statement of Kant's "Copernican Revolution" in his own words. The basic idea is that just as Copernicus suggested we switch our assumption from the sun revolving around the earth to the earth around the sun, so too Kant suggested we switch from the mind conforming to objects to the objects conforming to mind. There is a very simple way to state this in terms of the physical dimension; however, the example may be easily misunderstood if we attempt to extend it too far: Think of how there are things external to us that—even though they are there—we cannot see them, for example germs or x-rays. This suggests that whatever it is that we are seeing, the reason we are seeing it is because we have the capacity to see it. The more naïve way to explain the situation would be to say we see it because it is there; however, we know now that there may be many things in front of us presently which we cannot see because we do not have the capacity to see them.

 As a criticism of Hume, what Kant's revolution does is it provides a way to account for *a priori* knowledge, that is, knowledge of such aspects of reality as "causation" without using the principle of empiricism. How Kant accomplishes this is by noting that the understanding of "causation" derives from the very structure of ψυχή to which objects must conform if they are to be experienced by humans. We will have a bit more to say about this when answering the next question. In terms of Aristotle's "word-concept-thing" understanding of signification, it is as if Kant has provided a Leibnizian "Mental Activity" reading of Aristotle resulting in what may be called an "extra-dimensional" reading of the "way of ideas." That is to say, just as Leibniz granted the presence of "petite perceptions" toward which we are unconscious, so too Kant's revolution uses "thing" to refer to that which conforms to ψυχή's structures *before* it has conformed. After conforming to ψυχή's structures, then it is an "*object* of experience." Thus, words and concepts only refer to things insofar as we can know them; however, in the act of knowing them they are no longer things, they are objects of our knowing. Again, as we move through the rest of the questions this explication of Kant's revolution should gain clarification.

*Question 2: What method does Kant originate, and what are its consequences for subsequent psychology?* As Kant himself referred to it—it is the method of "Transcendental Logic." Transcendental logic originated with Kant, and he contrasted it with "formal logic," noting that formal logic pertains to forms of *thought* and transcendental logic is the science of the forms which are the conditions for the possibility of *objects* (Kant 1998: A50–57/B74–82). Whereas earlier thinkers applied rationality in the attempt to understand ψυχή, as if it were an observable object, Kant rationally organized Aristotle's (by way of Leibniz's) principles of potentiality and actuality to reveal the *a priori* aspects which logically, that is, necessarily, must be a part of ψυχή's structure for humans to have objective experience in general. On the one hand, the consequences of Kant's "transcendental method" have been acknowledged across the sciences (cf. Monod 2004; cf. Makkreel 2003; cf. Cevalley 1994).

On the other hand, there is another standard comment made—yet without significant clarification—regarding Kant in nearly every History and Systems of Psychology textbook. After noting the issue in general we will discuss its clarification. "Kant himself was clear in denying the possibility of traditional rational psychology and in expounding the irrelevance of empirical psychology to his project in the first *Critique*" (Hatfield 1992: 209; cf. Kant 1998: A 741/B 769). Thus, the issue seems to be that Kant would not have consider viable many of the post-Kantian approaches to psychology which have actualized in the history of Western psychology. However, it is interesting to realize that "there have been readers of [Kant's first *Critique*], from the time of its publication down to the present, who have contended that it is primarily a work in psychology." (Hatfield 1992: 209; cf. Schmidt 2008).

To clarify Kant's disparaging remarks about psychology, then: On the one hand, some emphasize the historical-context of Kant's understanding of the term "empirical psychology," and go on to point out that even a cursory comparison of the respective tables of contents from Kant's *Anthropology* (cf. Kant 2006) and contemporary Introduction to Psychology textbooks show striking similarity—in fact, some suggest that Kant's anthropology textbook, by contemporary standards, counts as a psychology textbook (cf. Hatfield 1998: 424). Moreover, given terminological differences between eighteenth century Germany and twenty-first century America, perhaps Kant would not be so disparaging in regard to these psychological methodologies today (cf. Schmidt 2008). On the other hand, some commentators understand Kant's disparaging remarks about rational and empirical psychology as critically directed at their methodology, that is, the inability of the "way of ideas," namely "introspection" and the "sensory verification" of empirical psychology, to reach ψυχή's Transcendental dimension. Certainly, the latter understanding would be consistent with the *logic* of Kant's philosophy; in order to have an empirical science there must be something that you can experience through the senses to subsequently study; however, as the *a priori* condition for the possibility of experience, it is not possible to experience ψυχή directly through the senses; therefore, *technically*, there can be no empirical science of psychology—just like there can be no empirical science of formal logic. As a result, what today goes by the name empirical psychology, Kant considered philosophical anthropology (cf. Hatfield 1992; cf. Kitcher 1993; cf. Makkreel 2003).

*Question 3: According to Kant, what is the structure and function of ψυχή?* The answer to this question invokes the structural models noted above, especially those of Aristotle and Wolff. Basically, just as we noted a distinction in Aristotle's psychology between the animal and the rational intellectual ψυχή, Wolff's Leibnizian conception divided ψυχή into sensation and imagination (Body) and understanding and reasoning (Mind). Kant's structure of experience, then, maps directly onto these divisions; however, it does so in the context of the Kantian Copernican Revolution. That is to say, Kant's structure of ψυχή, divides initially into "sensibility" and "understanding." Often given the multiple uses of the word "understanding," at this level of dividing ψυχή structurally into the "two stems" of experience, the latter stem is called "the understanding broadly construed." This clarification makes more sense in the context of Kant's discussion of the function of ψυχή.

Keeping in mind (1) that the structure under consideration is the structure to which things must conform to be experienced as objects and (2) that Kant is participating in the "Mental Activity" response to the "new philosophy," the rest of the structure of ψυχή may be most easily seen through a discussion of the activity constituting its functioning. Now, though psychologists say that "Functionalism" began with John Dewey and "The Chicago School," philosophers say it began with Kant, since, for Kant, the structure of ψυχή is essentially a complex of capacities—similar to the intense folds in Leibniz. Moreover, Kant understood the activity (think "Mental Activity" response) to which objects conform to be the function of "synthesis," and understood the intelligibility of this synthetic activity in terms of "judgment." That is to say, for a human to have an objective experience is for ψυχή to perform a judgment (cf. Keller 1998: 46; cf. Paton 1997; cf. Allison 2004). When thinking involves intuitions from sensibility, then that use of reason is called "impure," and when thinking does not involve intuitions from sensibility, then that use of reason is called "pure reason." On the one hand, notice it is from this essential distinction that the title of Kant's book derives, that is, the *Critique of Pure Reason*. On the other hand, this makes sense of Kant's claim to critique knowledge to "make room for faith" (Kant 1998: Bxxx), which is consistent with the idea that there can be no sensory verification of God through the natural powers of human sensation.

In this way, we can divide the two structural "stems" of experience further in terms of function. In the stem of sensibility we find the pure intuitions of space and time "at the bottom" of the structure of ψυχή and, then, the "threefold" synthesis of the "power of imagination." In the stem of the understanding broadly construed we find conceptual understanding and, then, thinking, and both of these activities function in terms of different types of judgment, which also correspond with subjectivity, objectivity, and certainty regarding *objective* mind-external reality. One of the most important parts of the *Critique of Pure Reason* for understanding these elements under discussion is the section called the "Transcendental Deduction." Further, there are two pieces left to discuss in order to more fully answer the question: according to Kant, what is the structure and function of ψυχή? Yet, these two pieces—in conjunction with what has already been said—answer the next two questions, respectively. Therefore, we will pick up the rest of this answer as we differentiate Kant from Descartes in the next two questions. Incidentally, it is worth noting that one of the most common mistakes encountered in regard to Kant's thinking is that some psychologists tend to suggest there is no difference between his thinking and that of Descartes'. However, the attempt to read Kant as Descartes radically misses Kant; the two areas most relevant for the history of Western psychology are Descartes' Mind-Body problem and the difference in the ways they understand subjectivity.

*Question 4: How does Kant solve Descartes' Mind-Body Problem?* There are only two ways to solve the Mind-Body problem. The first is to deny the problem; for example, by formulating a monist ontology, which ultimately denies any, but perhaps a "property," dualism on which to base the Mind-Body problem. The second is to follow Kant's "Transcendental Deduction." Kant's deduction specifically, and the *Critique of Pure Reason* generally, may be read as a demonstration—deriving from a dialectic involving the (initially hypothetical) first principle of the Kantian Revolution—in accordance with Transcendental logic, and it is so systematic that its structure provides a place for, that is, a self-encompassing account of, both demonstration and dialectic. Thus, anticipating what will be considered more fully in the next chapter, a fundamental component of dialectic for Kant is that it must not be one of "pure reason." Otherwise, despite any logical consistency within a dialectic of pure reason, it will ultimately lead, according to Kant, to "Transcendental Illusion" (cf. Guyer 1989; cf. Henrich 1969; cf. Paton 1931; cf. Ameriks 2003).

Now, in regard to Descartes' Mind-Body problem, the problem derives from the "heterogeneity" of the two substances. In other words, there are material beings and there are non-material beings, and the problem inquires in regard to how they are supposed to be connected. Kant's way to solve the Mind-Body problem, then, derives from the synthetic activity constituting an experience. As noted above, the two stems being combined which correspond with body and mind in Descartes are "sensibility" and "understanding" in Kant. We also noted that sensibility contains "pure" intuitions of space and time. These intuitions function like forms in which sensory content constitutes the material of a, thereby, perceptual (matter-form) composite. Further, the concepts of the understanding are "pure." Hence, when the synthetic activity of judgment combines sensory (body) content with the "higher" (in the structure) forms of understanding (i.e. mind), for Kant the two parts being combined are not heterogeneous. They are homogenous as pure intuitions synthesized with pure concepts. Notice how, in this way, the structure of ψυχή functions like a kind of "filter" in regard to mind-external *things*. Only the things which can con-*form* to the filter are picked up by the filter and experienced as objects. Thus, the Kantian Revolution solves Descartes' Mind-Body problem.

*Question 5: How is Kant's theory of subjectivity different from Descartes?* This question is not about the subjective aspects of experience, rather this question is about the subject of experience, that is, the subject undergoing an experience. See the previous two sections for a fuller discussion of Descartes' theory of the subject. To begin recall that "judgment" according to Descartes is an "idea" and according to Kant is a "synthetic activity." In order to understand Kant's theory of the subject we must again look at the Transcendental Deduction. Just as sensibility was associated with the body and understanding with the mind, so too sensibility is associated with empiricism and understanding with rationalism. Notice, then, it is the synthetic activity that points to the Kantian subject. Moreover, the Cartesian subject would be located in the understanding section of Kant's structural account of ψυχή. In other words, this is one way to notice that Descartes is a rationalist and Kant is not. The synthetic activity points beyond empiricism and rationalism to—you guessed it—the Transcendental dimension.

In other words, Transcendental logic points out that if there is an actualization of a synthetic power, then there must be a potential for that actualization. We know there is such actualization, so the actualization itself points to the potentiality. The unity of this pointing is called by Kant the "Transcendental Unity of Apperception." Using the term "apperception" indicates that it is possible to gain an awareness of one's self as that *thing* which is performing the synthetic action. The term "thing" is only used here to indicate its structural position, or rather its position beyond the structure, insofar as it is the power conditioning experience which manifests experience in terms of the structure. Just like the seeing eye cannot see itself, so too the subject revealed by Kant is Transcendental. Which, returning to the earlier methodological point, is why there can be no direct empirical investigation of Transcendental ψυχή. Thus, *because this revelation* of ψυχή *depends on the Kantian revolution and Transcendental logic, this understanding of* (Transcendental) *subjectivity cannot be Descartes'—or that of any one doing psychology before Kant.*

Moreover, this is not the self-conscious apperception of Leibniz or the self-consciousness discussed by Descartes, Locke, and so on, this is the self-consciousness of the Transcendental be-ing of the self. Think Plato; Kant's method has re-discovered the Transcendental dimension of ψυχή, and just as we saw it was possible in Plato to envision physically embodied experience from the point of view of the Transcendental dimension, so too Kant's Transcendental Unity of Apperception is that point of view insofar as we can uncover it through Transcendental logic. Kant himself paid homage to Plato (1998: B 370) and Plato's awareness of the Transcendental dimension; however, we can look back over the previous chapters to see just how different Kant's subject is from Plato's. The following quote from Kant may add further clarity.

> The consciousness of the ego proves that life is not located in the body, but in a special principle differing from the body; that as a consequence this principle can continue to exist without body, and that its life is not thereby diminished but augmented. This is the sole proof that can be given *a priori*,

and one drawn from the knowledge and nature of the soul [ψυχή] compre-
hended *a priori* by us. (Kant 2001: 176–177)

Thus, Kant avoids Solipsism, and despite his continued use of terms such
as "subject" and "ego," he avoids the Egoism associated with the ego-
centric shift accomplished by the "way of ideas."

Lastly, notice how Kant's description of his position in general differentiates him from the thinkers of the "way of ideas" associated with the
"new philosophy." In the section of the *Critique of Pure Reason* titled "On
the Amphiboly of Concepts of Reflection," distancing himself from
Leibniz and Locke, Kant famously claimed Leibniz "intellectualized
appearances" just as Locke "sensualized all of the concepts of understanding." (1998: A 271/B 327; cf. Deleuze 1984). Further, in regard to
Descartes and Berkeley, Kant noted that his and theirs are "Idealist" positions; however, here is how he differentiated himself from them: "The
dogmatic idealist would be one who denies the existence of matter, the
skeptical idealist one who doubts them because he holds them to be
unprovable." (1998: A 377). Whereas the former is Berkeley, the latter is
Descartes (cf. 1998: B 274). Finally, in regard to his own position, that is,
Transcendental Idealism, Kant pointed out regarding appearances "that
they are all together to be regarded as mere representations and not as
things in themselves, and accordingly that space and time are only sensi-
ble forms of our intuition, but not ... something given in themselves
(independent of our sensibility)." (1998: A 369). This also differentiates
Kant from Hume, for example, Kant noted "The transcendental idealist,
on the contrary, can be an empirical realist, hence ... he can concede the
existence of matter without going beyond mere self-consciousness and
assuming something more than the certainty of representations" (1998:
A 370). Notice, Kant's certainty is not based on the Cartesian methodology
of the "new philosophy" culminating in the *Cogito*, it is based on Kant's
methodology of Transcendental *logic* (cf. Allison 2004; cf. Ameriks 1982,
cf. Cicovacki 1997; cf. Deleuze 1984).

*Question 6: What is Kant's theory of Personhood?* In what amounts to an
overview of Kant's developmental theory of psychology, he claimed
regarding the human predisposition to self-fulfillment "We may conve-
niently divide this predisposition, with respect to function, into three

divisions, to be considered as elements in the fixed character and destiny of man." (Kant 1960: 33). Notice, of course, Kant's clarification that this division is "with respect to function." The three divisions are: (1) "The predisposition to *animality* in man, taken as a *living* being; [2] The predisposition to *humanity* in man, taken as a living and at the same time a *rational* being; [3] The predisposition to *personality* in man, taken as a rational and at the same time an *accountable* being." (Ibid.). Kant further clarified these three developmental characterizations of function by invoking something which sounds a good deal like the *Scala Amoris* from Plato. That is, Kant associated one's developmental actualization with self-love, and he cross-referenced them with the above divisions regarding predisposition.

(1) "The predisposition to *animality* in mankind may be brought under the general title of physical and purely *mechanical* [deterministic] self-love, wherein no reason is demanded." (2) "The predisposition to humanity can be brought under the general title of a self-love which is physical and yet *compares* … [i.e.] we judge ourselves happy or unhappy only by making comparison with others. Out of this self-love springs the inclination *to acquire worth in the opinion of others*." (3) The predisposition to *personality* is the capacity for respect for the moral law as *in itself a sufficient incentive of the will*." (Kant 1960: 34). Notice, then, just as Aristotle's animal ψυχή is without rationality, so too Kant's "animality" indicates a kind of love in which "no reason is demanded." The second type of self-love stems from the rational capacity of the human, and because rationality reveals *ratios*, this type of self-love is based on comparisons derived by illuminating various ratios between one's self and others. Finally, the last type of self-love belongs to Personhood, and one has, according to Kant, self-actualized to the level of being a "person" when one is able to have self-love based on being accountable to Moral Law. Thus, persons for Kant have self-respect by respecting themselves as a part of the Moral Law, and this will receive further clarification regarding the next question.

*Question 7: How does Kant make Free Will compatible with Mechanism?* Given all that has been said thus far we may be brief here. Notice from the previous question "mechanism" is associated with animality, first and foremost, and even humanity insofar as ego-based comparison is natural and mechanical unless one is able to transcend such triviality by means of self-respect. Just as the person, then, is able to relate to itself as a Transcendental be-ing, it is able to relate to nature as determined by laws. This is a resurgence of what was previously called the "Natural Law." Ultimately, then, the person understands that it is *free* to perform synthetic activity based on different understandings of situations (think Aristotle's "Character Types" again), and yet, when ψυχή relates to situations in terms of its lower capacities—like a "self-imposed immaturity" (Kant 1983: 41), then it does not respect the law-like nature of the situations. That is to say, in psychological terms such arrested development may be read in terms of teleological and soteriological non-self-actualization. Thus, it is free to either follow the Moral Law or not, according to Kant. This is related to Kant's famous "Categorical Imperative," especially the first of its three formulations; however, though it is beyond our current scope, we should point out that the reason our personal choices are supposed to be according to maxims which are universalizable is because the Natural Law applies universally. Hence, Kant's moral theory cannot be paraphrased by the "Golden Rule" (cf. Walsh et al. 2014: 138).

# Notes

1. I express this notion in the classroom by saying: Your external perception is a reflection of your internal perfection. Given Leibniz's metaphysics it would also be accurate to say: Your external perception is an expression of your internal perfection. Perfection here, of course, means "completion" in the sense of teleology (and soteriology).

# Bibliography

Allison, Henry E. 2004. *Kant's Transcendental Idealism*. New Haven, CT: Yale University Press.
Ameriks, Karl. 1982. *Kant's Theory of Mind: An Analysis of the Paralogisms of Pure Reason*. Oxford: Clarendon Press.
———. 2003. *Interpreting Kant's Critiques*. Oxford: Oxford University Press.

Angell, James Rowland. 1904. *Psychology: An Introductory Study of the Structure and Functions of Human Consciousness*. New York: Holt.

Balibar, Étienne. 1992. A Note on 'Consciousness/Conscience' in the *Ethics*. *Studia Spinozana* 8: 37–53.

Baudrillart, Alfred. 1907. *The Catholic Church: The Renaissance and Protestantism*. London: Kegan Paul.

Bering, Jesse M. 2006. The Folk Psychology of Souls. *Behavioral and Brain Sciences* 29 (5): 453–498.

Berkeley, George. 1910. *A Treatise Concerning the Principles of Human Knowledge*. Chicago: Open Court.

———. 1979. In *Three Dialogues Between Hylas and Philonous*, ed. R.M. Adams. Indianapolis, IN: Hackett Publishing.

Brennan, James F. 2003. *History and Systems of Psychology*. Upper Saddle, NJ: Prentice Hall.

Brentano, Franz. 1966. *The True and the Evident*, ed. O. Kraus. New York: The Humanities Press.

Bricke, John. 1980. *Hume's Philosophy of Mind*. Princeton, NJ: Princeton University Press.

Bruno, Giordano. 1998. *Cause, Principle and Unity and Essays on Magic*. Trans. R. De Luca. Cambridge: Cambridge University Press.

———. 2004. *The Expulsion of the Triumphant Beast*. Trans. A.D. Imerti. Lincoln, NE: University of Nebraska Press.

Burckhardt, Jacob. 1995. *The Civilization of the Renaissance in Italy*. New York: Modern Library.

Byron, Michael. 2015. *Submission and Subjection in Leviathan: Good Subjects in the Hobbesian Commonwealth*. London: Palgrave Macmillan.

Cassirer, Ernst. 1963. *The Individual and the Cosmos in Renaissance Philosophy*. New York: Harper & Row.

Cevalley, Catherine. 1994. Niels Bohr's Words and the Atlantis of Kantianism. In *Niels Bohr and Contemporary Philosophy*, ed. J. Faye and H. Folse, 33–59. Dordrecht: Kluwer.

Cicovacki, Predrag. 1997. *Anamorphosis: Kant on Knowledge and Ignorance*. Oxford: Oxford University Press.

de Condillac, Étienne Bonnot. 2001. *Essay on the Origin of Human Knowledge*. Trans. H. Aarsleff. Cambridge: Cambridge University Press.

Cornford, F.M. 2013. Mathematics and Dialectic in the *Republic*. In *Studies in Plato's Metaphysics*, ed. R.E. Allen, 61–96. New York: Routledge.

Crombie, A.C. 1996. *The History of Science from Augustine to Galileo*. Vol. I & II. New York: Dover Publications.

Deleuze, Gilles. 1984. *Kant's Critical Philosophy: The Doctrine of the Faculties.* Trans. H. Tomlinson. Minneapolis: University of Minnesota Press.

Deleuze, Gilles. 1993. *The Fold: Leibniz and the Baroque.* Trans. T. Conley. Minneapolis: University of Minnesota Press.

———. 2005. *Expressionism in Philosophy: Spinoza.* Trans. M. Joughin. New York: Zone Books.

Drake, Stillman, and Trevor H. Levere. 1999. *Essays on Galileo and the History and Philosophy of Science: Volume I.* Toronto, Canada: Toronto University Press.

Descartes, René. 1998. *Discourse on the Method for Conducting One's Reason Well and for Seeking Truth in the Sciences.* Trans. D.A. Cress. Indianapolis, IN: Hackett Publishing.

———. 2006. *Meditations, Objections, and Replies.* Ed. and Trans. R. Ariew and D. Cress. Indianapolis, IN: Hackett Publishing.

Edgerton, Samuel Y. 2009. *The Mirror, the Window, and the Telescope: How Renaissance Linear Perspective Changed Our Vision of the Universe.* Ithaca, NY: Cornell University Press.

Edwards, Michael. 2013. *Time and the Science of the Soul in Early Modern Philosophy.* Leiden: Brill.

Foucault, Michel. 1988. *Madness and Civilization: A History of Insanity in the Age of Reason.* Trans. A. Sheridan. New York: Vintage Books.

Frost, Samantha. 2005. Hobbes and the Matter of Self-Consciousness. *Political Theory* 33 (4): 495–517.

Gallie, Roger D. 2010. *Thomas Reid: Ethics, Aesthetics and the Anatomy of the Self.* Dordrecht: Kluwer Academic Publishers.

Gibson, A. Boyce. 2017. *The Philosophy of Descartes.* Vol. I & II. London: Routledge.

Guyer, Paul. 1989. Psychology and the Transcendental Deduction. In *Kant's Transcendental Deduction: The Three Critiques and the Opus postumum*, ed. E. Förster. Stanford, CA: Stanford University Press.

Hatfield, Gary. 1992. Empirical, Rational, and Transcendental Psychology: Psychology as Science and as Philosophy. In *The Cambridge Companion to Kant*, ed. P. Guyer. Cambridge: Cambridge University Press.

———. 1998. Kant and Empirical Psychology in the 18th Century. *Psychological Science* 9 (6): 423–428.

Henrich, Dieter. 1969. The Proof-Structure of Kant's Transcendental Deduction. *The Review of Metaphysics* 22 (4): 640–659.

Hume, David. 1985. *A Treatise of Human Nature.* London, England: Penguin.

————. 1993. *An Enquiry Concerning Human Understanding*. Indianapolis, IN: Hackett Publishing.

Johnstone, Albert A. 1991. *Rationalized Epistemology: Taking Solipsism Seriously*. Albany, NY: SUNY.

Kant, Immanuel. 1960. *Religion Within the Limits of Reason Alone*. Trans. T.M. Greene and H.H. Hudson. New York: Harper & Row.

————. 1983. *Perpetual Peace and Other Essays*. Trans. T. Humphrey. Indianapolis, IN: Hackett Publishing.

————. 1998. *Critique of Pure Reason*. Trans. P. Guyer and A. W. Wood. Cambridge: Cambridge University Press.

————. 2001. *Lectures on Metaphysics*. Trans. K. Ameriks and S. Naragon. Cambridge: Cambridge University Press.

————. 2006. *Anthropology from a Pragmatic Point of View*. Ed. and Trans. R.B. Louden. Cambridge: Cambridge University Press.

Kantor, J.R. 1969. *The Scientific Evolution of Psychology*. Vol. II. Granville, OH: The Principia Press.

Keller, Pierre. 1998. *Kant and the Demands of Self-Consciousness*. Cambridge, England: Cambridge University Press.

Kitcher, Patricia. 1993. *Kant's Transcendental Psychology*. Oxford: Oxford University Press.

Knight, David. 1982. Religion and the 'New Philosophy'. *Renaissance and Modern Studies* 26 (1): 147–166.

Kristeller, Paul Oskar. 1964. *Eight Philosophers of the Italian Renaissance*. Stanford, CA: Stanford University Press.

de La Mettrie, Julien Offray. 2003. *Machine Man and Other Writings*. Trans. A. Thomason. Cambridge: Cambridge University Press.

Leibniz, Gottfried Wilhelm. 1989. The Principles of Philosophy, or, the Monadology (1714). In *G.W. Leibniz: Philosophical Essays,* eds. and trans. R. Ariew and D. Garber. Indianapolis, IN: Hackett Publishing.

————. 1997. *New Essays on Human Understanding*. Ed. and Trans. P. Remnant and J. Bennett. Cambridge: Cambridge University Press.

Leijenhorst, Cees. 2010. Bernadino Telesio (1509–1588): New Fundamental Principles of Nature. Trans. B. McNeil. In *Philosophers of the Renaissance*, ed. P.R. Blum, 168–180. Washington, DC: The Catholic University of America Press.

Lewis, C.S. 1960. *Studies in Words*. Cambridge: Cambridge University Press.

Locke, John. 1841. *An Essay Concerning Human Understanding*. London: Thomas Tegg.

Makkreel, Rudolf A. 2003. The Cognition-Knowledge Distinction in Kant and Dilthey and the Implications for Psychology and Self-Understanding. *Studies in History and Philosophy of Science Part A* 34 (1): 149–164.

Menn, Stephen. 1998. The Intellectual Setting. In *The Cambridge History of Seventeenth-Century Philosophy*, ed. D. Garber and M. Ayers, vol. I, 33–86. Cambridge: Cambridge University Press.

Miller, Ted H. 2011. *Mortal Gods: Science, Politics, and the Humanist Ambitions of Thomas Hobbes.* University Park, PA: Penn State University Press.

Monod, Emmanuel. 2004. Einstein, Heisenberg, Kant: Methodological Distinction and Conditions of Possibilities. *Information and Organization* 14 (2): 105–121.

Nichols, Shaun. 2004. The Folk Psychology of Free Will: Fits and Starts. *Mind & Language* 19 (5): 473–502.

Olson, Michael J. 2014. The Camera Obscura and the Nature of the Soul: On a Tension Between the Mechanics of Sensation and the Metaphysics of the Soul. *Intellectual History Review* 25 (3): 279–291.

Parkinson, G.H.R. 1982. The Internalization of Appearances. In *Leibniz: Critical and Interpretive Essays*, ed. M. Hooker. Minneapolis, MN: Minnesota University Press.

Paton, Herbert James. 1931. The Key to Kant's Deduction of the Categories. *Mind* 40 (159): 310–329.

———. 1997. *Kant's Metaphysic of Experience.* Vol. 1. Sterling, VA: Thoemmes Press.

Plato. 1997. *Republic.* Trans. G. M. A. Grube and Rev. C. D. C. Reeve. In *Plato: Complete Works*, ed. John M. Cooper. Indianapolis, IN: Hackett Publishing.

Reid, Thomas. 1853. *Essays on the Intellectual Powers of Man.* London: Longmans and Company.

Riskin, Jessica. 2002. *Science in the Age of Sensibility: The Sentimental Empiricists of the French Enlightenment.* Chicago: University of Chicago Press.

Rorty, Richard. 1979. *Philosophy and the Mirror of Nature.* Princeton, NJ: Princeton University Press.

Scalambrino, Frank. 2015. The Temporality of Damnation. In *The Concept of Hell*, ed. R. Arp and B. McCraw, 66–82. New York: Palgrave Macmillan.

Schmidt, Claudia M. 2008. Kant's Transcendental and Empirical Psychology of Cognition. *Studies in History and Philosophy of Science Part A* 39 (4): 462–472.

Thiel, Udo. 2011. *The Early Modern Subject: Self-Consciousness and Personal Identity from Descartes to Hume.* Oxford: Oxford University Press.

Walsh, Richard T., Thomas Teo, and Angelina Baydala. 2014. *A Critical History and Philosophy of Psychology: Diversity of Context, Thought, and Practice.* Cambridge: Cambridge University Press.

Waxman, Wayne. 1994. *Hume's Theory of Consciousness.* Cambridge: Cambridge University Press.

Yates, Frances A. 1964. *Giordano Bruno and the Hermetic Tradition.* Chicago: University of Chicago Press.

Yolton, John W. 1984. *Thinking Matter: Materialism in Eighteenth-Century Britain.* Minneapolis, MN: Minnesota University Press.

# 5

# Modernism to Post-Modernism: Method as Archimedean Point

## 5.1   Principles of Post-Kantian Speculation and Naturalization

The stage set by the "new philosophy" and the struggle against Solipsism and Egoism associated with Early Modern philosophy produced an array of methodological options for Late Modern psychologists. Recalling that the problem of Solipsism belongs to the general category of skeptical problems and that Descartes initiated his method in relation to skepticism, the following blurb from a history of Western psychology textbook accurately depicts the "Post-Kantian" situation:

> [Psychologists] thought that a way of escape had been opened up from the skeptical positon … But the Hegelian elaboration of certain metaphysical aspects of Kant's thinking, aspects which are not essential to it, brought us to a full stop … In their discouragement many trooped back past Kant to the neighborhood of Hume's position. (Metzger 1971: 331)

This is an important historical insight with which to begin our "Post-Kantian" discussion, because otherwise it would be quite natural to wonder why so much conflict and disagreement continues despite Kant's

© The Author(s) 2018
F. Scalambrino, *Philosophical Principles of the History and Systems of Psychology*,
https://doi.org/10.1007/978-3-319-74733-0_5

success regarding the problems of the "new philosophy." Moreover, one of the major differences between the Pre-Modern to Modern and the Modern to Post-Modern division of Western history is the sheer amount of potentially relevant information for psychology. As a result, an even greater amount of compression of historical data will be necessary, if we are to keep to the path from which we will be capable of thinking through the history and systems of Western psychology.

In his *Contemporary Theories and Systems in Psychology*, Benjamin Wolman (1908–2000) confidently, and rightly, declared, "These are the three main sources of contemporary psychology: Pavlov, Freud, and neo-Kantianism." (1960: 21). If we look at the same categories of principles involved in these three sources, for example in regard to methodology and the structure and function of ψυχή, then we will be able to both clarify the similarities, differences, and incommensurabilities across these "sources" of Contemporary systems and provide a classification at the "highest level of philosophical specification" possible, prior to examining the Post-Modern criticisms of essential distinctness, on the one hand, and the Post-Modern criticisms of systems of psychology in general, on the other. Anticipating what will be considered more fully below, the mention here of a few historical events in the West will provide helpful context. The Age of Enlightenment is standardly said to have run from c.1685–c.1815; Kant published the first edition of the *Critique of Pure Reason* in 1781; the French Revolution lasted from 1789–1799, Romanticism is standardly said to have run from c.1800–c.1850, and "the high priest of Romanticism," Jean-Jacques Rousseau, lived from 1712–1778.

On the one hand, as the title of this section suggests, three (3) main "post-Kantian" approaches to Kant's Revolution can be discerned: (a) the attempt to return to some pre-Kantian Revolution style of thinking, or attempts to use Kant as a point of departure for dialectical approaches, which would ultimately (b) "naturalize" Kant or push his thought into (c) "speculative" thinking. On the other hand, by the end of this chapter, we will examine the four (4) major paradigms (i.e. systems) which emerged to historically constitute Contemporary psychology, and, as we will see, these paradigms emerged with clearly definable incommensurability constituting their uniqueness. Thus, the beginning of this chapter illustrates the manner in which post-Kantian approaches to Kant's revolution will influence the solidification the four (4) major paradigms of Contemporary Western psychology. Specifically, the first two (2) of these paradigms emerge from the first of the post-Kantian approaches and through Pavlov and Freud; the approach closest to Kant's own will constitute the "neo-Kantian" third paradigm, and the dialectical approaches to Kant's revolution will constitute the fourth paradigm.

Whereas this section of the chapter will discuss the latter two of the main post-Kantian approaches to Kant's writings, the next section will discuss the first approach insofar as it finds expression in the "new psychology" of the late nineteenth and early twentieth centuries. Of course, there may have been much—even unbeknownst to all historians—cross-influencing of theorists by theories and theorists; however, the paradigms which emerged may still be characterized as unique categories of principles, if seen in the light of the philosophical principles which constitute its incommensurability. On the one hand, these categories are generally classified in terms of Natural or Human science approaches to the study of ψυχή. On the other hand, these categories are specifically characterized by the Pavlovian, Freudian, and neo-Kantian approaches to the study of ψυχή—with the fourth paradigm becoming solidified near the midpoint of the twentieth century.

Recall, from above, that we have already seen how categorization-by-way-of-incommensurability functioned in the Pre-Modern Period regarding the principle of ψυχή's freedom or free will. Similarly, the neo-Kantian paradigm, or category of principle clusters, affirms the principle of ψυχή's freedom, while the Pavlovian and Freudian paradigms do not. However, because we will be encountering the Postmodernism of the Contemporary Period, we will witness attempts—we especially have Freudian Psychoanalysis in mind here—to "read" the major theoretical approaches to the study of ψυχή differently than they were originally intended by their authors. Again, it is not impossible to re-read or re-interpret theoretical approaches in psychology; this, as we mentioned above in Chap. 2 and will discuss further below, is an aspect of what has been called the "Death of the Author" in Contemporary philosophy. Yet, at the same time, there are constraints to such activity.

That is to say, when the re-reading changes the original theory's constitutive cluster of principles in such a way as to make the re-reading incommensurable with the theory of which it purports to be a re-reading, then it cannot simultaneously appeal to, for example, the methodological principles with which it is now incommensurable, simply by giving itself the name of the previous theory. For instance, if we are given a Dr. Seuss book and told that it is a manual for assembling a car engine, *even if we believe that it is such a manual*, we will not be able to use it to assemble a car engine. Trying to argue that *Freud's theory* can belong to any paradigm one likes in the history of psychology is not just silly, it is intellectually dishonest. That is to say, Freud appeared at a specific point in history, and based on primary and secondary sources we can get, at least, an approximate-enough sketch of Freudian psychoanalysis as a system to identify true incommensurabilities between Freudian Psychoanalysis and other systems in the history of Western psychology—claiming otherwise (most likely as an inauthentic marketing tactic or a lack of courage to commit to, and stand by, a set of principles) is like claiming Dr. Seuss wrote manuals for assembling car engines.

Johann Friedrich Herbart (1776–1841) is standardly referred to as "Kant's immediate successor." However, Herbart's denial of Kant's position regarding the unknowability of things essentially marks a regression to the philosophy of Leibniz. Two ideas which indicate the category which Herbart will occupy, then, are his emphasis on "the unconscious" and his "mental mechanics." According to one commentary,

> Every idea, according to Herbart, has the tendency to maintain itself and to drive out ideas with which it is incompatible; and ideas vary in strength … An idea that is weak may gain admittance to consciousness, and maintain itself there, if the ideas above the threshold are congenial with it … Mental life is thus mainly a struggle between ideas, each of which is active, each of which strives to attain and maintain a place in consciousness, and each of which tends to repel all ideas except those with which it is compatible. (Heidbreder 1933: 66)

Now, from the perspective of historiography there are many ways to discuss Herbart given one's various political affiliations and whatever issues regarding which one chooses to focus; however, our purpose here is not to argue whether Freud's theory of unconscious activity is or is not like Herbart's, etc. Our purpose is to identify the categories of principles into which these systems would fit based on their principles, and, of course, Herbart's will fit in the category associated with Freud.

After Herbart the next "neo-Kantian" discussions of ψυχή would be those associated with German Idealism, which is dated—if including Kant—from c.1781–c.1849. The two thinkers we need to include are Arthur Schopenhauer (1788–1860) and G.W.F. Hegel (1770–1831). We begin with Schopenhauer because he belongs to the same general category as Herbart. Schopenhauer's discussion of "will" in nature may be understood as an attempt to naturalize—despite its speculative nature—Kant's Transcendental Idealism. The basic idea is that ψυχή should be understood as subject to the forces of nature; nature may speculatively be said to have a "will" of its own to which individual ψυχή's are subjected, for example Schopenhauer discussed the urge toward sexual activity and eating in terms of the "will-to-live." Further, he sought to categorize the ways in which this will of nature produces illusions for its own sake; for example, Schopenhauer infamously characterized "love" as an illusion produced by nature to ensure the survival of the species. Yet, ψυχή, of course, is, initially at least, unconscious to the illusory nature of such experiences (cf. Schopenhauer 2005: 35–36).

Of all that could be said about Hegel, we should at least acknowledge his *Phenomenology of Spirit*, published in 1807, as a neo-Kantian work regarding ψυχή (cf. Hegel 1977). Hegel develops the Kantian dialectic—though in a way that Kant actually anticipated and argued against—toward a political, religious, and cultural theory of history. Whereas Hegel's discussion regarded, of course, "spirit," his is the same dialectic which Karl Marx (1818–1883) famously "turned upside down" (he thought to stand it on its feet) to discover "historical *materialism*." In both cases, we may see their theories as not only constituted by a principle of socio-historical ontological priority but also individual ψυχή—especially in terms of consciousness and self-consciousness—is characterized as an object determined by the respective socio-historical forces. Whatever influence on psychology these theorists had in immediate proximity to the publication of their ideas, their influence on psychology was even more significant—as we will see—in the Post-Modern Period. However, in regard to the categories under discussion, Hegelian and Marxist thinking participate in the constitution of another neo-Kantian approach to psychology.

There are two more influences from the nineteenth century whose selection of principles contribute to the categorization of the essentially distinct (incommensurability-based) Contemporary psychological systems. They are the evolutionary theories of Jean-Baptiste Lamarck (1744–1829) and Charles Darwin (1809–1882) and the nineteenth-century "existentialist" theories of Søren Kierkegaard (1813–1855) and Friedrich Nietzsche (1844–1900). Notwithstanding Nietzsche's provocative claims that he was the "first psychologist" in the West, the next section will discuss the systems standardly characterized as the "new psychology." Moreover, just as the terms "new philosophy" and "new psychology" truly were used at their respective places in history, so too something of a repetition may be discerned from what clearly amounts to a direct analogy between their applications in history—whether intended by the later authors or not. Moreover, recall we are not concerned to include as much information and name-dropping as possible; thus, for instance, the relationship between Darwin and Alfred Russel Wallace (1823–1913) is not within the scope of our concern presently.

The standard way to discuss Darwin's contribution to Modern psychology is in contrast to Kant; usually stated in terms of two principles, it is the first of which that is supposed to make Darwin's contribution revolutionary. The principles are: the elimination of final causes regarding development and materialism (cf. Weinert 2009). As the standard explication goes, Darwin provides a model for biology which is different from any of the previous philosophers discussed, since all of them believed in Aristotelian Final Causes, that is, purpose-driven nature. However, as is relevant for the next section, E. B. Titchener (1867–1927) repeatedly laments throughout his *Systematic Psychology: Prolegomena* that most of the "new psychologies" fall back into "teleological" theorizing, despite their avowal of "Darwinism." (Titchener 1927). The second principle is "materialism," which we have already discussed. What needs clarification, then, is the distinction between the evolutionary theories of Darwin and Lamarck.

The essential distinction between Darwin and Lamarck can be stated in terms of the difference between the "mechanism of natural selection" and the "mechanism of use-inheritance," respectively. The classic example regards giraffes. On the one hand, for Lamarck, giraffes stretched their necks to reach tree leaves, and thus the characteristic long neck of the giraffe developed over time and was passed on to subsequent generations. On the other hand, for Darwin, giraffes with short necks, since they could not reach the food source, eventually died out, and therefore, the surviving giraffes are the ones with long necks. Again, despite the clear preference for Darwin's explanation over Lamarck's, the latter's principle of use-inheritance, as we shall see, will find traction and enthusiasm in Postmodernism. Finally, two further principles follow from the principle of (the mechanism of) natural selection: "the principle of variation" and "the principle of the correlation of growth." The former principle suggests that there will be variation to the species produced over-time, some of which—depending on natural selection—may be incorporated into the future expressions of the species. The latter principle suggests: "Organisms are integrated systems and adaptive change in one part can lead to non-adaptive modification of other features." (Darwin 1859: 182). In other words, though giraffes developed longer necks due to natural selection, their longer necks may be beneficial in regard to functions other than the one(s) involved in the natural selection, that is, (in this case) eating.

Lastly, then, existentialism is standardly said to arise with Kierkegaard and Nietzsche; further, it is clear from the primary and secondary sources that both of these thinkers were reacting to Post-Kantian innovations. Whereas Hegel was read as emphasizing the community and collective spirit over the individual, Kierkegaard emphasized—to borrow a phrase from Heidegger—the *mineness* of existence. What this means is that even if there is a predictable pattern that every human goes through given some historical, geographical, and socio-economic status, for example, Kierkegaard would still emphasize the value of the personal choices and first-person perspective traversing the pattern. Though we could say his is an emphasis on the "subjective" point of view, the "personal" point of view better characterizes it—Kierkegaard was not concerned with such "subjective" aspects of experience as color perception, etc. Likewise, though more avowedly directed at Schopenhauer, Nietzsche also advocated for the individual. Whereas Schopenhauer's philosophy was pessimistic and tragic—depicting life as full of illusion and, ultimately, total loss, Nietzsche advocated for an interpretation of life as an adventure and a contest (cf. Kierkegaard 2009, 1998, 1980, 1988; cf. Nietzsche 1967, 1974, 1977, 1979, 1989; cf. Scalambrino 2015a). Moreover, because "existentialism," takes the focus off of universal spirit and the will of nature, respectively, placing it on the individual—"personalistic," rather than "naturalistic"[1]—and the individual's freedom and self-realization, is in multiple ways a return to the spirit of Kant's philosophy.

## 5.2    Principles of the "New" Psychology: The Birth of the Laboratory

For better or for worse, as every psychologist should know, the idea upon which the discipline of psychology's independence was finally established was the idea that psychology could be an experimental science. In other words, it was supposed that psychology could be a science like physics or biology, that is, a natural science (cf. Adams 1931: 8; Ash 2005: 100; cf. Dewey 1884). Recalling Feigl's joke noted above in Section 5, though the rhetoric of experimental science succeeded in establishing psychology as its own discipline, the idea that psychology is a natural science today, is more the idea that biology (especially neuroscience) should be the discipline which studies "psychology." Be that as it may, what we need to be sure to keep in mind when thinking through the principles of the systems of psychology as they emerged in this historical period of the West is that these systems, despite their differences, were vying for the claim to the title of "psychology as a natural science."

Keeping in mind that Sigmund Freud's (1856–1939) *Project for a Scientific Psychology* appeared in 1895 and the Russian physiologist Ivan Pavlov (1849–1936) did not win his "Nobel Prize in Physiology or Medicine" for "classical conditioning" until 1904, two of the "three main sources of contemporary psychology" have not yet emerged in the year 1870. Thus, "introspection," "extraspection," and "association" characterize the methods of the "new psychology" initially, as the non-Kantian principles inherited from Descartes, Hobbes, Locke, Leibniz, and Hume settle into a method distinctive of the "new psychology." It is worth quoting at length *A History of Experimental Psychology* from 1929:

> There was something fresh and exciting in the 1870s about the new experimental psychology that Wundt called "physiological psychology." It has all the status of a new scientific endeavor. It was something more than the sensory experiments of physiologists, like E.H. Weber's and Johannes Müller's discoveries. It was more than the philosophers' turning toward science as an aid, than Herbart's use of mathematics, than Lotze's writing a 'medical' psychology. There was really something new here, a scientific activity with its own name. It is true that most of the new research was on perception, but even so there was hope for a complete experimental psychology as soon as there had been time. Fechner had already provided new methods of measurement. Helmholtz was showing how researches in vision and hearing were to be done, and he was not alone. (Boring 1950: 384)

It is clear from this excerpt that its author—Edwin G. Boring (1886–1968)—provides a progressive reading of the history of Western psychology, according to which the "physiological psychology" of Wilhelm Wundt (1832–1920) quite literally and actually ushered in a "new psychology." Moreover, as Boring emphasized, for the "new psychology" Wundt provided "its structure and form, its self-consciousness, its name, its first formal laboratory, its first experimental journal, as well as the systematic patter with respect to which the experiments could be formulated and given their significance." (Ibid.). The question we should be asking, then, is: How did Pavlov and Freud come to eclipse Wundt?

In regard to the principles at work across these systems "between psychophysical methods and physiological theories" (cf. Sinatra 2006) vying for the claim to the title of "psychology as a natural science," each of the different psychologists may be understood (philosophically) as thinking through the methodological, structural, and functional principles regarding ψυχή with which to characterize the "new psychology." Thus, as we will see, Wundt's methodological choice was neither extraspective or deterministic enough for Behaviorism nor reductionistic or unconscious-oriented enough for Psychoanalysis. It is worth quoting Boring at length one last time regarding the principles of the "new psychology." Thus, initially, this new psychology was introspective, sensationistic, elementistic and associationistic. It was *introspective* because consciousness was its subject-matter ... It was *sensationistic* because sensation shows what the nature of consciousness is. The imageless thoughts were not to claim status until the century had changed. It was *elementistic*, because the whole conception at the start was of a mental chemistry, and it seemed as if sensations, images and feelings might well be the elements which make up those compounds that are the stuff of psychology. And it was *associationistic* because association is the very principle of compounding ... Later this sort of psychology came to be called the *psychology of content*, in contradistinction to the *psychology of act* which bore Brentano's label ... Experimental psychology knew what to do, more or less, with a psychology of content. The acts ... were elusive and did not stand up to observation like the contents. (1950: 385)

Wundt's "new psychology" has been called "voluntarism"—not to be confused with the philosophical-theological position—because he still embraced a non-deterministic principle of agency; this may be understood as either too Leibnizian or too Kantian to square with a natural science understanding of ψυχή. For, following the "Mental Activity" approach of Leibniz and Kant, Wundt theorized experience in terms of "apprehension," "apperception," and "volition." That is to say, a voluntary, that is, intentional, use of the will is the condition for apprehending sensation within the apperception of consciousness—or, "attention" for short (cf. Wundt 1904). As a result of adhering to this principle, Wundt understood individual psychology along the lines of a natural science or *Naturwissenschaften* and social psychology along the lines of moral philosophy, that is, a human science, or *Geisteswissenschaften* (cf. Danziger 1979: 207; cf. Scalambrino 2018).

However, the eclipse of Wundt's system began with his student (and English translator) E. B. Titchener, that is, his student's more positivistic approach to the method of introspection; thus, though beyond our present scope, a spectrum of uses of the term "introspection" may be identified from Descartes through Titchener, despite the general sameness of the meaning in opposition to extraspection (cf. Araujo 2016: 154–167; cf. Gillespie 2006; cf. Singh 1999: 100). Just as objective experimentation could take place by way of extraspection, so too could experimentation take place by way of introspection with the aid of instruments to objectify various aspects of experience. As a result, "experimental introspection" names the method of asking individual's to verify, based on self-report, the experience of various sensations (cf. Boring 1953; cf. Hilgard 1987). Of course, the goal was to make the natural science of psychology as much like a purely "physical science" as possible. According to Titchener, "Physical science, then, explains by assigning a cause; mental science explains by reference to those nervous processes which correspond with the mental processes that are under observation." (Titchener 1910: 41). Recalling the distinction between *Naturwissenschaften* explanation and *Geisteswissenschaften* description, "We may bring these two modes of explanation together if we define explanation itself as the statement of the proximate circumstances or conditions under which the described phenomenon occurs." (Ibid.). Titchener, then, provided the following illustration: "Dew is formed under the condition of a difference of temperature between the air and the ground; ideas are formed under the condition of certain processes in the nervous system. Fundamentally, the object and the manner of explanation, in the two cases, are one and the same." (Ibid).

Moreover, in this way, introspection could be combined with even more positivistic principles regarding the structure and function of ψυχή. For example, by allowing for the phenomena of experience to be based on the "nervous system," rather than "sensation," the previous French "sensorium-positivism" evolved into the "phenomenal-positivism" associated with Ernst Mach (1838–1916) and Richard Avenarius (1843–1896). In fact, under the label of "save the appearances" (by not inferring them away in favor of an unobservable *a priori*) and consistent with a line of thought running from Hume's to John Stuart Mill's (1806–1873) associationism, the influence of "Machism" continued into the 1920's influencing the establishment of "The Vienna Circle" and later "Logical Positivism." (cf. Blackmore and Itagaki 2013: 2–3). Thus, the embrace of positivistic principles (whether phenomenally or materialistically understood) can be seen in Titchener's "Positivistic Structuralism," the psychophysics of Ernst H. Weber (1795–1878) and Gustav T. Fechner (1801–1887), and in Hermann Ebbinghaus' (1850–1909) use of the methods of the "new psychology" regarding associationism (cf. Robinson

1964) differentiate them from Wundt's "Voluntarism" (cf. Baker 1992; cf. Danziger 1979).

Lastly, Titchener's *Systematic Psychology* provides a good explanation of the principles which differentiate his "Positivistic Structuralism" from "Pragmatic Functionalism." According to Titchener,

> These, then, seem to be the four main characteristics of the functional systems. The subject-matter of psychology is duplicated, though [1] function is preferred to content; [2] consciousness is a solver of problems; [3] the whole course of the mental life is regarded teleologically; and [4] psychology is written as a preface to philosophy or some practical discipline. (1927: 193)

Importantly, we should clarify the second principle which he attributed to "Pragmatic Functionalism." Titchener's clarification itself involved quoting James R. Angell's (1869–1949) *Psychology: An Introductory Study of the Structure and Functions of Human Consciousness* (1904), "conscious activities emerge at the point where reflex acts are found inadequate to meet the needs of particular situations"; "if the reflexes and the automatic acts were wholly competent to steer the organism throughout its course, there is no reason to suppose that consciousness would ever put in an appearance." (Angell 1904: 50; cf. Titchener 1927: 183). Of course Dewey's discussion of Pragmatic Functionalism as a "new psychology" involved not only an avowal of the principles of Darwinian evolution but also a criticism of "introspection" (Dewey 1884). Yet, as Titchener pointed out, "A view of this sort seems, indeed, to be logically bound up with the view that consciousness is primarily and actively a matter of function, and only secondarily and passively a matter of content." (1927: 184). Thus, Titchener accused Pragmatic Functionalism of reducing "consciousness" to mere instrumentality.

Interestingly, a direct analogy may be seen regarding scientific methodology, revolution, and the relation between the emergence of the "new philosophy" and the "new psychology." This "Renaissance cycle" of rejecting positions previously considered authoritative will cycle yet again in the transition from Modernity to Post-Modernity. In sum, we have seen how the principles of methodology, structure and function regarding ψυχή shaped the systems characteristic of the "new psychology." This sets the stage to discuss the "three main sources of contemporary psychology: Pavlov, Freud, and neo-Kantianism." (Wolman 1960: 21). Moreover, the criticism of Pragmatic Functionalism from Titchener's Positivistic Structuralism shall prove prophetic in the culmination of the "new psychology" and essential eclipse of the systems of psychology just discussed. That is to say, anticipating what will be considered more fully below, the idea—noted above—that "there is no reason to suppose that consciousness would ever put in an appearance" may retrospectively read as if it were a suggestion to Pavlov and Freud.

## 5.3    Constitutive Principles of the "Four Forces of Psychology"

The purpose of this section is to state the "highest," so to speak, four (4) categories into which early-twentieth-century Western psychological systems may be placed. As noted above, these may be understood as "paradigms," but should be thought of as categorizations of clusters of principles, which emerged with clearly definable incommensurability constituting their uniqueness. Thus, it is precisely *not* the purpose of this section to list all of the different variations within a category or the textbooks and times associated with each alteration. Such would be the purpose for a history textbook; however, our purpose is to gain a vision of the history and systems of Western psychology, at the level of systems, so as to think through the principles and essential distinctions regarding their constitution. Because we have been moving toward the "Information Age" the proliferation of many different systems of contemporary psychology could be articulated—some argue that just as there are lists of over 250 different kinds of psychotherapy (cf. Corsini 2001), there could be just as many different psychologies. It is neither our intention to take a stance in opposition to such proliferation of psychological systems nor do we believe that every one of however many systems there may be are essentially incommensurable with one another.

Hence, by rising to the level of essential incommensurability, we arrive at: (1) a way to categorize a proliferation of psychological systems, (2) a way to think about and talk about different systems, and (3) a ground from which to be critical. This last aspect is quite important because without it psychology loses its identity, and though from the perspective of some political allegiances those words might sound good, the problem is that the disciplines willing to take over the domain and funding, etc. of psychology are not "losing their identity." For example, if you pride yourself as a psychoanalyst, you should be able to state the principles of your position and be able to identify how you are not a behaviorist. Moreover, from the point of view of philosophy, if you cannot identify what your position is *not*, then you do not really know your position. Is the activity of eating a sandwich psychoanalysis? If you think so, then you do not truly understand psychology.

The "Four Forces" of Psychology are: Behaviorism, Psychoanalysis, Neo-Kantianism, and "General Systems Theory." The progenitors of these systems are respectively: Ivan Pavlov (1849–1936), Sigmund Freud's (1856–1939) Immanuel Kant (1724–1804), and Ludwig von Bertalanffy (1901–1972). Rather than consider any one of Kant's "neo-Kantian" innovators as the progenitor of the "third force" of psychology, it solves a number of problems to refer the category directly to Kant. Consistent with the manner in which the historical systems of psychology have been discussed in the previous sections, this section will consider the principles of the Four Forces which will reveal their essential incommensurabilities, that is, the methodological, structural and functional principles regarding ψυχή. Also, it is important to keep in mind that we are considering these categories as original, that is, prior to the influence of any innovators, and prior to the influence of the "Cognitive Revolution." As needed, innovations and influences will be addressed later.

Behaviorism's methodology is extraspective. As John B. Watson opened his seminal paper of 1913, "Psychology as the behaviorist views it is a purely objective experimental branch of natural science." (Watson 1913: 158). It is environment-centric in that it considers the organism's relation to things in the environment. In that ontological priority is assigned to behavior, it retains an essentially mechanistic vision for psychology, revealing its connection with the Early Modern French sensorium-positivists, and its emphasis on the principles of reflex, conditioning, and habit-formation reveal its connection to the earlier associationist thinking. The fact that consciousness need not put in an appearance, reveals the extent to which it is amenable to materialistic monism and the phenomenalism of Hume. Lastly, in regard to function, just as there is no need for consciousness to put in an appearance, so too there is no need for "freedom of the will" to put in an appearance. As we concluded above in regard to this issue: logical, radical and methodological Behaviorism amount to an understanding of the "contingencies" found within a "physical system," and "It is in the nature of an experimental analysis of human behavior that it should strip away the *functions* previously assigned to autonomous man and transfer them one by one to the controlling environment [emphasis added]." (Skinner 1971: 194).

Freudian Psychoanalysis occupies a different category of methodological principles from Behaviorism, not because it is not extraspective; rather, introspection too has a place in Freudian Psychoanalysis, and Freud was clearly willing to consider a patient (or analysand's) "free associations." Thus both extraspection and introspection have a place in the methodology of Freudian Psychoanalysis, so long as both are grounded in his understanding of what the science of psychoanalysis is. For example, if we take the "Project" of 1895 to indicate the beginning of his psychoanalytic writing and the posthumously published *An Outline of Psychoanalysis* (1940) to indicate the end of his psychoanalytic writing, then from beginning to end Freud gave the same characterization of psychoanalysis: Freudian psychoanalysis is a natural science.

For Freud, "the intellect and the mind are objects for scientific research in exactly the same way as any non-human things." (Freud 1933: 159). Thus, in the beginning,

> The intention of this project is to furnish us with a psychology which shall be a natural science: its aim, that is, is to represent psychical processes as quantitatively determined states of specifiable material particles and so to make them plain and void of contradiction. (Freud 1895: 355)

And, at the end, "Psychoanalysis is a part of the mental science of psychology ... Psychology, too, is a natural science. What else can it be?"

(1940: 282; cf. Grünbaum 1984; cf. Macmillan and Crews 1997; cf. Sulloway 1992; cf. Zepf 2016). Anticipating what will be considered again below, taking the word "contradiction" as a point of departure for interpreting Freud's "Project," some have located a "dialectic of desire" in Freud's system. Tracing a line of thought from Jean-Martin Charcot's (1825–1893) student Pierre Janet (1859–1947) in which he used a distinction originating from Maine de Biran (1766–1824) between the immediate data of consciousness—reminiscent of the "bare sensation" of Early Modern French sensorium-positivism—and "the self" as an active energy, Freud's "dialectic of desire" may be understood as his attempt to provide a *naturalistic account* of this line of thought.

That is, Janet saw an "antithesis" between "the automatism of subconscious acts" of ψυχή and the "personalized apprehension of things" which was picked up in Henri Bergson's (1859–1941) theorizing. From there:

> To "mechanism" the philosopher of creative evolution [Bergson] opposes "dynamism," a principle which is allied to vitalism so soon as it suggests a creative force in life. Dynamism ... is based upon a dialectic of mind and matter. This dialectic leads it straight toward the problems of knowledge and reality ... The dynamical principles of Freud are of the same general character as those which we have found in Janet and Bergson. (Bentley 1921: 10)

Moreover, a naturalization or "materialization" of the dialectic is, of course, possible, as Darwin and Marx have shown (cf. Skoll 2014: esp. Ch. 3). Thus, as we will see, the innovators of Freud who read the "dialectic of desire" not in terms of natural science are actually shifting to the French (Maine de Biron, Janet, and Bergson) position, instead of Freud's.

In regard to structure, Freud offered multiple models of ψυχή, for example the "structural" and "topographical." However, for the purpose of identifying a principle which makes Freudian Psychoanalysis incommensurable with the other "Forces" of psychology, we may simply notice that he gave "the unconscious"—biologically construed—ontological priority (cf. Freud 1915; cf. Sulloway 1992). Further, his bio-organism-centric psychoanalysis espoused an "identity theory of mind," aka "type physicalism" or "reductive materialism." (cf. Smith

1999: 49–57; cf. Smith 2001: 405–406; cf. Solomon 1974). Freud's system also evidences incommensurability in relation to Behaviorism regarding function; however, since the question of free will may be said to characterize the central principle regarding function, we will need to look beyond the surface to see the incommensurability between Freudian Psychoanalysis and Behaviorism regarding function.

What makes the issue complicated in Freud's theorizing is the presence of both an affirmation of teleology and an affirmation of determinism. On the one hand, whether one approaches the question of free will in Freud by way of his infamous claim that "anatomy is destiny" (1961: 178, 1957: 189) or by way of his "psychosexual stages," (1953) he seems to suggest that there are progressive stages at which to arrive—or not—, and, therefore, it seems like individuals may have freedom in the actualization of stages. On the other hand, Freud was explicitly and avowedly a determinist; noting, for example, "You nourish the illusion of there being such a thing as psychical freedom, and you will not give it up. I am sorry to say I disagree with you categorically over this." (Freud 1963: 49).

Not surprisingly Freud linked this position with the accomplishment of the "new psychology," that is, "I ventured to tell you that you nourish a deeply rooted faith in undetermined psychical events and in free will, but that this is quite unscientific and must yield to the demand of a determinism whose rule extends over mental life." (Ibid: 106). Further, note well that he characterized even rational deliberation about the future as "the unfulfilled but possible futures to which we still like to cling *in phantasy*, all the strivings of the ego ... which nourish in us *the illusion of Free Will* [emphasis added]" (1955: 236). Moreover, it makes sense that, as Thomas Szasz (1920–2012) pointed out, "although an entire volume of the Standard Edition of Freud's collected works is devoted to an index, there is no entry for *responsibility* in it." (2001: 237).

Ultimately, the "Third Force" of psychology is grounded in Kant's philosophy; that is, it is not a psychology grounded in the thinking of, for example, Descartes, Locke, or Hume. The term "Third Force" psychology comes from the psychologists Abraham H. Maslow (1908–1970) and Carl R. Rogers (1902–1987). The name was supposedly derived as a reaction to Psychoanalysis as a "First Force" and Behaviorism as a "Second Force" in psychology. Two of the twentieth-century "Existentialist" philosophers whose work has clearly influenced Third Force psychology are Martin Heidegger (1889–1976) and Jean-Paul Sartre (1905–1980). In many ways, the Third Force is the diametrical opposite of the other two "forces." In terms of structure the first two forces were mechanistic and materialistic; in terms of function they were deterministic, and in terms of methodology they were reductionistic, if not positivistic, that is, exemplary of *Naturwissenschaften*.

Thus, in discussing the "Third Force" of psychology, there will be three key features which differentiate it from the other forces. The first, which may be considered structural, is that the Third Force gives ontological priority to the conscious individual human-person. On the one hand, this immediately differentiates it from all of the other forces in that by relating to ψυχή in terms of the conscious individual human-person, consciousness very much makes an appearance—to turn a locution referring to Titchener's portent phrase above. On the other hand, this may be seen as an affirmation of two Renaissance principles. First, the Third Force of psychology affirms the principle of Individualism by recognizing the individual's ability to self-actualize its unique, or "ownmost," potential. Second, it affirms the principle of Humanism by recognizing the dignity and primacy of the person over, for example, unconscious deterministic forces or environment-based reflexes. There are, of course, different *perspectives* within Third Force psychology on how to understand the affirmation of these principles; a topic to be addressed below.

It is in terms of function that the various interpretations and approaches within the Third Force of psychology appear most unified. This principle of function, then, is "freedom." That is to say, two principles are needed to differentiate Third Force psychology from the other forces in terms of incommensurability: Third Force psychology is non-deterministic, and Third force psychology gives ontological priority to the individual person. Whereas the former differentiates the Third Force from Freudian Psychoanalysis and Behaviorism, the latter differentiates it from all of the other forces, that is, the "Fourth Force" as well. In this way, Third Force psychology affirms notions such as "responsibility" and "commitment" (cf. Rogers 1964). Regarding the "Humanists," whereas for Rogers the way to "develop an acceptable self-concept, to realize one's potential, [and] to achieve self-actualization" was through "a process of self-discovery and self-acceptance," for Maslow "self-actualization requires the satisfaction of lower order physiological needs, and needs for safety, love, and self-esteem." (Kimble 1985: 15).

Moreover, recall that according to the account of ψυχή revealed through Kant's Transcendental Logic, a "predisposition to *personality* is the capacity for respect for the moral law as *in itself a sufficient incentive of the will.*" (Kant 1960: 34). Because the human will has the potential to be non-mechanical in its relation to the environment, its embodiment, and its own existence, the person is free. Psychologists working within this system may or may not contextualize this freedom in terms of morality and theology (cf. DuBose 2013; cf. Camus 1991, 1992). This idea— as we will see more clearly regarding methodology—has been elaborated into the idea of "meaning-making," and, in this way, the Third Force of psychology emphasizes the manner in which individuals "create themselves" and the meaning of their existence through their own choices, that is, their use of freedom (cf. Maslow 1943, 1968, 1970a, b; cf. Rogers 1961, 1963a, b, 1965, 1979, 1995; cf. Frankl 2006; cf. Spinelli 2005).

Whereas the perspective of function emphasized unity across the various interpretations and approaches within the Third Force of psychology, the perspective of methodology emphasizes diversity. We must not confuse the diversity of methodology with an anarchic-eclecticism. For example, inspired by Existentialism and Humanism and frustrated with the de-personalizing agendas of Freudian Psychoanalysis and Behaviorism, many psychologists from diverse methodological backgrounds were unified by the structural and functional principles of the Third Force of psychology; in fact, some were "psychoanalysts who left the Freudian fold because they were dissatisfied with its blind allegiance to the natural scientific account of the mind." (Burston 2003: 312; cf. Pandora 2002: 38). Thus, of the innovators of Freud's system, we must ask whether they embrace the structural and functional principle of the Third Force of psychology, and it is an either/or situation, that is, there is a genuine incommensurability between Freudian psychoanalysis and the Third Force of psychology in terms of their constitutive principles. Anticipating what will be considered more fully below, because the Third Force of psychology has a human science or *Geisteswissenschaften* orientation, one of the methods associated with the meaning-making activities of ψυχή is the study of Hermeneutics. So, in the Post-Modern Period we will see what is considered by many to be a Hermeneutic Psychoanalysis, which is also a human science. The only point to make here is that, to the extent that such an approach is truly a human science, then it is incommensurable with Freudian Psychoanalysis.

The diverse methodologies of the Third Force of psychology have often been called "Qualitative Methods." This is unfortunate for Third Force psychologists, since it implies that they are somehow barred from using "Quantitative Methods," which is simply not true—such thinking stems from a lack of understanding the principles constituting the Third Force's incommensurability with other systems. Despite the vagueness of the term "holism," in general, we may distinguish between the essence of Third Force psychology's methodology and the essence of Freudian Psychoanalysis and Behaviorism in that the Third Force is non-reductionistic, that is, it embraces "holism" by regarding the whole person as "greater than the sum of its parts." In doing this it respects the dignity of the person's humanity and avoids "de-personalizing" the individual. The primary three methods involved are: Phenomenology, Phenomenography, and Hermeneutics.

There are many variations across these categories; however, in general we may say that when a researcher is interested in the merely subjective aspects of the person's experience, then the methodology of "Phenomenography" is involved; that is, questions like: "What was your experience of the event?" are asked, and the researcher is not interested in investigating the objective nature of the person's experience (cf. Husserl 1977, 1970; cf. Marton 1981, 1986; cf. Svensson 1997). The principle distinguishing between "Phenomenology" and "Phenomenography" is directly analogous to the difference between Kantian and Cartesian subjectivity, respectively (cf. Heidegger 1962b, 1997; cf. Rockmore 2011). That is to say, though it is true that Phenomenology studies the subjective structure of human experience, it does so for the purpose of explicating the psychological structures determining the *object* of that subject's experience. To clarify, one: Consider the APA Dictionary's definition, "phenomenology should be distinguished from introspection as it is concerned with the relationship between acts of consciousness and the objects of such acts." (VandenBos 2007: 695). Two, following from the "Mental

Activity" tradition, the human sensorium dynamically overflows—in that it has more potential content than it can "process," and, therefore, a distinction is to be made between the "intentional" acts of *consciousness* (noesis) and the content (noema) selected from out of the overflow by the acts. Phenomenology describes this intentional selection process in terminology developed out of Kant (cf. Scalambrino 2015b), not "in terms of their relationship to events in the body or in the external world." (VandenBos 2007: 695; cf. Husserl 1983: 211–233 & 181).

Hence, when psychologists are not concerned with the subject's conditions for experiencing an object as much as with the manner in which the subject characterizes its own experience, then such psychologists are not performing Phenomenology, they are performing Phenomenography; to mix the two up is to commit the logical fallacy of "Psychologism" (Scalambrino 2015b). As the *phenomenologist* Edmund Husserl (1859–1938) explained it: "the expression psychologism" applies to "any interpretation which converts objectivities into something psychological in the proper sense" (Husserl 1969: 169; cf. Hopkins 2006). In other words, the objective aspects of human experience are "psychologized" when "their objective sense, their sense as a species of objects having a peculiar essence, is denied in favor of the subjective mental occurrences, the data in immanent or psychological temporality" (Husserl 1969: 169; cf. Scalambrino 2015b). At any moment of some human subject's experience of the content *of that moment* may be differentiated between the objective and subjective aspects *of the experience*, and one is guilty of psychologism when one treats the objective (universalizable) aspects of the experience as if they are merely subjective. Though different subjects have different perspectives, to claim the reality of a situation is not universally true because it rather depends on the subjective determination of subjects is to commit the fallacy of psychologism.[2]

Also in regard to the methodology of phenomenology, Gestalt psychology features prominently as another "neo-Kantian" source of contemporary psychology with its principles of "retrospection," "imageless thought," and the principle (what they call "the Law") of "*Prägnanz*." Gestalt psychology has been characterized as the "antithesis of Wundtian Structuralism." (Sahakian 1975: 155). Retrospection adds to introspection and extraspection: looking "backward," rather than "inward" or "outward." And, it was used to reveal the principle of "imageless thought." That is, the "Würzburg School," led by Oswald Külpe (1862–1915) produced experiments in which they would ask participants if they agree with some of Nietzsche's aphorisms. For example, do you agree with §115 from *Beyond Good & Evil*: "The sense of the tragic gains and wanes with sensuality." (Nietzsche 1989: 90), or §175: "In the end one loves one's desire and not what is desired." (Ibid: 93)? After recording a response, participants were asked to "retrospect" and notice whether any images consistently corresponded to such activities as "affirmation" or "denial" (cf. Mayer and Orth 1901; cf. Seel 2011: 1366–1371; cf. Köhler 1970; cf. Perls et al. 1994).

On the one hand, this seems to indicate that some kinds of thinking can occur without being accompanied by images. Finally, this led to the idea that such—what Kant would have called "synthetic transcendental"—activity takes place outside of awareness. Thus, on the other hand, this allows for discussion both of such *conditions for the possibility of* conscious human experience and the principle of "*Prägnanz.*" The latter idea being, then, that even if given fragmented or fragmentary sensory input, Gestalt phenomenology reveals that "acts of consciousness" fill-in or complete what is lacking, and are, therefore, "organizing" and active beyond mere recognition of what things may be environmentally present. The principle of "*Prägnanz*" is, of course, holistic, then—keeping in mind the "imageless" contributions to experience—in that it suggests the whole of experience is greater than the sum of its analytically identifiable parts (cf. Scalambrino 2014). This will also be relevant for the methodology of Hermeneutics regarding the agency of the species-specific meaning-making actions of ψυχή.

Last of the three primary methods of the Third Force is "Hermeneutics." Because Section 6 above is dedicated to a discussion of Hermeneutics, we may be brief here. Recall that the term "hermeneutics" points to the study of different ways of describing or "interpreting," as opposed to a process of essential specification. This is different from Phenomenology and Phenomenography, though it may incorporate information from both. Hermeneutics is associated with "meaning-making," for example narrative descriptions of a person's lived-experience. A basic premise holds for the use of Hermeneutics in psychology that when we have an experience we provide a description of the experience to ourselves; further, we incorporate the description of the experience into our "life story." As we noted above regarding Kant's philosophy, just as we have regulative ideas, which mediate our experience and influence the meaning we find in existence, so too "a person functions in terms of a creative representation of the world rather than in terms of a passive reaction to the physical environment." (Kimble 1985: 16). Hermeneutics, in regard to psychology, studies how persons make meaning, choose their actions, and dwell in a meaningful "world" (cf. Smith and Osborn 2003). Anticipating what will be considered more fully below, a concluding discussion of the Hermeneutic method below will help us understand two (2) different historical "turns" of the late twentieth century. That is, emphasis may be placed on the historicity of the language through the performance of which one "makes meaning." Or, emphasis may be placed on the performance itself.

The question of Hermeneutics relates in interesting ways to the question of the relationship between Existentialism and Humanism. Though beyond the scope of our present discussion, anticipating its presence in the background of our conclusion, we should at least note the following. Not only because "Existentialists" tend to have an inherent aversion to "isms," but also disagreements among them, make the "Existentialist" idea of "Freedom" difficult to characterize beyond its Kantian-base. Famously Heidegger and Sartre disagreed on the relationship between Existentialism and Humanism, and this may be understood in terms of how to characterize Freedom. Whereas Sartre in his writings *Being & Nothingness* and especially "The Humanism of Existentialism," aka "Existentialism is a Humanism," seemed to believe he was explicating Heidegger's position from *Being & Time*, Heidegger's explicit disagreement appeared in his "Letter on Humanism" (cf. Sartre 1992, 1993; cf. Heidegger 1962a, 1993). Thus, in regard to the Hermeneutic question of meaning-making, Sartre seemed to emphasize absolute freedom as "inescapably dreadful," despite any "deterministic excuses," and Heidegger seemed to emphasize freedom in regard to what may be accomplished given our situatedness within historical-expressions of Be-ing. Roughly, the Humanism of Sartre's position may be likened to the idea that you are only as limited as your imagination and knowledge or "where there's a will there's a way." Yet, Heidegger's emphasis on language as "the house of Being" and his concern that we are the "shepherds of Be-ing" suggests a greater focus on one's present existential conditions than perhaps is found in Sartre's approach (cf. Heidegger 2001; cf. Guignon and Adams 2003; cf. Scalambrino 2015d; cf. Solomon 1987).

In regard to the "Fourth Force," then, there is a straightforward way to illuminate its incommensurability from the other "forces"; however, given the nature of the Fourth Force, it may be the most difficult of the four to tell apart from the others at first glance. Ultimately, because the Fourth Force gives ontological priority to systems, it differs from the other forces insofar as those forces give ontological priority to the individual, and insofar as they do not, then the Fourth Force sets out to subsume them. For example, Behaviorism is enviro-centric; however, by focusing on the conditioning of the individual, it reduces the environment to its involvement regarding the conditioning of the individual, rather than the individual as a part of the environment as a systemic whole.

Bertalanffy suggested, regarding the essential distinction between the animal and the human-person found in the history of Western philosophy, that one cannot simply choose one pole of the opposition and assign ontological priority to it. Rather, it is the system of which both the animal and the human-person are parts to which, according to the psychological application of General Systems Theory, must be given ontological priority (cf. von Bertalanffy 1967, 1968, 1969, 1981). For example, in terms of family or couples therapy, it is not individuals as much as it is the family or the couple, as a systemic entity, which is "in therapy," that is, toward which the therapy is oriented. Systems may be "closed" (we are able to know all the variables and functions involved in the system) or "open" (we can know the system essentially in terms of its operable variables and functions, but not the totality). Thus, in either case, the metaphors of "Laplace's Demon" or the "Limitless" idea from popular American culture are relevant for the Fourth Force of psychology (von Bertalanffy 1967: 128).

Along with the shift in ontological priority comes a shift of emphases regarding multiple principles of philosophical psychology—the two most prominent being the principles of "Emergence" and "Multiple

Realizability." As noted above regarding these principles, their emphasis brings forth a different methodological relation to causation. In other words, "A stimulus (i.e. a change in external conditions) does not cause a process in an otherwise inert system; it only modifies processes in an autonomously active system" (Ibid: 129). Thus, the principle of homeostasis found, for example, in mechanistic theories such as the Freudian hydraulic model, opens onto cultural terrain beyond the hedonistic principle. Further, the Fourth Force emphasizes the principle of difference or differentiation. That is to say, the pre-systems principle of individuation is transformed into the principle of differentiation (since everything remains "within" the system), and from the perspective of the system as a whole, differentiation is understood as transformation into a more "heterogeneous" condition (Ibid: 130; cf. Deleuze 1994).

Bertalanffy is clear that "Organisms *are* not machines"; however, "they can to a certain extent *become* machines, congeal into machine." (von Bertalanffy 1967: 131; cf. Deleuze and Guattari 1980). He referred to this way in which organisms may be differentiated as "the principle of progressive mechanization." (von Bertalanffy 1967: 131). According to the principle of "boundary regulation," then, it is still possible to speak of ψυχή, though in terms of differentiated phases of change in the system (cf. de Mul 2016). What is more, though Bertalanffy emphasizes a kind of human dignity—in that human organisms include "symbolic activities" and, therefore, cannot be reduced to mere "biologistic notions"—he also recognized the manner in which the principle of progressive mechanization leaves even the human organism susceptible to control regarding its *functions* in the system. Such "control theory," though the impulse for which may be seen in Bacon and Descartes, in terms of General Systems Theory is called "cybernetics." Interestingly, this term comes from the Greek for "steersman," and therefore is directly analogous to Aristotle's discussion of ψυχή as the sailor or "ship's captain." Yet, from the Systems perspective, the control is directed at the system, and, therefore, at the individual, by way of the system.

As Norbert Wiener explained it in his seminal *Cybernetics; or, Control and Communication in the Animal and Machine* (1965): "the newer study of automata, whether in the metal or in the flesh, is a branch of communication engineering," and this involves a "quantity of information and

[a] coding technique" (Wiener 1965: 42). For example, as W. Ross Ashby's *An Introduction to Cybernetics* characterizes it, the "unpredictable behavior of an insect that lives in and about a shallow pond, hopping to and fro among water, bank, and pebble, can illustrate a machine in which the state transitions correspond to" a probability-based pattern that can be analyzed statistically (Johnston 2008: 31; Heidegger 1976; cf. Scalambrino 2015c; cf. von Uexküll 2010). With such principles and innovations in methodology, the study of ψυχή was able to shift further toward neuroscience. For instance, Evan Thompson's *Mind in Life* (2007) provides an excellent summary of the present state of this shift.

Moreover, just as General Systems Theory has a way of subsuming previously opposed "variables," such as those of "mind" and "body," so too the Fourth Force of psychology seemingly can incorporate the methodologies of the other forces, for example association, introspection, phenomenography, phenomenology, and hermeneutics; however, because the results of these methods are used to characterize correlations from the perspective of the system (even if it is the "neuro-system" of the individual as dynamic differentiation of the environment), the incommensurability between the clusters of principles constituting the "forces" of Western psychology still stands. Yet, it is especially through such power of Systems methodology to subsume the methods of the other forces that it brought about what is known as the "Cognitive Revolution" in Western psychology (cf. O'Donahue et al. 2003). We will conclude this discussion below in regard to the "Cognitive Turn" in the history of Western psychology, since the "Cognitive Revolution" in psychology is really the "Systems Revolution" in philosophy.

# Notes

1. As a compromise among different readings of Nietzsche's often epigrammatical writings, I have taken to referring to Nietzsche's philosophy as a kind of "ecstatic naturalism." Yet, for the purpose of Nietzsche's "existential" philosophy as a neo-Kantian influence on Contemporary psychology, his emphasis on the individual and the value of life-affirmation

suffices, and, therefore, the question of how to interpret his philosophy in relation to "naturalism" need not be decided here.

2. Depending upon the attitude of the psychologist reading this: one may celebrate my pointing out that many of the so-called phenomenological psychologists commit "psychologism" by making the above noted mistake regarding phenomenology; further, one may celebrate my pointing out that the distinction between phenomenology and phenomenography will fix that mistake. Or, one may be enraged that I am saying something which goes against the political-psychological-establishment regarding "phenomenological psychology." However, I assure you (dear reader), the fundamental failure of "phenomenological psychologists" to differentiate between phenomenology and phenomenography has led to their theoretical stagnation. For, when you have reached the point at which you are willing to denounce all objectivity, then you have reached a point at which you are completely out of touch with reality. These psychologists need to realize that it can be simultaneously true that the psychological products of your subjective relation to some event or thing may be *subjectively* valid, while also being *objectively* wrong. Jurisprudence dismisses, every day without hesitation, the kinds of judgments that cause these psychologists to falter. For example, someone kills another person; no matter how the perpetrator articulates the subjective aspects of the action, no articulation will be grounds for doubting the objectivity of the action—the victim is still dead. Suppose the perpetrator says, "When I did it the color red was present to me" or "I thought the plumber had my sandwich," regardless of what the perpetrator says, it does not change the objective truth that the victim is dead. Now, how the perpetrator articulates the subjective aspects of their performance of the action may influence how the action is characterized—first degree murder, man slaughter, self-defense, Not Guilty by Reason of Insanity, and so on. However, if it is true that the perpetrator killed another person, then no subjective description of that action will change its objective truth. An example even more to the point: despite the feelings of some psychologists about what I am saying, what I am saying about the fallacy of psychologism and the distinction between phenomenology and phenomenography is still true.

# Bibliography

Adams, Grace. 1931. *Psychology: Science or Superstition?* New York: Covici-Friede.

Angell, James Rowland. 1904. *Psychology: An Introductory Study of the Structure and Functions of Human Consciousness.* New York: Holt.

Araujo, Saulo de Freitas. 2016. *Wundt and the Philosophical Foundations of Psychology: A Reappraisal.* Dordrecht: Springer.

Ash, Mitchell G. 2005. The Uses and Usefulness of Psychology. *The Annals of the American Academy of Political and Social Science* 600 (1): 99–114.

Baker, William J. 1992. Positivism Versus People: What Should Psychology Be About? In *Positivism in Psychology: Historical and Contemporary Problems*, ed. C.W. Tolman, 9–16. Dordrecht: Springer.

Bentley, Madison. 1921. Dynamical Principles in Recent Psychology. In *Psychological Monographs: Critical and Experimental Studies in Psychology*, ed. M. Bentley, vol. 30.6, 1–16. Lancaster, PA: Psychological Review Company.

von Bertalanffy, Ludwig. 1967. General Theory of Systems: Application to Psychology. *Social Science Information* 6 (6): 125–136.

———. 1968. *General Systems Theory: Foundations, Developments, Applications.* New York: Braziller.

———. 1969. *Robots, Men and Minds: Psychology in the Modern World.* New York: Braziller.

———. 1981. *A Systems View of Man.* Boulder: Westview Press.

Blackmore, J.T., and R. Itagaki. 2013. *Ernst Mach's Vienna 1895–1930: Or Phenomenalism as Philosophy of Science.* Dordrecht: Kluwer.

Boring, Edwin G. 1950. *A History of Experimental Psychology.* Bombay: The Times of India Press.

———. 1953. A History of Introspection. *Psychological Bulletin* 50 (3): 169–189.

Burston, Daniel. 2003. Existentialism, Humanism and Psychotherapy. *Existential Analysis* 14 (2): 309–319.

Camus, Albert. 1991. *The Myth of Sisyphus and Other Essays.* Trans. J. O'Brien. New York: Vintage Books.

———. 1992. *The Rebel: An Essay on Man in Revolt.* Trans. A. Bower. New York: Vintage Books.

Corsini, Raymond J. 2001. *Handbook of Innovative Therapy.* Hoboken, NJ: Wiley-Blackwell.

Danziger, Kurt. 1979. The Positivist Repudiation of Wundt. *Journal of the History of the Behavioral Sciences* 15 (3): 205–230.

Darwin, Charles. 1859. *On the Origin of Species by Means of Natural Selection.* London, England: John Murray.

Deleuze, Gilles. 1994. *Difference & Repetition.* Trans. Paul Patton. New York: Columbia University.

Deleuze, Gilles, and Félix Guattari. 1980. *A Thousand Plateaus.* Trans. B. Massumi. Vol. II. of *Capitalism and Schizophrenia.* (1972–1980). London: Continuum.

Dewey, John. 1884. The New Psychology. *Andover Review* 2: 278–289.

DuBose, Todd. 2013. Let the Kierkegaardian Comedy Resume: Faith-Phobia and Faithful Leaning in Evidence-Based Criteria for Therapeutic Care. *Existential Analysis* 24 (1): 70–81.

Frankl, Viktor E. 2006. *Man's Search for Meaning.* Trans. I. Lasch. Boston, MA: Beacon Press.

Freud, Sigmund. 1895. The Project for a Scientific Psychology, Trans. J. Strachey. In *The Standard Edition of the Complete Psychological Works of Sigmund Freud,* vol. 1. London: Vintage Classics.

———. 1915. The Unconscious. Trans. J. Strachey. In *The Standard Edition of the Complete Psychological Works of Sigmund Freud,* vol. 14. London: Vintage Classics.

———. 1933. The Question of a Weltanschauung. Trans. J. Strachey. In *The Standard Edition of the Complete Psychological Works of Sigmund Freud,* vol. 22. London: Vintage Classics.

———. 1940. An Outline of Psychoanalysis. Trans. J. Strachey. In *The Standard Edition of the Complete Psychological Works of Sigmund Freud,* vol. 23. London: Vintage Classics.

———. 1953. Three Essays on Sexuality. Trans. J. Strachey. In *The Standard Edition of the Complete Psychological Works of Sigmund Freud,* vol. 7. London: The Hogarth Press.

———. 1955. The "Uncanny". Trans. J. Strachey. In *The Standard Edition of the Complete Psychological Works of Sigmund Freud,* vol. 17. London: The Hogarth Press.

———. 1957. On the Universal Tendency to Debasement in the Sphere of Love. Trans. J. Strachey. In *The Standard Edition of the Complete Psychological Works of Sigmund Freud,* vol. 11. London: The Hogarth Press.

———. 1961. The Dissolution of the Oedipus Complex. Trans. J. Strachey. In *The Standard Edition of the Complete Psychological Works of Sigmund Freud,* vol. 19. London: The Hogarth Press.

———. 1963. Introductory Lectures on Psycho-Analysis (Parts I and II). Trans. J. Strachey. In *The Standard Edition of the Complete Psychological Works of Sigmund Freud*, vol. 15. London: The Hogarth Press.

Gillespie, Alex. 2006. Descartes' Demon: A Dialogical Analysis of 'Meditations on First Philosophy'. *Theory & Psychology* 16 (6): 761–781.

Grünbaum, Adolf. 1984. *The Foundations of Psychoanalysis: A Philosophical Critique*. Berkeley, CA: University of California Press.

Guignon, Charles, and Robert Merrihew Adams. 2003. *The Existentialists: Critical Essays on Kierkegaard, Nietzsche, Heidegger, and Sartre*. London: Rowman & Littlefield.

Hegel, G.W.F. 1977. *Phenomenology of Spirit*. Trans. A.V. Miller. Oxford: Oxford University Press.

Heidbreder, Edna. 1933. *Seven Psychologies*. New York: Appleton-Century-Crofts.

Heidegger, Martin. 1962a. *Being and Time*. Trans. J. Macquarrie and E. Robinson. New York: Harper & Row

———. 1962b. The Phenomenological Method of Investigation. In *Being and Time*. Trans. J. Macquarrie and E. Robinson, 49–62. New York: Harper & Row.

———. 1976. Nur noch ein Gott kann uns retten. *Der Spiegel* 31 (May): 193–219. Trans. W. Richardson as "Only a God Can Save Us. In (1981) *Heidegger: The Man and the Thinker*, ed. T. Sheehan, 45–67. New York: Transaction Publishers.

———. 1993. Letter on Humanism. Trans. D.F. Krell. In *Basic Writings*, ed. D. F. Krell, 213–266. New York: Harper Collins Publishers.

———. 1997. *Phenomenological Interpretation of Kant's* Critique of Pure Reason. Trans. P. Emad and K. Maly. Bloomington, IN: Indiana University Press.

———. 2001. *Poetry, Language, Thought*. Trans. A. Hofstadter. New York: Harper Collins Perennial Classics.

Hilgard, Ernest R. 1987. *Psychology in America: A Historical Survey*. San Diego, CA: Harcourt Brace Jovanovich.

Hopkins, Burt C. 2006. Husserl's Psychologism, and Critique of Psychologism, Revisited. *Husserl Studies* 22: 91–119.

Husserl, Edmund. 1969. *Formal and Transcendental Logic*. Trans. D. Cairns. The Hague: Martinus Nijhoff Publishers.

———. 1970. Clarification of the Origin of the Modern Opposition Between Physicalistic Objectivism and Transcendental Subjectivism. In *The Crisis of*

*European Sciences and Transcendental Phenomenology*. Evanston, IL: Northwestern University Press.

————. 1977. *Phenomenological Psychology: Lectures, Summer Semester, 1925*. Trans. J. Scanlon. The Hague: Martinus Nijhoff Publishers.

————. 1983. *Ideas Pertaining to a Pure Phenomenology and to a Phenomenological Philosophy*, vol. I. Trans. F. Kersten. The Hague: Martinus Nijhoff Publishers.

Johnston, John. 2008. *The Allure of Machinic Life: Cybernetics, Artificial Life, and the New AI*. Cambridge, MA: MIT Press.

Kant, Immanuel. 1960. *Religion Within the Limits of Reason Alone*. Trans. T.M. Greene and H.H. Hudson. New York: Harper & Row.

Kierkegaard, Søren. 1980. *The Sickness Unto Death*. Trans. H.V. Hong and E.H. Hong. Princeton, NJ: Princeton University Press.

————. 1988. *Stages on Life's Way*. Trans. H.V. Hong and E. H. Hong. Princeton, NJ: Princeton University Press.

————. 1998. *The Point of View*. Trans. H.V. Hong and E.H. Hong. Princeton, NJ: Princeton University Press.

————. 2009. *"The Moment" and Late Writings*. Trans. H.V. Hong and E.H. Hong. Princeton, NJ: Princeton University Press.

Kimble, Gregory A. 1985. Overview: The Chronology. In *Topics in the History of Psychology*, ed. G.A. Kimble and K. Schlesinger, vol. II, 1–18. Hillsdale, NJ: Lawrence Erlbaum Associates.

Köhler, Wolfgang. 1970. *Gestalt Psychology: The Definitive Statement of Gestalt Theory*. New York: Liveright Publishing Company.

Macmillan, Malcolm, and Fred Crews. 1997. *Freud Evaluated: The Completed Arc*. Cambridge, MA: MIT Press.

Marton, Ference. 1981. Phenomenography—Describing Conceptions of the World Around Us. *Instructional Science* 10 (2): 177–200.

————. 1986. Phenomenography—A Research Approach Investigating Different Understandings of Reality. *Journal of Thought* 21 (2): 28–49.

Maslow, Abraham H. 1943. A Theory of Human Motivation. *Psychological Review* 50 (4): 370–396.

————. 1968. *Toward a Psychology of Being*. New York: Van Nostrand Reinhold.

————. 1970a. The Farther Reaches of Human Nature. *Journal of Transpersonal Psychology* 1 (1): 1–9.

————. 1970b. *Motivation and Personality*. New York: Harper & Row.

Mayer, A., and J. Orth. 1901. Zur qualitativen untersuchung der associationen. *Zeitschrift für Psychologie* 26: 1–13.

Metzger, Wolfgang. 1971. The Historical Background for National Trends in Psychology: German Psychology. In *Historical Perspectives in Psychology: Readings*, ed. V.S. Sexton and H. Misiak, 329–353. Pacific Gove, CA: Brooks Cole Publishing.

de Mul, Elize. 2016. Existential Privacy and the Technological Situation of Boundary Regulation. In *Social Epistemology and Technology: Toward Public Self-Awareness Regarding Technological Mediation*, ed. F. Scalambrino, 69–79. London: Rowman & Littlefield International.

Nietzsche, Friedrich. 1967. *The Birth of Tragedy Out of the Spirit of Music*. Trans. W. Kaufmann. New York: Vintage Books.

———. 1974. *The Gay Science*. Trans. W. Kaufmann. New York: Vintage Books.

———. 1977. Homer's Contest. Trans. W. Kaufmann. *The Portable Nietzsche*. London: Penguin.

———. 1979. On Truth and Lies in a Nonmoral Sense. In *Philosophy and Truth: Selections from Nietzsche's Notebooks of the Early 1870's*, ed. and trans. D. Breazeale, 79–97. Atlantic Highlands, NJ: Humanities Press.

———. 1989. *Beyond Good & Evil: Prelude to a Philosophy of the Future*. Trans. W. Kaufmann. New York: Vintage Books.

O'Donahue, William, Kyle E. Ferguson, and Amy E. Naugle. 2003. The Structure of the Cognitive Revolution: An Examination from the Philosophy of Science. *The Behavior Analyst* 26 (1): 85–110.

Pandora, Katherine. 2002. *Rebels Within the Ranks: Psychologists' Critique of Scientific Authority and Democratic Realities in New Deal America*. Cambridge: Cambridge University Press.

Perls, Frederick S., Ralph Hefferline, and Paul Goodman. 1994. *Gestalt Therapy: Excitement and Growth in the Human Personality*. Gouldsboro, ME: The Gestalt Journal Press.

Robinson, Edward S. 1964. *Association Theory Today: An Essay in Systematic Psychology*. New York: Hafner Publishing Company.

Rockmore, Tom. 2011. *Kant and Phenomenology*. Chicago: University of Chicago Press.

Rogers, Carl R. 1961. *On Becoming a Person*. Boston: Houghton Mifflin.

———. 1963a. The Actualizing Tendency in Relation to "Motives" and to Consciousness. In *Nebraska Symposium on Motivation*, ed. M. Jones, 1–24. Lincoln, NE: University of Nebraska Press.

———. 1963b. The Concept of the Fully Functioning Person. *Psychotherapy: Theory, Research and Practice* 1 (1): 17–28.

———. 1964. Freedom and Commitment. *The Humanist* 24 (2): 37–40.

————. 1965. A Humanistic Conception of Man. In *Science and Human Affairs*, ed. R.E. Farson, 18–31. Palo Alto, CA: Science & Behavior Books.

————. 1979. Foundations of the Person-Centered Approach. *Education* 110 (2): 98–107.

————. 1995. *A Way of Being*. Boston: Houghton Mifflin.

Sahakian, William S. 1975. *History and Systems of Psychology*. London: Wiley.

Sartre, Jean-Paul. 1992. *Being and Nothingness*. Trans. H.E. Barnes. New York: Washington Square Press.

————. 1993. The Humanism of Existentialism. In *Essays in Existentialism*, 31–62. New York: Citadel Press.

Scalambrino, Frank. 2014. Review of *Perception Beyond Inference* by L. Albertazzi, G. J. van Tonder, D. Vishwanath, eds.. *Philosophical Psychology* 27(5), 764–768.

————. 2015a. *Full Throttle Heart: Nietzsche, Beyond Either/Or*. New Philadelphia, OH: The Eleusinian Press.

————. 2015b. Phenomenological Psychology. *Internet Encyclopedia of Philosophy*. http://www.iep.utm.edu/phen-psy/. Accessed 3 May 2017.

————. 2015c. The Vanishing Subject: Becoming Who You Cybernetically Are. In *Social Epistemology & Technology*, ed. F. Scalambrino, 197–206. London: Roman & Littlefield International.

————. 2015d. What Control? Life at the Limits of Power Expression. In *Social Epistemology & Technology*, ed. F. Scalambrino, 101–112. London: Roman & Littlefield International.

————. 2018. *Geisteswissenschaften*. In *The Wiley-Blackwell Encyclopedia of Social Theory*, eds. B. Turner, C. Kyung-Sup, C. Epstein, P. Kivisto, J.M. Ryan and W. Outhwaite, vol. II, 1st edn, 912–913. London: Wiley-Blackwell.

Schopenhauer, Arthur. 2005. *Philosophical Writings*. Trans. W. Schirmacher. New York: Continuum.

Seel, Norbert M. 2011. Gestalt Psychology of Learning. In *Encyclopedia of the Sciences of Learning*, ed. N.M. Seel, 1366–1371. New York: Springer.

Sinatra, Maria. 2006. The Birth of Experimental Psychology in Germany Between Psychophysical Methods and Physiological Theories. *Physis; rivista internazionale di storia della scienza* 43: 91–131.

Singh, Arun K. 1999. *Comprehensive History of Psychology*. Jawahar Nagar, Delhi: Motilal Banarsidass.

Skinner, B.F. 1971. *Beyond Freedom and Dignity*. Indianapolis, IN: Hackett Publishing.

Skoll, Geoffrey R. 2014. *Dialectics in Social Thought: The Present Crisis*. New York: Palgrave Macmillan.

Smith, David L. 1999. *Freud's Philosophy of the Unconscious*. Dordrecht: Kluwer Academic Publishers.

Smith, Noel W. 2001. *Current Systems in Psychology: History, Theory, Research, and Applications*. Stamford, CT: Wadsworth Publishing.

Smith, Jonathan A., and Mike Osborn. 2003. Interpretative Phenomenological Analysis. In *A Practical Guide to Research Methods*, ed. J.A. Smith. London: Sage.

Solomon, Robert C. 1974. Freud's Neurological Theory of Mind. In *Freud: A Collection of Critical Essays*, ed. R. Wollheim. Garden City, NY: Anchor Press.

———. 1987. *From Hegel to Existentialism*. Oxford: Oxford University Press.

Spinelli, Ernesto. 2005. *The Interpreted World: An Introduction to Phenomenological Psychology*. London: Sage.

Sulloway, Frank. 1992. *Freud, Biologist of the Mind: Beyond the Psychoanalytic Legend*. Cambridge, MA: Harvard University Press.

Svensson, Lennart. 1997. Theoretical Foundations of Phenomenography. *Higher Education Research & Development* 16 (2): 159–171.

Szasz, Thomas. 2001. *Insanity: The Idea and Its Consequences*. Syracuse, NY: Syracuse University Press.

Thompson, Evan. 2007. *Mind in Life: Biology, Phenomenology, and the Sciences of Mind*. Cambridge, MA: Harvard University Press.

Titchener, Edward B. 1910. *A Textbook of Psychology*. New York: Macmillan.

———. 1927. *Systematic Psychology: Prolegomena*. Ithaca, NY: Cornell University Press.

von Uexküll, Jakob. 2010. *A Foray Into the Worlds of Animals and Humans: With a Theory of Meaning*. Trans. J.D. O'Neil. Minneapolis, MN: Minnesota University Press.

VandenBos, Gary R. 2007. *APA Dictionary of Psychology*. Washington, DC: American Psychological Association.

Watson, John B. 1913. Psychology as the Behaviorist Views It. *Psychological Review* 20 (2): 158–177.

Weinert, Friedel. 2009. *Copernicus, Darwin, & Freud*. Hoboken, NJ: Wiley-Blackwell.

Wiener, Norbert. 1965. *Cybernetics, Or, the Control and Communication in the Animal and the Machine*. Cambridge, MA: MIT Press.

Wolman, Benjamin B. 1960. *Contemporary Theories and Systems in Psychology*. New York: Harper & Brothers Publishers.

Wundt, Wilhelm. 1904. *Principles of Physiological Psychology*. Trans. E.B. Titchener, vol. 1. New York: Macmillan.

Zepf, Siegfried. 2016. Psychoanalysis as a Natural Science: Reconsidering Freud's 'Scientistic' Self-Misunderstanding. *International Forum of Psychoanalysis* 25: 157–168.

# 6

# Conclusion: Post-Modern Turning Away from Method

## 6.1 The Linguistic Turn: Agency's Slide from Discursive to Postmodern Condition

In this concluding chapter we will consider the major "turns," aka "revolutions" depending on your perspective, regarding the Contemporary Period of Western psychology. In general the history of these turns may be characterized in three ways. First, there are those who support the continuing influence and presence of the Fourth Force of psychology, for example, by attempting to find the most appropriate way to characterize "the system" from within which ψυχή may be examined. Second, there are those who are critical of the Fourth Force of psychology by being "anarchist" regarding its principles—though in this way its criticizers also essentially criticize the other "forces" also. Third, there are those who are critical of the Fourth Force of psychology by attempting a re-turn or produce a reconstruction of a different "force" of psychology, that is, one of the first three "forces." It is important to keep these two types of criticism distinct, since the one rejects and the other embraces principles. Further, such characterizations allow us to indicate how a criticism may invoke Freud, for example, in either a destructive or constructive (respectively)

© The Author(s) 2018
F. Scalambrino, *Philosophical Principles of the History and Systems of Psychology*,
https://doi.org/10.1007/978-3-319-74733-0_6

dialectic. That is to say, are you invoking Freud merely to attack the principles of the Fourth Force, or are you invoking Freud to advocate for the First Force over the Fourth?

The "Linguistic Turn" refers to a movement which began taking shape in the early twentieth century. In the context of understanding its relevance for the history of Western psychology, note that it may be seen as an attempt to provide an identity to the "system" of the Fourth Force of psychology. In other words, the study of humans and the study of ψυχή was thought to be best approached methodologically through the study of language (cf. de Saussure 2011; cf. Austin 1975; cf. Wittgenstein 1969, 1980, 1982, 2001; cf. Valsiner and Rosa 2007). This may be understood in a Modern or a more Post-Modern way (cf. Rorty 1992b). The former interpretation holds as closely as possible to a science of language as a "system." The idea here is that there is enough universality and objectivity in the human use of language to form a solid base for psychology. The latter interpretation emphasizes the relativity of language use, that is, "actions speak louder than words" (cf. Henle 1992). Whereas in the former interpretation this relativity still accounts for the objectively subjective uses of language, in the latter interpretation the relativity is read as politically based, not psychologically based. That is to say, your language use reflects not your "inner" psychology as much as your "outer" political affiliations and socio-economic, geographic, and historical situation.

There are three points we need to draw from the "Linguistic Turn" for the History and Systems of Western psychology. First, the above distinction between the objective and the subjective use of language is an essential and irreducible distinction, so long as we take "Language" as the primary system which psychology studies. This distinction often invokes discussion of the "Humpty Dumpty" theory of language, since both sides of the distinction are illustrated in Chap. 6, the "Humpty Dumpty" chapter of *Through the Looking-Glass*, with Alice taking the objective-side and "Humpty" taking the subjective-side (cf. Carroll 2006). Second, though it does not resolve the distinction, if we are to understand linguistic utterances (some might say: if an utterance is to truly count as a linguistic *communication*), then the principles of Hermeneutics become operable once again. On the objective-side it is as if each individual is a poem, or continuous poetic-expression, of the language-system within which it operates—recall the discussion of different styles of reading from Sect. 2.2 above. This is not to be understood as a surface effect, but rather as including the individual's self-reflection. That is to say, depending upon the grammar and vocabulary you use to "reflect upon yourself," then that vocabulary may be said to constrain your "reflections" to the point of possibly even itself determining your self-understanding.

Third, as it threatens to become a fully biological or cognitive-behavioral "Medical Model" based science, the defenders of Humpty Dumpty charge the scientists with being first and foremost a cultural force. That is to say, defenders of the subjective-side (and one individual may be seen supporting different "sides" depending on the issue in question) argue that what the "objective-side" is actually attempting to accomplish is a kind of hegemony in regard to what may and may not be considered "psychology." Of course, on some level this is true, and the question we should be asking is does its truth warrant some type of ethical restraint? After all, we usually do not attempt to restrain scientists for "being right." However, there are instances regarding bio-ethics (cf. Scalambrino 2018) in which political restraints are explicit, so the argument that a certain type of psychology is "destructive for society" may be able to gain some political-traction. Moreover, it is interesting to notice how this "move" on the part of the subjective-side supporters is a re-turn to the times when psychology and morality were not considered separable.

In sum, the distinction between the objective and subjective use of language initiates the concern to find some other system in which to possibly ground language. The major candidates who emerged in this regard were Ludwig Wittgenstein (1889–1951)—this aspect of Wittgenstein's work is often referred to as the "after the *Philosophical Investigations* period" or his "later period"—and Martin Heidegger (1889–1976)—this aspect of Heidegger's work is often referred to as his "middle period" or, depending on your perspective, his "later period." Whereas Wittgenstein sought to ground language in "agreement" and agreement in "form of life," Heidegger sought to ground language in Be-ing, or, again depending on your perspective, he may have considered language equi-primordial with Be-ing. Interestingly, then, the work of both of these philosophers has been appropriated by General Systems Theory or the Fourth Force of psychology. However, as we will see in the next section, the "Linguistic Turn" gives way to the "Performative Turn" precisely because of the oscillation between the sides of the objective and subjective understanding of language *use*.

## 6.2    The Performative Turn: The Essence of Postmodernism

Just as the principle of Hermeneutics re-emerged in the Linguistic Turn, the principle of Freedom or free will and agency receives emphasis in the Performative Turn (cf. Petit 2001). This is especially the case regarding identity, for example by way of culture, and the capacity to be critical of non-freely determined characterizations of actions and events. On the one hand, the idea is quite simple. Regardless of *whatever term is used* to identify "the system," many individuals will still believe they are free, despite whatever extent to which they may be part of such a system. Thus, resistance to the hegemony of the system—however identified— indicates the impulse of the Performative Turn. However, on the other hand, because the various expressions of the Performative Turn are— given its essence—necessarily localized, that is, not "universal" performances, and they often resist being even philosophically systematized, discussions of the Performative Turn can become quite complicated.

As noted above, the anarchic impulse—the attempt to avoid association with any principles at all—reaches its zenith in the Performative Turn. In fact, the "Performative Turn" refers to Postmodernism in its most purified expression. Thus, Postmodernism represents a revival of an antiauthoritarian Renaissance posture; however, this time (after Darwin, Marx, Freud, and Nietzsche) it often may be seen attempting to resist even the "authority" of rationality, and especially "absolute truth." It is important, then, to notice that when various thinkers such as Freud are invoked that it may not be in the service of propping up some sort of "Freudian system" as much as it may be the attempt to provide arguments against "the system," or even any system. This is often why the *ad hominem* argument, which is fallacious from a rational perspective, circulates like a kind of Postmodern currency in the Performative Turn. That is to say, some Postmodern anarchists like to launch localized attacks on the supporters of the objective-science systems approach to psychology, as if a psychoanalytic description of a scientist's motivations would debunk the findings of science. Of course, if the findings are objective, "fit" the theory, and "work," then no psychoanalytic description—no matter how accurate, incidentally—would debunk the scientific findings. Yet, what such *ad hominem* attacks might accomplish is the reduction of the political influence of those findings; that is to say, in the Performative Turn, psychology performs "Cultural Criticism," and, in this way, (social) psychology finds itself in the service of culture and politics.

Perhaps no theory has critically re-emerged during the Performative Turn with as confusing-effects in psychology as Freud's psychoanalytic theory. For example, there are those who now claim Freudian psychoanalytic theory is a "Human Science"—it is not. We will examine two different lines of thought here insofar as they are relevant to the Performative Turn and the principles of Western psychology in the Contemporary Period. First, the theoretical account of Freudian psychoanalysis as a *Geisteswissenschaften* alternative *system* of psychology congealed through the work of Paul Ricoeur (1913–2005) and Jürgen Habermas (b.1929). Second, perhaps psychology found its purest Postmodern performance in the irony and parody expressed—and mostly without "breaking character"—in the likes of Jacques Lacan (1901–1981). That is, from his self-selected costumes to his bent cigars, it is because of him—and we should, therefore, give him the credit, that is, this is not an *ad hominem* statement—that Lacan and other Postmodern figures are now referred to as "clowns" (cf. Tobias 2007; cf. Little 2002).

In regard to Freudian psychoanalysis as a "Human Science," Adolf Grünbaum (b. 1923) has conclusively shown that such an understanding of Freudian psychology is wrong (cf. Grünbaum 1984, 1990). However, because the Performative Turn is—like Humpty Dumpty—more interested in subjective use than objective truth, that such an interpretation of Freudian psychoanalysis is both theoretically incoherent and would have gone even against Freud's wishes, noted above, has not stopped academics from continuing to celebrate such an interpretation (cf. Habermas 1972: 246; cf. Jaspers 1974: 91; cf. Ricoeur 1970: 359, 1981: 271). On the one hand, these theorists, especially Habermas, are self-aware of the "transgressive" nature of their reading of Freud, also known in general as: the "violence of interpretation" (cf. Aulagnier 2001), and they also seem to recognize two essential steps in shifting Freud from nature to nurture: articulate a theory of "desire" and extend his ideas to culture (cf. Ricoeur 1981: 7).

Thus, the question becomes: if we follow such a "Hermeneutic" appropriation of Freudian theory to the context of culture, then what work is there for such theorizing to do that may still be called "psychology"? Ultimately, either the answer is none (and we have left the field of psychology for politics or political activism) or this is a place from which psychologists can engage in "cultural criticism." Moreover, as Deleuze and Guattari infamously pointed out in regard even to those psychologists who use such Hermeneutic appropriations of Freudian theory in the clinic with individual patients, those "psychoanalysts" are criticizing— and helping the analysand learn to self-criticize—the cultural identity they express as a part of its system. Of course, we must keep in mind that "culture criticism" is rhetorical; that is to say, it does not need to be a fact-based discourse, that is, facts are just one way to accomplish its goal which is *persuasion*. (cf. Szasz 1998, 2010). Yet, since as it is often said that social evolution is "Lamarckian," much is at stake in terms of the culture which we perpetuate. Also, it is important to keep in mind that in the context of cultural criticism, as noted above, culture, specifically its performance, is given ontological priority as "the system," that is, from a Fourth Force of psychology perspective (cf. Biernacki 2000; cf. Brodsky and LaBrada 2017; cf. Möhring 2003).

Lacan, then, represents an extreme example of the Hermeneutic appropriation of Freudian theory to the context of culture. "Reorienting Freud to a postmodern context, Lacan carries forward certain of his principles and reconciles in his best efforts psychoanalysis to postmodern language and social theory." (Martin and Pesta 2016: 132; cf. Nancy and Lacoue-Labarthe 1992; cf. Žižek 1987). Though Hermeneutics may be operative with any psychology which engages in "interpretation," Lacan's theorizing in regard to subject constitution (for example, cf. 1991, 1977), suggests a characterization of his appropriation of Freud in terms of Saussure and Surrealism (cf. Lacan 1965; cf. Greely 2001; cf. Suleiman 1990; cf. Williams 1981). According to Lacan, "Hieroglyphics of hysteria ... enigmas of inhibition, oracles of anxiety ... these are the hermetic elements that our exegesis resolves" (1982: 69–70). Moreover, it is in this way that—beyond merely the subject's word choice—everyday life may be understood in terms of dreaming and fantasizing *à la* Surrealism (think Marx's notion of "false consciousness"). Thus, on the one hand, Fourth Force (so-called) psychoanalytic theory functions as cultural criticism, since culture is the ground of these dreams and fantasies; and, on the other hand, Lacan's roguish and clownish performances may be seen as a resistance to be subject to the culture-system (cf. Elliott 2004; cf. Peters and Ceci 1980). For a similar example of Postmodern irony and parody "without breaking character" see *Dancing with Cats* (Silver and Busch 2014).

For a different understanding of the Performative Turn, psychologists may look to the work of Gilles Deleuze (1925–1995). What Deleuze offers psychology in relation to the Fourth Force may be characterized as a return to Kant; further, it may be understood as a return "through the systems perspective" in that it gives ontological priority to the transcendental dimension by way of the (recall the term from above) "differentiated individual," and this individual is understood as a systematic part of its environment from the very Transcendental point indicating the origin of its differentiation. In this way, Deleuze provides a theory which remains *continuously new* in that it subsumes any attempt to identify it with a generalization. (cf. Deleuze 1994, 2004; cf. Deleuze and Guattari 2004, 1980). Simply put, Deleuze's "systems theory" re-turns psychology to the Transcendental dimension. There are only two brief points we need consider here to understand how Deleuze relates to the Performative Turn and the "Cognitive Revolution" of General Systems Theory, which we will consider in the following section.

First, Deleuze offers a theory, beyond "Structuralism," for psychology by emphasizing the function of "intensity" as the Transcendental condition constituting structures. In other words, Deleuze offers us a method for theorizing that which is always already different from its identifiable manifestations. However, this is more profound than any re-turn to the, or a, "Unconscious." Recall that from a systems perspective the individual is constituted through a principle of difference; rather than understand this ontologically most primordial be-ing as language, Deleuze characterizes it as Difference-in-Itself; that is to say, it is that which is always already different from any general characterization in terms of a system. Notice how on the one hand, this characterization carries its capacity to be a critical theory embryonically within itself, so to speak, since every characterization of it is necessarily contextual and temporary. Difference-in-Itself is different from itself (cf. Deleuze 1994). One way to understand this difference is in terms of "intensity" and another is in terms of ψυχή. The principle of freedom applies, *whatever term is used* to identify "the system," regarding the agency of that which we call "ψυχή," though it be involved as a part or portion of the system (cf. Phillips 2006). On the other hand, Deleuze's theory represents a kind of perfection of dynamic process theorizing in that it allows for and anticipates the re-coding and phase changes characteristic of systems.

Second, Deleuze's work may be seen as attempting to provide us with a vocabulary of continual appropriation. In this way, it is as if he is onto-logically theorizing "Be-coming," rather than "Being." Thus, the indi-vidual as an already differentiated assemblage of the system is always already in the process of be-coming a differently expressed assemblage of the system. A particularly helpful expression of Deleuze's vocabulary may be found in his two volume set titled *Capitalism and Schizophrenia* writ-ten with Félix Guattari (1930–1992). Envisioning environmental inter-actions in terms of coding and re-coding—for example the way the body might adjust itself to catch a falling object which has unexpectedly slipped from your hand—provides a context within which the kinds of "Computationalism" and "Connectionism" associated with the "Cognitive Revolution" might widen their horizons (cf. Bachmann-Medick 2016: 95). In other words, Deleuze's re-turn to the Transcendental dimension and Transcendental philosophy invokes a deeper holism beyond even the contemporary politicized characterization of neurosci-entific research in terms of pluralism and inter-disciplinary studies (cf. Thompson 2007).

## 6.3    The Cognitive Turn: Almost "Normal Science" in Psychology

To be sure, the "psychology of cognition" was not new in the 1950s. For example, we find the following definition indicating that practitioners of the "new psychology" were already working toward an explication of the "Psychology of Cognition." The following comes from 1874:

> Cognition is a general name which we may apply to all those mental states in which there is made known in consciousness either some affection or activity of the mind itself, or some external quality or object. The Psychology of Cognition analyzes knowledge into its primary elements, and seeks to ascertain the nature and laws of the processes through which all our knowledge passes in progressing from its simplest to its most elaborate condition. (Jardine 1874: 1–2)

Yet, "the nature and laws of the processes through which all our knowledge passes" would not find its most productive context until the control-based theories of information-processing and cybernetics took shape (cf. Shannon and Weaver 1949; cf. Miller 2003; cf. Gardner 1987: 19–32; cf. Thompson 2007: 8). However, we must keep in mind, as was noted above, that cybernetics may apply even to the First and Second Forces of psychology and does not of necessity apply to the Fourth Force. That is to say, General Systems Theory—as Bertalanffy characterized it—may or may not be understood in terms of cybernetics. Thus, importantly, there may still be room within the Fourth Force of psychology for the principle of free will.

The term "Normal Science" is used in "Paradigm Theory" to denote the paradigm through which practitioners understand the work they are performing within a discipline when the discipline has essentially and universally "settled," so to speak, on that paradigm. Though the emergence of General Systems Theory has undeniably influenced the discipline of psychology as a whole, there is sufficient resistance to General Systems Theory that it would be unfair to conclude "Cognition" refers to the paradigm upon which contemporary psychology has settled. At the same time, the Cognitive Turn has been so influential across the Humanities in general that it used to be referred to as the "Cognitive Revolution" (cf. cf. Hobbs and Burman 2009; cf. Knapp and Robertson 2017; cf. Dember 1974; cf. Weimer and Palermo 1973; cf. Joynson 1970). At this point, as we are now witnessing the push-back against the Cognitive Turn across the disciplines of the Humanities, it is easy to find historical research calling the use of the term "revolution" into question. However, there clearly has taken place within the history and systems of Western psychology a "Cognitive Turn."

The Cognitive Turn is usually described as having two (2) different phases. There is little disagreement about how to identify the "first phase" of the Cognitive Turn, as it was the first phase which provided us with the "computer processing" metaphor for the materialist reduction of psychology to "the brain" (cf. Dehaene 2014; cf. Boden 2006; cf. Harré 1995; cf. Evans 1992; cf. Gardner 1987;). However, the "second phase" essentially may be seen as an echo of the distinction between the Linguistic and the Performative Turns. That is to say, the second phase has been characterized, on the one hand, as the "Discursive Turn" and, on the other, as the "Agential Turn" (cf. Harré 1995: 26; cf. Rottschaefer 1997: 125). From the perspective of those who resist understanding psychology as a "Cognitive Science," there are a number of options—just as there were regarding what belongs "outside" structure in the tension between language and performance—including affect, volition, and the Transcendental dimension. However, for those who embrace psychology as a Cognitive Science, retrospective efforts may be found attempting to locate the emergence of Cognitive Science from the work of Descartes (cf. Chomsky 2004: 607). This complexity, of course, contributes to whatever confusion there may be about the identity of the Contemporary study of ψυχή.

As a result, it is, at least, helpful to understand what may have been a "Cognitive Revolution" outside of psychology—in culture and the Humanities in general—as a "Cognitive Turn" regarding the Fourth Force within psychology. In this way, "Computationalism" and "Connectionism" become emphasized functional principles along with Multiple Realizability and the ontological and structural principles of Eliminative Materialism and Reductionism. Moreover, the concerns which were prominent regarding the principles of realism, phenomenalism conceptualism, and nominalism may be seen as operable again insofar as in order to "reduce" some phenomena of experience to an observable system of cognitive processing, we must have some understanding of what it is we are reducing. From the perspective of these principles, then, we may see that it was the combination of a "psychology of cognition"—more Cartesian and mechanistic than Kant's—with technology and General Systems thinking which conditioned the Cognitive Turn.

Moreover, the presence of the influence of General Systems Theory may be noticed immediately in the "neural network" descriptions regarding structure in the Cognitive Turn and the "connectionist" descriptions regarding function.

Connectionist models assume that information processing takes place through the interaction of large numbers of simple processing units that pass activation through connection weights. Knowledge is stored in connection weights that modulate the transfer of activity from one unit to the next. Learning occurs typically by presenting a network of units with a set of inputs and outputs and utilizing error-correction algorithms to change the connection weights such that the input predicts the output. (Schneider and Graham 1992: 513)

On the one hand, such "Computationalism" in regard to "connection weights" has been referred to as "machine functionalism" invoking Bertalanffy's principle—and the Early Modern notion—of mechanization. The tension, then, found in the oscillation between structure and function and language and use, reemerges. Yet, just as General Systems Theory is said to bridge the methods of extraspection and introspection, so too advocates for "Connectionist models" follow Bertalanffy's suggestion that systems may be articulated so as to affirm or deny the principle of Freedom, and, thereby, the principle may be seen producing an essential distinction within the Cognitive Turn between, on the one side, the "Soft Determinists" or "Compatibilists" and Libertarians, and, on the other, the "Incompatibilists" and multiple-realizability-oriented "Hard Determinists" (cf. Tryon 2014: 114; Dreyfus 1992; cf. Knapp and Roberston 2017; cf. Chipman 2017). Recall, the principle of Freedom differentiated the *Geisteswissenschaften* or human sciences of the Third Force from the *Naturwissenschaften* or natural science-oriented Behaviorism and Freudian Psychoanalysis.

## 6.4    The Historical Turn: Self-Reflective Thinking Through Psychology Beyond Postmodernism

The "Historical Turn," aka the "Historic Turn," has been announced in both the natural and the human sciences (cf. Bird 2008; cf. Griffiths 1996; cf. McDonald 1996; cf. Spiegel 2005; cf. Glock 2013). What perhaps stands out most about the Historical Turn is that it does not emerge as an answer to a question—for example, what is the "normal science" paradigm of psychology? – as much as it emerges to formulate questions and "think through" possible answers. Recalling the first two sections of the Introduction to this book, the Historical Turn is understood as the activation of a capacity for practitioners of a discipline to be "self-reflective." On the one hand, it is as if it is not possible for practitioners of psychology to not have a principled point of view regarding ψυχή. As we suggested above, from the perspective of the history and systems of Western psychology, that is, from the standpoint of a Historical Turn, to be consistently an "anarchist" is to consistently act in accordance with the principle(s) of disavowing principles. Thus, the Historical Turn provides the kind of univocity which, at least, allows for productive communicative action across paradigms, despite the necessarily enduring incommensurabilities and the twists and Turns associated with Contemporary Western psychology.

On the other hand, as we also briefly discussed above, since solutions to problems, legitimacy, and progress toward becoming the "normal science" paradigm (even if "transgressively" from within a Performative Turn) are foundational elements for the discourses and narratives of psychology outside of a Historical Turn, it is within a Historical Turn that the various contextualizations of events and things receive a disciplinary-specific context. Keeping in mind the standpoints of anarchism, progress to "normal science," and "eclecticism," this context is important for psychology to retain its integrity as a discipline. That is to say, even if the various approaches constituted by differently selected clusters of principles sustain incommensurable disagreement regarding the identity of ψυχή, the tradition and the practice of the study of ψυχή upon which such disagreement stands is affirmed in a Historical Turn, and that affirmation may be the last bastion and rallying point for psychology against the leveling effects of cybernetics and Postmodernism. In other words, psychology's Historical Turn is the point at which psychology affirms its integrity.

It is, of course, important to recognize the difference between the affirmation of psychology's integrity and its dis-integration. Whereas the former affirms incommensurability the latter seeks to deny incommensurability in any number of ways. In general—from the perspective of the Historical Turn in Contemporary Western psychology—there seems to be three general options. First, we either accept the pluralism constituted by the incommensurability between systems or paradigms in psychology, or we attempt to reduce the incommensurabilities. The second two options relate to the latter strategy. Second, then, we use various principles associated with the Performative Turn to reduce or eliminate incommensurability, not for the sake of establishing psychology's identity as much as for the sake of the principles of equality or anarchy. That is to say, a popular Postmodern strategy is to simply ignore any purported truth if it does not fit with the political principles you embrace. A clear anarchy example of such a strategy is to talk as if any activity can be considered an activity of psychology, since we do not want to "marginalize" any interpretations. A clear eclecticism example is to talk as if a psychologist cannot be inconsistent or incorrect in the practice of psychology, for example in performing clinical experiments or psychotherapy, because psychologists may want to think of themselves as above reproach. Incommensurability, then, may be inconvenient for such psychologists. Third, it is clear that some practitioners of psychology are working toward the establishment of a "normal science" system or paradigm for psychology. Of course, were this option to be accomplished, it would provide, and affirm the integrity of, a new identity for the study of ψυχή.

It is in the light of incommensurability where we may most clearly see the importance of principles of selection from which thinking through psychology and performing activities consistent with an integrity-sustaining understanding of psychology may occur; the Historical Turn provides the appropriate prism for such light. At the same time, the Historical Turn is self-reflective enough that it can sustain the tension between Historicism and Presentism which was at the basis of major rifts in other contexts. For example, in regard to the evolution of systems, "Selection processes are historical because the relative fitness of characters is a function of the historical conditions in which selection takes place" (Griffiths 1996: 515). Yet, notice that the historical conditions operable at the moments of principle selection do not eclipse our capacity to think through the selected principles, within the historical context, despite any Presentist opacity which may otherwise influence our understanding of those historical conditions.

For, "Historicizing is nothing more nor less than the constant asking of questions about how something came to be and about what effects things have had over time. To historicize is to accept that" historical narratives about the past are constructed (McDonald 1996: 32). If nothing else, we can see that the history of psychology is a historiographical construction regarding the past choices made by practitioners pertaining to principles.

> It is in this sense that the "linguistic turn" is giving way to the "historical turn," since historicism—understood as an acknowledgement of the contingent, temporally, and socially situated character of our beliefs, values, institutions, and practices—subtends both the retention of an attenuated concept of discourse as that which creates the conditions of possibility for, and the constituents of, a given culture … (Spiegel 2005: 25)

If the principles are essential, then the historiography may be characterized by Mild Presentism, and if the principles are merely cultural, eclectic, or anarchically denied, then such Postmodern, and social constructionist historiography may be characterized by Strong Presentism. Further, as we noted above, whereas the Performative Turn may justify the re-structuring of knowledge and hegemonic power systems based on the idea that the structure is not grounded in an essential explanation, the Historical Turn "deconstructively" reveals that whatever knew structure takes the place of the old structure, the new structure will itself not be grounded in an essential distinction; moreover, going beyond Postmodernism, the new structure will be grounded in a historiographical construction, that is, history (cf. Glock 2013; cf. Kane 2000).

Thus, the question emerges for Contemporary Western psychology: Just as "psychology as the Behaviorist views it" is not "psychology as the Psychoanalyst views it," and neither is "psychology as the Existentialist views it," how may Contemporary psychology philosophically sustain both pluralism and incommensurability? Again, the Historical Turn itself emerged not so much directly toward an answer to this question, as toward a context with which to appropriately formulate the question; that is, the "Historical Turn" may refer to the accomplishment of a context in which to regard the principles selected throughout the history of Western psychology without either privileging a paradigm of psychology as a point of view or reducing psychology to a different discipline. Moreover, the Historical Turn provides a context in which we can see the incommensurabilities between the clusters of principles constituting the multiple systems and paradigms of psychology; in this way, when we "think through" the multiple systems in regard to ψυχή and when we enact, or "perform," activities from one of the standpoints of the multiple systems in regard to ψυχή, we are able to do so with a principled, systematic, self-reflective awareness, and integrity. It is as if, invoking the analogy of the night sky from the Introduction, with the Historical Turn, we emerge from Postmodernism, to see—once more—the stars.

# Bibliography

Aulagnier, Piera. 2001. *The Violence of Interpretation*. Trans. A. Sheridan. London: Routledge.

Austin, J.L. 1975. *How to Do Things with Words*. Cambridge, MA: Harvard University Press.

Bachmann-Medick, Doris. 2016. *Cultural Turns: New Orientations in the Study of Culture*. Trans. A. Blauhut. Berlin: Walter de Gruyter.

Biernacki, Richard. 2000. Language and the Shift from Signs to Practices in Cultural Inquiry. *History and Theory* 39 (3): 289–310.

Bird, Alexander. 2008. The Historical Turn in the Philsoophy of Science. In *Routledge Companion to the Philosophy of Science*, ed. S. Psillos and M. Curd, 67–77. London: Routledge.

Boden, M.A. 2006. *Mind as Machine: A History of Cognitive Science*. Oxford: Clarendon Press.

Brodsky, Claudia, and Eloy LaBrada. 2017. *Inventing Agency: Essays on the Literary and Philosophical Production of the Modern Subject.* New York: Bloomsbury Academic.

Carroll, Lewis. 2006. *Alice's Adventures in Wonderland and Through the Looking-Glass.* New York: Bantam Dell.

Chipman, Susan E.F. 2017. *The Oxford Handbook of Cognitive Science.* Oxford: Oxford University Press.

Chomsky, Noam. 2004. *Language and Politics.* Montreal: Black Rose Books.

Dehaene, Stanislas. 2014. *Consciousness and the Brain: Deciphering How the Brain Codes Our Thoughts.* New York: Viking.

Deleuze, Gilles. 1994. *Difference & Repetition.* Trans. Paul Patton. New York: Columbia University.

———. 2004. The Method of Dramatization. In *Desert Islands and Other Texts, 1953–1974*, ed. D. Lapoujade and trans. M. Taormina, 94–116. New York: Semiotext(e).

Deleuze, Gilles, and Félix Guattari. 1980. *A Thousand Plateaus.* Trans. B. Massumi. Vol. II. of *Capitalism and Schizophrenia.* (1972–1980). London: Continuum.

———. 2004. *Anti-Oedipus.* Trans. R. Hurley, M. Seem, & H. R. Lane. Vol. I. of *Capitalism and Schizophrenia.* (1972–1980). London: Continuum.

Dember, William N. 1974. Motivation and the Cognitive Revolution. *American Psychologist* 29: 161–168.

Dreyfus, Hubert. 1992. *What Computers Still Can't Do.* Cambridge, MA: MIT Press.

Elliott, Anthony. 2004. *Subject to Ourselves: Social Theory, Psychoanalysis and Postmodernity.* Boulder, CO: Paradigm Press.

Evans, Fred J. 1992. *Psychology and Nihilism: A Genealogical Critique of the Computational Model of Mind.* Albany, NY: SUNY Press.

Gardner, Howard E. 1987. *The Mind's New Science: A History of the Cognitive Revolution.* New York: Basic Books.

Glock, Hans-Johann. 2013. The Owl of Minerva: Is Analytic Philosophy Moribund? In *The Historical Turn in Analytic Philosophy*, ed. E.H. Reck. New York: Palgrave Macmillan.

Greely, Robin Adèle. 2001. Dalí's Fascism; Lacan's Paranoia. *Art History* 24 (4): 465–492.

Griffiths, Paul E. 1996. The Historical Turn in the Study of Adaptation. *British Journal for the Philosophy of Science* 47 (4): 511–532.

Grünbaum, Adolf. 1984. *The Foundations of Psychoanalysis: A Philosophical Critique.* Berkeley, CA: University of California Press.

————. 1990. 'Meaning' Connections and Causal Connections in the Human Sciences: The Poverty of Hermeneutic Philosophy. *Journal of the American Psychoanalytic Association* 38 (3): 559–577.

Habermas, Jürgen. 1972. *Knowledge & Human Interests.* Trans. J.J. Shapiro. Boston: Beacon Press.

Harré, Rom. 1995. Emotion and Memory: The Second Cognitive Revolution. In *Philosophy, Psychology and Psychiatry*, ed. A.P. Griffiths. Cambridge: Cambridge University Press.

Henle, Paul. 1992. Do We Discover Our Uses of Words? In *The Linguistic Turn: Essays in Philosophical Method*, ed. R. Rorty, 218–223. Chicago: University of Chicago Press.

Hobbs, Sandy, and Jeremy T. Burman. 2009. Looking Back: Is the Cognitive Revolution a Myth? *The British Psychological Society* 22: 812–815.

Jardine, Robert. 1874. *Elements of the Psychology of Cognition.* London: Macmillan.

Jaspers, Karl. 1974. Causal and "Meaningful" Connections Between Life, History and Psychosis. Trans. G. Hoenig. In *Themes and Variations in European Psychiatry*, eds. S. Hirsch and M. Shepard, 80–93. Bristol, CT: John Wright & Sons.

Joynson, Robert B. 1970. The Break-Down of Modern Psychology. *Bulletin of the British Psychological Society* 23: 261–269.

Kane, Anne. 2000. Reconstructing Culture in Historical Explanation: Narratives as Cultural Structure and Practice. *History and Theory* 39 (3): 311–330.

Knapp, Terry J., and Lynn C. Robertson. 2017. *Approaches to Cognition: Contrasts and Controversies.* London: Routledge.

Lacan, Jacques. 1965. Hommage fait à Marguerite Duras, du *Ravissement de Lol V. Stein. Cahiers Renaud-Barrault* 52: 7–15.

————. 1977. *The Four Fundamental Concepts of Psychoanalysis.* Trans. A. Sheridan. New York: W.W. Norton & Co.

————. 1982. *Ecrits: A Selection.* Trans. A. Sheridan. New York: W.W. Norton & Co.

————. 1991. *The Ego in Freud's Theory and in the Technique of Psychoanalysis, 1954–1955*, vol. II. Trans. S. Tomaselli. New York: W.W. Norton & Co.

Little, Kenneth. 2002. Pitu's Doubt: Entrée Clown Self-Fashioning in the Circus Tradition. In *Popular Theatre: A Sourcebook*, ed. J. Schechter, 138–148. London: Routledge.

Martin, Thomas L., and Duke Pesta. 2016. *The Renaissance and the Postmodern: A Study in Comparative Critical Values.* London: Routledge.

McDonald, Terrence J. 1996. Is Vice Versa? Historical Anthropologies and Anthropological Histories. In *The Historic Turn in the Human Sciences*, ed. T.J. McDonald, 17–52. Ann Arbor, MI: University of Michigan Press.

Miller, George A. 2003. The Cognitive Revolution: A Historical Perspective. *Trends in Cognitive Sciences* 7 (3): 141–144.

Möhring, Maren. 2003. Performanz und historische Mimesis. In *Geschichtswissenschaft und "Performative Turn"*, ed. J. Martschukat and S. Patzold. Vienna: Böhlau Verlag.

Nancy, Jean-Luc, and Philippe Lacoue-Labarthe. 1992. *The Title of the Letter: A Reading of Lacan*. Trans. F. Raffoul and D. Pettigrew. Albany, NY: SUNY Press.

Peters, Douglas P., and Stephen J. Ceci. 1980. A Manuscript Masquerade. *The Sciences* 20 (7): 16–19.

Petit, Philip. 2001. *A Theory of Freedom: From the Psychology to the Politics of Agency*. Oxford: Oxford University Press.

Phillips, John. 2006. Agencement/Assemblage. *Theory, Culture & Society* 23 (2–3): 108–109.

Ricoeur, Paul. 1970. *Freud and Philosophy*. Trans. D. Savage. New Haven, CT: Yale University Press.

———. 1981. *Hermeneutics and the Human Sciences: Essays on Language, Action and Interpretation*. Trans. J.B. Thompson. Cambridge: Cambridge University Press.

Rorty. 1992b. *Wittgenstein, Heidegger, and the Reification of Language. Essays on Heidegger and Others. Vol II of Philosophical Papers*, 50–66. Cambridge: Cambridge University Press.

Rottschaefer, William A. 1997. *The Biology and Psychology of Moral Agency*. Cambridge: Cambridge University Press.

de Saussure, Ferdinand. 2011. *Course in General Linguistics*. Eds. P. Meisel and H. Saussy, Trans. W. Baskin. New York: Columbia University Press.

Scalambrino, Frank. 2018. Futurology in Terms of the Bioethics of Genetic Engineering: Proactionary and Precautionary Attitudes Toward Risk with Existence in the Balance. In *Social Epistemology and Futurology: Precautionary & Proactionary Perspectives*, ed. S. Fuller. London: Rowman and Littlefield International. (In Press).

Schneider, Walter, and David J. Graham. 1992. Introduction to Connectionist Modeling in Education. *Educational Psychologist* 27 (4): 513–530.

Shannon, Claude E., and Warren Weaver. 1949. *The Mathematical Theory of Communication*. Urbana, IL: University of Illinois.

Silver, Burton, and Heather Busch. 2014. *Dancing with Cats*. San Francisco: Chronicle Books.

Spiegel, Gabrielle M. 2005. Introduction. In *Practicing History: New Directions in Historical Writing After the Linguistic Turn*, ed. G.M. Spiegel, 1–32. London: Routledge.

Suleiman, Susan R. 1990. *Subversive Intent: Gender, Politics, and the Avant-Garde*. Cambridge, MA: Harvard University Press.

Szasz, Thomas. 1998. *Manufacture of Madness: A Comparative Study of the Inquisition and the Mental Health Movement*. Syracuse, NY: Syracuse University Press.

———. 2010. *The Myth of Mental Illness*. New York: Harper Perennial.

Thompson, Evan. 2007. *Mind in Life: Biology, Phenomenology, and the Sciences of Mind*. Cambridge, MA: Harvard University Press.

Tobias, Ashley. 2007. The Postmodern Theatre Clown. In *Clowns, Fools and Picaros: Popular Forms in Theatre, Fiction and Film*, ed. D. Robb, 37–56. Amsterdam: Rodopi.

Tryon, Warren W. 2014. *Cognitive Neuroscience and Psychotherapy: Network Principles of a Unified Theory*. Oxford: Elsevier Science.

Valsiner, Jaan, and Alberto Rosa. 2007. *The Cambridge Handbook of Sociocultural Psychology*. Cambridge: Cambridge University Press.

Weimer, Walter B., and David S. Palermo. 1973. Paradigms and Normal Science in Psychology. *Science Studies* 3 (3): 211–244.

Williams, Linda. 1981. *Figures of Desire: A Theory and Analysis of Surrealist Film*. Berkeley, CA: University of California Press.

Wittgenstein, Ludwig. 1969. *On Certainty*. Trans. G.E.M. Anscombe. New York: Harper & Row Publishers.

———. 1980. *Remarks on the Philosophy of Psychology*. Vol. 2. Chicago: University of Chicago Press.

———. 1982. Conversations on Freud; Excerpt from 1932–3 Lectures. In *Philosophical Essays on Freud*, ed. R. Wollheim and J. Hopkins. Cambridge: Cambridge University Press.

———. 2001. *Philosophical Investigations*. Trans. G.E.M. Anscombe, P.M.S. Hacker, and J. Schulte. Hoboken, NJ: Wiley-Blackwell.

Žižek, Slavoj. 1987. Why Lacan Is Not a Post-Structuralist. *Newsletter of the Freudian Field* 1 (2): 31–39.

# Bibliography

Adams, Grace. 1931. *Psychology: Science or Superstition?* New York: Covici-Friede.

Allison, Henry E. 2004. *Kant's Transcendental Idealism*. New Haven, CT: Yale University Press.

Ameriks, Karl. 1982. *Kant's Theory of Mind: An Analysis of the Paralogisms of Pure Reason*. Oxford: Clarendon Press.

———. 2003. *Interpreting Kant's Critiques*. Oxford: Oxford University Press.

Angell, James Rowland. 1904. *Psychology: An Introductory Study of the Structure and Functions of Human Consciousness*. New York: Holt.

———. 1907. The Province of Functional Psychology. *Psychological Review* 14 (2): 61–91.

Anton, John P. 1992. Plotinus and the Neoplatonic Conception of Dialectic. *The Journal of Neoplatonic Studies* 1 (1): 3–30.

Aquinas, Thomas. 1920. *The "Summa Theologica" of St. Thomas Aquinas*. Trans. Fathers of the English Dominican Province. London: Burns Oates & Washbourne.

———. 2012. *Commentary on the Letters of Saint Paul to the Corinthians*. Ed. The Aquinas Institute and Trans. F.R. Larcher. Lander, WY: The Aquinas Institute for the Study of Sacred Doctrine.

Araujo, Saulo de Freitas. 2016. *Wundt and the Philosophical Foundations of Psychology: A Reappraisal*. Dordrecht: Springer.

© The Author(s) 2018
F. Scalambrino, *Philosophical Principles of the History and Systems of Psychology*,
https://doi.org/10.1007/978-3-319-74733-0

Aristotle. 1937. *Parts of Animals*. Trans. W. Ogle. In *The Complete Works of Aristotle: The Revised Oxford Translation* (1995), ed. J. Barnes, vol. I, 994–1086. Princeton, NJ: Princeton University Press.

―――. 1950. *Physics*. Trans. W.D. Ross. R.P. Hardie and Revised by R.K. Gaye (Rev.). In *The Complete Works of Aristotle: The Revised Oxford Translation* (1995), ed. J. Barnes, vol. I, 315–446. Princeton, NJ: Princeton University Press.

―――. 1956a. *Categories*. Trans. J.L. Ackrill. In *The Complete Works of Aristotle: The Revised Oxford Translation* (1995), ed. J. Barnes, vol. I, 3–24. Princeton, NJ: Princeton University Press.

―――. 1956b. *On the Soul*. Trans. J.A. Smith. In *The Complete Works of Aristotle: The Revised Oxford Translation* (1995), ed. J. Barnes, vol. I, 641–692. Princeton, NJ: Princeton University Press.

―――. 1964a. *Posterior Analytics*. Trans. W.D. Ross. In *The Complete Works of Aristotle: The Revised Oxford Translation* (1995), ed. J. Barnes, vol. I, 114–166. Princeton, NJ: Princeton University Press.

―――. 1964b. *Prior Analytics*. Trans. A.J. Jenkinson. In *The Complete Works of Aristotle: The Revised Oxford Translation* (1995), ed. J. Barnes, vol. I, 39–113. Princeton, NJ: Princeton University Press.

―――. 1965. *Generation of Animals*. Trans. A. Platt. In *The Complete Works of Aristotle: The Revised Oxford Translation* (1995), ed. J. Barnes, vol. I, 1111–1218. Princeton, NJ: Princeton University Press.

―――. 1967. *Topics*. Trans. J. Brunschwig. In *The Complete Works of Aristotle: The Revised Oxford Translation* (1995), ed. J. Barnes, vol. I, 167–277. Princeton, NJ: Princeton University Press.

―――. 1984. *Metaphysics*. Trans. W.D. Ross. In *The Complete Works of Aristotle: The Revised Oxford Translation* (1995), ed. J. Barnes, vol. II, 1552–1728. Princeton, NJ: Princeton University Press.

―――. 2006. *On Memory & Recollection*. Trans. R. Sorabji. In *Aristotle on Memory*, ed. R. Sorabji, 47–60. Chicago, IL: University of Chicago Press.

―――. 2009. *Nicomachean Ethics*. Trans. R. Crisp. Cambridge: Cambridge University Press.

Ash, Mitchell G. 2005. The Uses and Usefulness of Psychology. *The Annals of the American Academy of Political and Social Science* 600 (1): 99–114.

Aulagnier, Piera. 2001. *The Violence of Interpretation*. Trans. A. Sheridan. London: Routledge.

Austin, J.L. 1975. *How to Do Things with Words*. Cambridge, MA: Harvard University Press.

Bachelard, Gaston. 2016. *The Dialectic of Duration.* Trans. M.M. Jones. London: Rowman & Littlefield International.

Bachmann-Medick, Doris. 2016. *Cultural Turns: New Orientations in the Study of Culture.* Trans. A. Blauhut. Berlin: Walter de Gruyter.

Baker, William J. 1992. Positivism Versus People: What Should Psychology Be About? In *Positivism in Psychology: Historical and Contemporary Problems*, ed. C.W. Tolman, 9–16. Dordrecht: Springer.

Balibar, Étienne. 1992. A Note on 'Consciousness/Conscience' in the *Ethics*. *Studia Spinozana* 8: 37–53.

Barnes, Jonathan. 1969. Aristotle's Theory of Demonstration. *Phronesis* 14 (2): 123–152.

Barthes, Roland. 1978. Death of the Author. Ed. and Trans. S. Heath, *Image, Music, Text*, 142–149. New York: Hill and Wang.

Baudrillard, Jean. 1994. *The Illusion of the End.* Stanford, CA: Stanford University Press.

———. 2006. The Precession of Simulacra. In *Simulacra and Simulation*, ed. and trans. S.F. Glaser 1–42. Ann Arbor, MI: University of Michigan Press.

Baudrillart, Alfred. 1907. *The Catholic Church: The Renaissance and Protestantism.* London: Kegan Paul.

Baydala, Angelina, and William E. Smythe. 2012. Hermeneutics of Continuity: Theorizing Psychological Understanding of Ancient Literature. *Theory & Psychology* 22 (6): 842–859.

Beck, Lewis White. 1969. *Early German Philosophy: Kant and his Predecessors.* Cambridge, MA: Harvard University Press.

Benjafield, John G. 2012. *Psychology: A Concise History.* Oxford: Oxford University Press.

Bentley, Madison. 1921. Dynamical Principles in Recent Psychology. In *Psychological Monographs: Critical and Experimental Studies in Psychology*, ed. M. Bentley, vol. 30.6, 1–16. Lancaster, PA: Psychological Review Company.

Berger, Peter L., and Thomas Luckmann. 1966. *The Social Construction of Reality: A Treatise in the Sociology of Knowledge.* New York: Anchor Books.

Bergson, Henri. 2004. *Matter and Memory.* Trans. Nancy Margaret Paul & W. Scott Almer. New York: Dover Publications.

Bering, Jesse M. 2006. The Folk Psychology of Souls. *Behavioral and Brain Sciences* 29 (5): 453–498.

Berkeley, George. 1910. *A Treatise Concerning the Principles of Human Knowledge.* Chicago: Open Court.

———. 1979. In *Three Dialogues Between Hylas and Philonous*, ed. R.M. Adams. Indianapolis, IN: Hackett Publishing.

von Bertalanffy, Ludwig. 1967. General Theory of Systems: Application to Psychology. *Social Science Information* 6 (6): 125–136.

———. 1968. *General Systems Theory: Foundations, Developments, Applications.* New York: Braziller.

———. 1969. *Robots, Men and Minds: Psychology in the Modern World.* New York: Braziller.

———. 1981. *A Systems View of Man.* Boulder: Westview Press.

Beckman, James. 1979. *The Religious Dimension of Socrates' Thought.* Waterloo, ON: Wilfrid Laurier University Press.

Beutler, Larry E. 1983. *Eclectic Psychotherapy: A Systematic Approach.* New York: Pergamon.

Biernacki, Richard. 2000. Language and the Shift from Signs to Practices in Cultural Inquiry. *History and Theory* 39 (3): 289–310.

Bird, Alexander. 2008. The Historical Turn in the Philsoophy of Science. In *Routledge Companion to the Philosophy of Science,* ed. S. Psillos and M. Curd, 67–77. London: Routledge.

Blackmore, J.T., and R. Itagaki. 2013. *Ernst Mach's Vienna 1895–1930: Or Phenomenalism as Philosophy of Science.* Dordrecht: Kluwer.

Blondell, Ruby. 2002. *The Play of Character in Plato's Dialogues.* Cambridge: Cambridge University Press.

Boden, M.A. 2006. *Mind as Machine: A History of Cognitive Science.* Oxford: Clarendon Press.

Boring, Edwin G. 1950. *A History of Experimental Psychology.* Bombay: The Times of India Press.

———. 1953. A History of Introspection. *Psychological Bulletin* 50 (3): 169–189.

Boys-Stones, George, and Christopher Rowe. 2013. *The Circle of Socrates: Reading in the First-Generation Socratics.* Indianapolis, IN: Hackett Publishing.

Brampton, C.K. 1964. Nominalism and the Law of Parsimony. *The Modern Schoolman* 41 (3): 273–281.

Brennan, James F. 2003. *History and Systems of Psychology.* Upper Saddle, NJ: Prentice Hall.

Brentano, Franz. 1966. *The True and the Evident,* ed. O. Kraus. New York: The Humanities Press.

———. 1973. *Psychology from an Empirical Standpoint.* London: Routledge.

Bricke, John. 1980. *Hume's Philosophy of Mind.* Princeton, NJ: Princeton University Press.

Brodsky, Claudia, and Eloy LaBrada. 2017. *Inventing Agency: Essays on the Literary and Philosophical Production of the Modern Subject*. New York: Bloomsbury Academic.

Brümmer, Vincent. 1981. *Theology & Philosophical Inquiry: An Introduction*. London: The Macmillan Press.

Bruno, Giordano. 1998. *Cause, Principle and Unity and Essays on Magic*. Trans. R. De Luca. Cambridge: Cambridge University Press.

———. 2004. *The Expulsion of the Triumphant Beast*. Trans. A.D. Imerti. Lincoln, NE: University of Nebraska Press.

Bruza, Peter D., Zheng Wang, and Jerome R. Busemeyer. 2015. Quantum Cognition: A New Theoretical Approach to Psychology. *Trends in Cognitive Science* 19 (7): 383–393.

Burckhardt, Jacob. 1995. *The Civilization of the Renaissance in Italy*. New York: Modern Library.

Burke, Peter. 2014. *The Italian Renaissance: Culture and Society in Italy*. Princeton, NJ: Princeton University Press.

Burkert, Walter. 1989. *Ancient Mystery Cults*. Cambridge, MA: Harvard University Press.

Burnyeat, Myles F. 1976. Plato on the Grammar of Perceiving. *The Classical Quarterly* 26 (1): 29–51.

Burston, Daniel. 2003. Existentialism, Humanism and Psychotherapy. *Existential Analysis* 14 (2): 309–319.

Butterfield, Herbert. 1931. *The Whig Interpretation of History*. London: George Bell.

———. 1949. *Christianity and History*. London: George Bell.

Byron, Michael. 2015. *Submission and Subjection in Leviathan: Good Subjects in the Hobbesian Commonwealth*. London: Palgrave Macmillan.

Cain, Rebecca Bensen. 2007. *The Socratic Method: Plato's Use of Philosophical Drama*. New York: Continuum International Publishing Group.

Camus, Albert. 1991. *The Myth of Sisyphus and Other Essays*. Trans. J. O'Brien. New York: Vintage Books.

———. 1992. *The Rebel: An Essay on Man in Revolt*. Trans. A. Bower. New York: Vintage Books.

Carroll, Lewis. 2006. *Alice's Adventures in Wonderland and Through the Looking-Glass*. New York: Bantam Dell.

Cassirer, Ernst. 1963. *The Individual and the Cosmos in Renaissance Philosophy*. New York: Harper & Row.

Cevalley, Catherine. 1994. Niels Bohr's Words and the Atlantis of Kantianism. In *Niels Bohr and Contemporary Philosophy*, ed. J. Faye and H. Folse, 33–59. Dordrecht: Kluwer.

Chalmers, David. 1996. *The Conscious Mind*. Oxford: Oxford University Press.

Chapman, Loren J., and Jean Chapman. 1982. Test Results Are What You Think They Are. In *Judgment Under Uncertainty: Heuristics and Biases*, ed. D. Kahneman, P. Slovic, and A. Tversky, 239–248. Cambridge: Cambridge University Press.

Chipman, Susan E.F. 2017. *The Oxford Handbook of Cognitive Science*. Oxford: Oxford University Press.

Chomsky, Noam. 1957. *Syntactic Structures*. The Hague: Mouton de Gruyter.

———. 1959. A Review of B.F. Skinner's *Verbal Behavior*. *Language* 35 (1): 26–58.

———. 2004. *Language and Politics*. Montreal: Black Rose Books.

Churchland, Paul M. 1981. Eliminative Materialism and the Propositional Attitudes. *The Journal of Philosophy* 78 (2): 67–90.

———. 1992. Activation Vectors Versus Propositional Attitudes: How the Brain Represents Reality. *Philosophy and Phenomenological Research* 52 (2): 419–424.

Cicero. 1967. *On the Nature of the Gods*. Trans. H. Rackham. Cambridge, MA: Harvard University Press.

Cicovacki, Predrag. 1997. *Anamorphosis: Kant on Knowledge and Ignorance*. Oxford: Oxford University Press.

Clark, Jonathan. 2004. *Our Shadowed Present: Modernism, Postmodernism, and History*. Stanford, CA: Stanford University Press.

de Condillac, Étienne Bonnot. 2001. *Essay on the Origin of Human Knowledge*. Trans. H. Aarsleff. Cambridge: Cambridge University Press.

Corlett, J. Angelo. 2005. *Interpreting Plato's Dialogues*. Las Vegas, NV: Parmenides Publishing.

Cornford, F.M. 2013. Mathematics and Dialectic in the *Republic*. In *Studies in Plato's Metaphysics*, ed. R.E. Allen, 61–96. New York: Routledge.

Corsini, Raymond J. 2001. *Handbook of Innovative Therapy*. Hoboken, NJ: Wiley-Blackwell.

Coulter, James A. 1976. *The Literary Microcosm: Theories of Interpretation of the Later Neoplatonists*. Leiden: Brill.

Crombie, A.C. 1996. *The History of Science from Augustine to Galileo*. Vol. I & II. New York: Dover Publications.

Csikszentmihalyi, Mihaly J. 1996. *Creativity: Flow and the Psychology of Discovery and Invention*. New York: Harper Collins.

Cunningham, Francis A. 1988. *Essence and Existence in Thomism: A Mental Vs the "Real Distinction?".* Lanham, MD: University Press of America.

Daniel, Stephen L. 1986. The Patient as Text: A Model of Clinical Hermeneutics. *Theoretical Medicine* 7 (2): 195–210.

Danziger, Kurt. 1979. The Positivist Repudiation of Wundt. *Journal of the History of the Behavioral Sciences* 15 (3): 205–230.

———. 1990. *Constructing the Subject: Historical Origins of Psychological Research.* Cambridge: Cambridge University Press.

Darwin, Charles. 1859. *On the Origin of Species by Means of Natural Selection.* London, England: John Murray.

Davidson, Donald. 1970. Mental Events. In *Experience and Theory,* ed. L. Foster and J.W. Swanson, 79–101. Amherst, MA: University of Massachusetts Press.

Dehaene, Stanislas. 2014. *Consciousness and the Brain: Deciphering How the Brain Codes Our Thoughts.* New York: Viking.

Deleuze, Gilles. 1983. Plato and the Simulacrum. Trans. R. Krauss. 27(October): 45–56.

———. 1992. Postscript on the Societies of Control. Trans. M. Sheridan. 59 (October): 3–7.

———. 1993. *The Fold: Leibniz and the Baroque.* Trans. T. Conley. Minneapolis: University of Minnesota Press.

———. 1994. *Difference & Repetition.* Trans. Paul Patton. New York: Columbia University.

———. 2004a. How Do We Recognize Structuralism? (1967). In *Desert Islands and Other Texts, 1953–1974,* ed. D. Lapoujade and trans. M. Taormina, 170–192. New York: Semiotext(e).

———. 2004b. The Method of Dramatization. In *Desert Islands and Other Texts, 1953–1974,* ed. D. Lapoujade and trans. M. Taormina, 94–116. New York: Semiotext(e).

———. 2005. *Expressionism in Philosophy: Spinoza.* Trans. M. Joughin. New York: Zone Books.

———. 2006. *Nietzsche and Philosophy.* Trans. H. Tomlinson. New York: Columbia University.

Deleuze, Gilles, and Félix Guattari. 1980. *A Thousand Plateaus.* Trans. B. Massumi. Vol. II. of *Capitalism and Schizophrenia.* (1972–1980). London: Continuum.

———. 2003. *What Is Philosophy?* Trans. G. Birchill and H. Tomlinson. New York: Verso.

———. 2004. *Anti-Oedipus*. Trans. R. Hurley, M. Seem, & H. R. Lane. Vol. I. of *Capitalism and Schizophrenia*. (1972–1980). London: Continuum.

Dember, William N. 1974. Motivation and the Cognitive Revolution. *American Psychologist* 29: 161–168.

Dennett, Daniel C. 1991. *Consciousness Explained*. Boston: Little Brown.

Descartes, René. 1998. *Discourse on the Method for Conducting One's Reason Well and for Seeking Truth in the Sciences*. Trans. D.A. Cress. Indianapolis, IN: Hackett Publishing.

———. 2006. *Meditations, Objections, and Replies*. Ed. and Trans. R. Ariew and D. Cress. Indianapolis, IN: Hackett Publishing.

Deslauriers, Marguerite. 2007. *Aristotle on Definition*. Leiden: Brill.

Derrida, Jacques. 1978. *Writing and Difference*. Trans. A. Bass. Chicago: University of Chicago.

Dewey, John. 1884. The New Psychology. *Andover Review* 2: 278–289.

———. 1886. Psychology as Philosophic Method. *Mind* 2 (42): 153–173.

———. 1896. The Reflex Arc Concept in Psychology. *The Psychological Review* 33 (4): 357–370.

Deleuze, Gilles. 1984. *Kant's Critical Philosophy: The Doctrine of the Faculties*. Trans. H. Tomlinson. Minneapolis: University of Minnesota Press.

Diamond, Stephen. 1996. *Anger, Madness, and the Daimonic*. New York: SUNY Press.

Dickinson, John Peter. 1986. *Science and Scientific Researchers in Modern Society*. Lanham, MD: Bernan Press.

Dilthey, Wilhelm. 1989. *Introduction to the Human Sciences*. Eds. and Trans. R.A. Makkreel and R. Rodi, *Wilhelm Dilthey: Selected Works*, vol. I. Princeton, NJ: Princeton University Press.

———. 2010. *Ideas for a Descriptive and Analytic Psychology (1894)*. Trans. R.A. Makkreel and D. Moore. In *Understanding the Human World*, eds. R.A. Makkreel and R. Rodi, *Wilhelm Dilthey: Selected Works*, vol. II, 115–210 Princeton, NJ: Princeton University Press.

Drake, Stillman, and Trevor H. Levere. 1999. *Essays on Galileo and the History and Philosophy of Science: Volume I*. Toronto, Canada: Toronto University Press.

Dreyfus, Hubert. 1992. *What Computers Still Can't Do*. Cambridge, MA: MIT Press.

DuBose, Todd. 2013. Let the Kierkegaardian Comedy Resume: Faith-Phobia and Faithful Leaning in Evidence-Based Criteria for Therapeutic Care. *Existential Analysis* 24 (1): 70–81.

Durant, Will. 1939. *The Story of Civilization: The Life of Greece*. New York: Simon & Shuster.

Edgerton, Samuel Y. 2009. *The Mirror, the Window, and the Telescope: How Renaissance Linear Perspective Changed Our Vision of the Universe*. Ithaca, NY: Cornell University Press.

Edwards, Michael. 2013. *Time and the Science of the Soul in Early Modern Philosophy*. Leiden: Brill.

Elliott, Anthony. 2004. *Subject to Ourselves: Social Theory, Psychoanalysis and Postmodernity*. Boulder, CO: Paradigm Press.

Engel, Andreas K., Karl J. Friston, and Danica Kragic. 2016. *The Pragmatic Turn: Toward Action-Oriented Views in Cognitive Science*. Cambridge, MA: MIT Press.

Entralgo, Lain. 1970. *The Therapy of the Word in Classical Antiquity*. New Haven: Yale University Press.

Epicurus. 1994. *The Epicurus Reader: Selected Writings and Testimonia*. Trans. L.P. Gerson and B. Inwood. Indianapolis, IN: Hackett Publishing.

Epictetus. 1998. *Encheiridion*. Trans. W.I. Matson. In *Classics of Philosophy*, L.P. Pojman, vol. I, 358–368. Oxford: Oxford University Press.

Evans, Fred J. 1992. *Psychology and Nihilism: A Genealogical Critique of the Computational Model of Mind*. Albany, NY: SUNY Press.

Feigl, Herbert. 1959. Philosophical Embarrassments of Psychology. *American Psychologist* 14 (3): 115–128.

Feyerabend, Paul. 1983. *Against Method*. New York: Verso.

———. 1987. *Farewell to Reason*. New York: Verso.

———. 2001. *Conquest of Abundance: A Tale of Abstraction Versus the Richness of Being*. Chicago, IL: University of Chicago Press.

Ficino, Marsilio. 1981. *Marsilio Ficino and the Phaedran Charioteer*. Trans. M.J.B. Allen. Berkeley, CA: University of California Press.

Finkelman, David. 1978. Science and Psychology. *American Journal of Psychology* 78 (91): 179–199.

Fleck, Ludwik. 1979. *Genesis and Development of a Scientific Fact*. Eds. T.J. Trenn and R.K. Merton and Trans. F. Bradley and T.J. Trenn. Chicago: University of Chicago Press.

Fodor, Jerry. 1968. *Psychological Explanation: An Introduction to the Philosophy of Psychology*. New York: Random House.

Foucault, Michel. 1971. *The Order of Things: An Archaeology of the Human Sciences*. Trans. A. Sheridan. New York: Pantheon Books.

———. 1988. *Madness and Civilization: A History of Insanity in the Age of Reason*. Trans. A. Sheridan. New York: Vintage Books.

————. 1994. *The Birth of the Clinic: An Archaeology of Medical Perception.* Trans. A. Sheridan. New York: Vintage Books.

Frankfurt, Harry. 2009. Freedom of the Will and the Concept of a Person. In *Free Will*, ed. D. Pereboom, 196–212. Indianapolis, IN: Hackett Publishing.

Frankl, Viktor E. 2006. *Man's Search for Meaning.* Trans. I. Lasch. Boston, MA: Beacon Press.

Frede, Dorothea. 1993. Out of the Cave: What Socrates Learned from Diotima. In *Nomodeiktes: Greek Studies in Honor of Martin Ostwald*, ed. R. Rosen and R. Farrell, 397–422. Ann Arbor, MI: University of Michigan Press.

Frede, Michael. 2011. *A Free Will: Origins of the Notion in Ancient Thought*, ed. A.A. Long. Berkeley, CA: University of California Press.

Freud, Sigmund. 1895. The Project for a Scientific Psychology, Trans. J. Strachey. In *The Standard Edition of the Complete Psychological Works of Sigmund Freud*, vol. 1. London: Vintage Classics.

————. 1915. The Unconscious. Trans. J. Strachey. In *The Standard Edition of the Complete Psychological Works of Sigmund Freud*, vol. 14. London: Vintage Classics.

————. 1933. The Question of a Weltanschauung. Trans. J. Strachey. In *The Standard Edition of the Complete Psychological Works of Sigmund Freud*, vol. 22. London: Vintage Classics.

————. 1940. An Outline of Psychoanalysis. Trans. J. Strachey. In *The Standard Edition of the Complete Psychological Works of Sigmund Freud*, vol. 23. London: Vintage Classics.

————. 1953. Three Essays on Sexuality. Trans. J. Strachey. In *The Standard Edition of the Complete Psychological Works of Sigmund Freud*, vol. 7. London: The Hogarth Press.

————. 1955. The "Uncanny". Trans. J. Strachey. In *The Standard Edition of the Complete Psychological Works of Sigmund Freud*, vol. 17. London: The Hogarth Press.

————. 1957. On the Universal Tendency to Debasement in the Sphere of Love. Trans. J. Strachey. In *The Standard Edition of the Complete Psychological Works of Sigmund Freud*, vol. 11. London: The Hogarth Press.

————. 1961. The Dissolution of the Oedipus Complex. Trans. J. Strachey. In *The Standard Edition of the Complete Psychological Works of Sigmund Freud*, vol. 19. London: The Hogarth Press.

————. 1963. Introductory Lectures on Psycho-Analysis (Parts I and II). Trans. J. Strachey. In *The Standard Edition of the Complete Psychological Works of Sigmund Freud*, vol. 15. London: The Hogarth Press.

Frost, Samantha. 2005. Hobbes and the Matter of Self-Consciousness. *Political Theory* 33 (4): 495–517.

Fuchs, Alfred H., Rand B. Evans, and Roger K. Thomas. 2007. History of Psychology: Recurring Errors Among Recent History of Psychology Textbooks. *The American Journal of Psychology* 120 (3): 477–495.

Fuchs, Alfred H., and Wayne Viney. 2002. The Course in the History of Psychology: Present Status and Future Concerns. *History of Psychology* 5 (1): 3–15.

Fukuyama, Francis. 1992. *The End of History and the Last Man*. New York: The Free Press.

Fuller, Steve, Marc De Mey, Terry Shinn, and Steve Woolgar, eds. 1989. *The Cognitive Turn: Sociological and Psychological Perspectives on Science*. Dordrecht: Springer.

Gadamer, Hans-Georg. 1980. *Dialogue and Dialectic: Eight Hermeneutical Studies on Plato*. Trans. P. Christopher Smith. New Haven, CT: Yale University Press.

———. 1989. *Truth and Method* (2nd rev). Trans. J. Weinsheimer and D.G. Marshall. New York: Continuum Press.

Galilei, Galileo. 1962. *Dialog Concerning the Two Chief World Systems*. Trans. S. Drake. Berkeley, CA: Berkeley University Press.

Gallie, Roger D. 2010. *Thomas Reid: Ethics, Aesthetics and the Anatomy of the Self*. Dordrecht: Kluwer Academic Publishers.

Gardner, Howard E. 1987. *The Mind's New Science: A History of the Cognitive Revolution*. New York: Basic Books.

Garrigou-Lagrange. 2015. *The Three Conversions in the Spiritual Life*. Charlottesville, NC: TAN Books.

Gazzaniga, Michael S. 2006. My Brain Made Me Do It. In *Ethical Brain*, ed. M.S. Gazzaniga The, 87–104. New York: Harper Collins.

Geelan, David R. 1997. Epistemological Anarchy and the Many Forms of Constructivism. *Science & Education* 6 (1–2): 15–28.

Gergen, Kenneth J. 1985. The Social Constructionist Movement in Modern Psychology. *American Psychologist* 40 (3): 266–275.

Geuter, Ulfried. 1983. The Uses of History for the Shaping of a Field: Observations on German Psychology. In *Functions and Uses Disciplinary Histories*, ed. L. Graham, W. Leneies, and P. Weingart. Dordrecht: Springer.

Gibson, A. Boyce. 2017. *The Philosophy of Descartes*. Vol. I & II. London: Routledge.

Gill, Christopher. 2006a. Psychophysical Holism in Stoicism and Epicureanism. In *Common to Body and Soul*, ed. R.A.H. King, 209–231. Berlin: Walter de Gruyter.

————. 2006b. *The Structured Self in Hellenistic and Roman Thought*. Oxford: Oxford University Press.

Gillespie, Alex. 2006. Descartes' Demon: A Dialogical Analysis of 'Meditations on First Philosophy'. *Theory & Psychology* 16 (6): 761–781.

Glenn, Paul J. 1939. *Ontology: A Class Manual in Fundamental Metaphysics*. St. Louis, MO: B. Herder Book Co.

Glock, Hans-Johann. 2013. The Owl of Minerva: Is Analytic Philosophy Moribund? In *The Historical Turn in Analytic Philosophy*, ed. E.H. Reck. New York: Palgrave Macmillan.

Gramsci, Antonio. 1971. *Selections from the Prison Notebooks*. Ed. and Trans. Q. Horare and G. N. Smith. London: Lawrence & Wishart.

————. 2013. *Quaderni dal carcere. Vol. IV: Passato e presente*. Torino: Giulio Einaudi.

Greely, Robin Adèle. 2001. Dalí's Fascism; Lacan's Paranoia. *Art History* 24 (4): 465–492.

Green, Stuart. 1994. The Problems of Learning to Think Like a Historian: Writing History in the Culture of the Classroom. *Educational Psychologist* 29 (2): 9–96.

Greenbaum, Dorian G. 2016. *The Daimon in Hellenistic Astrology: Origins and Influence*. Leiden: Brill.

Griffiths, Paul E. 1996. The Historical Turn in the Study of Adaptation. *British Journal for the Philosophy of Science* 47 (4): 511–532.

Grünbaum, Adolf. 1984. *The Foundations of Psychoanalysis: A Philosophical Critique*. Berkeley, CA: University of California Press.

————. 1990. 'Meaning' Connections and Causal Connections in the Human Sciences: The Poverty of Hermeneutic Philosophy. *Journal of the American Psychoanalytic Association* 38 (3): 559–577.

Guignon, Charles, and Robert Merrihew Adams. 2003. *The Existentialists: Critical Essays on Kierkegaard, Nietzsche, Heidegger, and Sartre*. London: Rowman & Littlefield.

Guyer, Paul. 1989. Psychology and the Transcendental Deduction. In *Kant's Transcendental Deduction: The Three Critiques and the Opus postumum*, ed. E. Förster. Stanford, CA: Stanford University Press.

Habermas, Jürgen. 1972. *Knowledge & Human Interests*. Trans. J.J. Shapiro. Boston: Beacon Press.

Hadot, Pierre. 1995. *Philosophy as a Way of Life*. Oxford: Oxford University Press.

————. 2002. *What Is Ancient Philosophy?* Cambridge, MA: The Belknap Press of Harvard University.

Harré, Rom. 1995. Emotion and Memory: The Second Cognitive Revolution. In *Philosophy, Psychology and Psychiatry*, ed. A.P. Griffiths. Cambridge: Cambridge University Press.

Hart, J.T. 1986. Functional Eclectic Therapy. In *Handbook of Eclectic Psychotherapy*, ed. J.C. Norcross, 201–225. New York: Brunner-Mazel.

Hart, F. Elizabeth. 2006. Performance, Phenomenology, and the Cognitive Turn. In *Performance and Cognition: Theater Studies and the Cognitive Turn*, ed. B. McConachie and F.E. Hart, 29–51. New York: Routledge.

Harris, Ben. 2009. What Critical Psychologists Should Know About the History of Psychology. In *Critical Psychology: An Introduction*, ed. D. Fox, I. Prilleltensky, and S. Austin, 20–35. London: Sage.

Hatfield, Gary. 1992. Empirical, Rational, and Transcendental Psychology: Psychology as Science and as Philosophy. In *The Cambridge Companion to Kant*, ed. P. Guyer. Cambridge: Cambridge University Press.

————. 1998. Kant and Empirical Psychology in the 18th Century. *Psychological Science* 9 (6): 423–428.

————. 2000. Descartes' Naturalism About the Mental. In *Descartes' Natural Philosophy*, ed. S. Gaukroger, J. Schuster, and J. Sutton, 630–658. London: Routledge.

Hawking, Stephen, and Leonard Mlodinow. 2007. *A Briefer History of Time*. New York: Bantam Dell.

Heal, Jane. 1986. Replication and Functionalism. In *Language, Mind, and Logic*, ed. J. Butterfield, 45–59. Cambridge: Cambridge University Press.

Hegel, G.W.F. 1901. *Philosophy of History*. Trans. J. Sibree. New York: P.F. Collier and Son.

————. 1977. *Phenomenology of Spirit*. Trans. A.V. Miller. Oxford: Oxford University Press.

Heidbreder, Edna. 1933. *Seven Psychologies*. New York: Appleton-Century-Crofts.

Heidegger, Martin. 1962a. *Being and Time*. Trans. J. Macquarrie and E. Robinson. New York: Harper & Row

————. 1962b. The Phenomenological Method of Investigation. In *Being and Time*. Trans. J. Macquarrie and E. Robinson, 49–62. New York: Harper & Row.

————. 1976. Nur noch ein Gott kann uns retten. *Der Spiegel* 31 (May): 193–219. Trans. W. Richardson as "Only a God Can Save Us. In (1981)

*Heidegger: The Man and the Thinker*, ed. T. Sheehan, 45–67. New York: Transaction Publishers.

———. 1993. Letter on Humanism. Trans. D.F. Krell. In *Basic Writings*, ed. D. F. Krell, 213–266. New York: Harper Collins Publishers.

———. 1997. *Phenomenological Interpretation of Kant's* Critique of Pure Reason. Trans. P. Emad and K. Maly. Bloomington, IN: Indiana University Press.

———. 2001. *Poetry, Language, Thought*. Trans. A. Hofstadter. New York: Harper Collins Perennial Classics.

———. 2003. *Plato's Sophist*. Trans. R. Rojcewicz and A. Schuwer. Bloomington, IN: Indiana University Press.

Hergenhahn, B.R., and Tracy Henley. 2013. *An Introduction to the History of Psychology*. Stamford, CT: Wadsworth Publishing.

Henle, Paul. 1992. Do We Discover Our Uses of Words? In *The Linguistic Turn: Essays in Philosophical Method*, ed. R. Rorty, 218–223. Chicago: University of Chicago Press.

Henrich, Dieter. 1969. The Proof-Structure of Kant's Transcendental Deduction. *The Review of Metaphysics* 22 (4): 640–659.

Henriques, Gregg R. 2004. Psychology Defined. *Journal of Clinical Psychology* 60 (12): 1207–1221.

Hergenhahn, B.R. 2009. *An Introduction to the History of Psychology*. Belmont, CA: Cengage.

Higgins, E. Tory. 1991. Expanding the Law of Cognitive Structure Actication: The Role of Knowledge Applicability. *Psychological Inquiry* 2 (2): 192–193.

Hilgard, Ernest R. 1987. *Psychology in America: A Historical Survey*. San Diego, CA: Harcourt Brace Jovanovich.

Hobbs, Sandy, and Jeremy T. Burman. 2009. Looking Back: Is the Cognitive Revolution a Myth? *The British Psychological Society* 22: 812–815.

Hopkins, Burt C. 2006. Husserl's Psychologism, and Critique of Psychologism, Revisited. *Husserl Studies* 22: 91–119.

Howard, Alex. 2000. *Philosophy for Counselling and Psychotherapy: Pythagoras to Postmodernism*. London: Macmillan Press.

Huby, Pamela. 1967. The First Discovery of the Freewill Problem. *Philosophy* 42 (162): 353–362.

Hurley, Susan. 2005. The Shared Circuits Hypothesis: A Unified Functional Architecture for Control, Imitation, and Simulation. In *Perspectives on Imitation: From Neuroscience to Social Science, Vol. I: Mechanisms of Imitation and Imitation in Animals*, ed. S. Hurley and N. Chater, 177–193. Cambridge, MA: MIT Press.

Husserl, Edmund. 1969. *Formal and Transcendental Logic.* Trans. D. Cairns. The Hague: Martinus Nijhoff Publishers.

———. 1970. Clarification of the Origin of the Modern Opposition Between Physicalistic Objectivism and Transcendental Subjectivism. In *The Crisis of European Sciences and Transcendental Phenomenology.* Evanston, IL: Northwestern University Press.

———. 1977. *Phenomenological Psychology: Lectures, Summer Semester, 1925.* Trans. J. Scanlon. The Hague: Martinus Nijhoff Publishers.

———. 1983. *Ideas Pertaining to a Pure Phenomenology and to a Phenomenological Philosophy,* vol. I. Trans. F. Kersten. The Hague: Martinus Nijhoff Publishers.

Hume, David. 1985. *A Treatise of Human Nature.* London, England: Penguin.

———. 1993. *An Enquiry Concerning Human Understanding.* Indianapolis, IN: Hackett Publishing.

Iamblichus. 2003. *On the Mysteries.* Trans. E.C. Clarke, J.M. Dillon, and J.P. Hershbell. Atlanta, GA: Society of Biblical Literature.

Iglesias, Maria R. Gómez. 2016. The Echoes of Eleusis: Love and Initiation in the Platonic Philosophy. In *Greek Philosophy and Mystery Cults,* eds. M.J. Martin-Velasco and M.J.G. Blanco. [Papers from the 2012 bimonthly meeting of the Iberian Society of Greek Philosophy.], 61–102. Newcastle upon Tyne: Cambridge Scholars Publishing.

Irwin, Terence H. 1990. *Aristotle's First Principles.* Oxford: Oxford University Press.

Jackson, Frank. 1986. What Mary Didn't Know. *Journal of Philosophy* 83 (5): 291–295.

James, William. 1918. *The Principles of Psychology.* Vol. 1. New York: Dover Publications.

Jardine, Robert. 1874. *Elements of the Psychology of Cognition.* London: Macmillan.

Jaspers, Karl. 1974. Causal and "Meaningful" Connections Between Life, History and Psychosis. Trans. G. Hoenig. In *Themes and Variations in European Psychiatry,* eds. S. Hirsch and M. Shepard, 80–93. Bristol, CT: John Wright & Sons.

Johnston, John. 2008. *The Allure of Machinic Life: Cybernetics, Artificial Life, and the New AI.* Cambridge, MA: MIT Press.

Johnstone, Albert A. 1991. *Rationalized Epistemology: Taking Solipsism Seriously.* Albany, NY: SUNY.

Jones, Mary McAllester. 1991. *Gaston Bachelard, Subversive Humanist: Text and Readings.* Madison, WI: University of Wisconsin Press.

Joynson, Robert B. 1970. The Break-Down of Modern Psychology. *Bulletin of the British Psychological Society* 23: 261–269.

Jung, C.G. 2001. *Modern Man in Search of a Soul*. Trans. W.S. Dell and C.F. Baynes. New York: Routledge.

———. 2014. *Psychology and Religion: West and East*. Trans. R.F.C. Hull. In *The Collected Works of C.G. Jung*, series eds. H. Read et al., vol. 11. Princeton, NJ: Princeton University Press.

Jung, C.G., and Carl Kerényi. 1969. *Essays on a Science of Mythology: The Myth of the Divine Child and The Mysteries of Eleusis*. Princeton, NJ: Princeton University Press.

Kagan, Jerome. 2013. Equal Time for Psychological and Biological Contributions to Human Variation. *Review of General Psychology* 17 (4): 351–357.

Kahn, Charles. 1996. *Plato and the Socratic Dialogue: The Philosophical Use of a Literary Form*. Cambridge: Cambridge University Press.

Kane, Anne. 2000. Reconstructing Culture in Historical Explanation: Narratives as Cultural Structure and Practice. *History and Theory* 39 (3): 311–330.

Kant, Immanuel. 1960. *Religion Within the Limits of Reason Alone*. Trans. T.M. Greene and H.H. Hudson. New York: Harper & Row.

———. 1982. *Kant's Theory of Mind: An Analysis of the Paralogisms of Pure Reason*. Oxford: Clarendon Press.

———. 1983. *Perpetual Peace and Other Essays*. Trans. T. Humphrey. Indianapolis, IN: Hackett Publishing.

———. 1998. *Critique of Pure Reason*. Trans. P. Guyer and A. W. Wood. Cambridge: Cambridge University Press.

———. 1999. *Critique of Practical Reason*. Trans. M. Gregor. Cambridge: Cambridge University Press.

———. 2001. *Lectures on Metaphysics*. Trans. K. Ameriks and S. Naragon. Cambridge: Cambridge University Press.

———. 2006. *Anthropology from a Pragmatic Point of View*. Ed. and Trans. R.B. Louden. Cambridge: Cambridge University Press.

Kantor, J.R. 1963. *The Scientific Evolution of Psychology*. Vol. I. Granville, OH: The Principia Press.

———. 1969. *The Scientific Evolution of Psychology*. Vol. II. Granville, OH: The Principia Press.

Keller, Pierre. 1998. *Kant and the Demands of Self-Consciousness*. Cambridge, England: Cambridge University Press.

Kierkegaard, Søren. 1980. *The Sickness Unto Death*. Trans. H.V. Hong and E.H. Hong. Princeton, NJ: Princeton University Press.

————. 1988. *Stages on Life's Way*. Trans. H.V. Hong and E. H. Hong. Princeton, NJ: Princeton University Press.

————. 1998. *The Point of View*. Trans. H.V. Hong and E.H. Hong. Princeton, NJ: Princeton University Press.

————. 2009. *"The Moment" and Late Writings*. Trans. H.V. Hong and E.H. Hong. Princeton, NJ: Princeton University Press.

Kim, Jaegwon. 1998. *Mind in a Physical World*. Cambridge: Cambridge University Press.

————. 2005. *Physicalism, Or Something Near Enough*. Princeton, NJ: Princeton University Press.

Kimble, Gregory A. 1985. Overview: The Chronology. In *Topics in the History of Psychology*, ed. G.A. Kimble and K. Schlesinger, vol. II, 1–18. Hillsdale, NJ: Lawrence Erlbaum Associates.

Kitcher, Patricia. 1993. *Kant's Transcendental Psychology*. Oxford: Oxford University Press.

Klagge, James C., and Nicholas D. Smith, eds. 1992. *Methods of Interprting Plato and His Dialogues*. Oxford: Clarendon Press.

Klein, D.B. 1970. *A History of Scientific Psychology*. New York: Basic Books.

Knapp, Terry J., and Lynn C. Robertson. 2017. *Approaches to Cognition: Contrasts and Controversies*. London: Routledge.

Knight, David. 1982. Religion and the 'New Philosophy'. *Renaissance and Modern Studies* 26 (1): 147–166.

Köhler, Wolfgang. 1970. *Gestalt Psychology: The Definitive Statement of Gestalt Theory*. New York: Liveright Publishing Company.

Kragh, Helge. 1989. *An Introduction to the Historiography of Science*. Cambridge: Cambridge University Press.

Kristeller, Paul Oskar. 1964. *Eight Philosophers of the Italian Renaissance*. Stanford, CA: Stanford University Press.

Krstic, Kruno. 1964. Marko Marulic—The Author of the Term 'Psychology'. *Acta Instituti Psychologici Universitatis Zagrabiensis* 36: 7–13.

Kugelmann, Robert. 2011. *Psychology and Catholicism: Contested Boundaries*. Cambridge: Cambridge University Press.

Kuhn, Thomas. 1969. Comment [On the Relations of Science and Art]. *Comparative Studies in Society and History* 11: 403–412.

————. 1996. *The Structure of Scientific Revolutions*. Chicago: University of Chicago.

Lacan, Jacques. 1965. Hommage fait à Marguerite Duras, du *Ravissement de Lol V. Stein*. *Cahiers Renaud-Barrault* 52: 7–15.

————. 1977. *The Four Fundamental Concepts of Psychoanalysis*. Trans. A. Sheridan. New York: W.W. Norton & Co.

————. 1982. *Ecrits: A Selection*. Trans. A. Sheridan. New York: W.W. Norton & Co.

————. 1991. *The Ego in Freud's Theory and in the Technique of Psychoanalysis, 1954–1955*, vol. II. Trans. S. Tomaselli. New York: W.W. Norton & Co.

Ladd, George Trumbull. 1892. Psychology as So-Called 'Natural Science. *The Philosophical Review* 1 (1): 24–53.

————. 1894. *Psychology: Descriptive and Explanatory*. New York: Charles Scribner's Sons.

Lamanna, Marco. 2010. On the Early History of Psychology. *Revista Filosófica de Coimbra* 19 (38): 291–314.

de La Mettrie, Julien Offray. 2003. *Machine Man and Other Writings*. Trans. A. Thomason. Cambridge: Cambridge University Press.

Lapointe, François H. 1973. The Origin and Evolution of the Term "Psychology". *Rivista Critica di Storia della Filosofia* 28 (2): 138–160.

Leibniz, Gottfried Wilhelm. 1989. The Principles of Philosophy, or, the Monadology (1714). In *G.W. Leibniz: Philosophical Essays,* eds. and trans. R. Ariew and D. Garber. Indianapolis, IN: Hackett Publishing.

————. 1997. *New Essays on Human Understanding*. Ed. and Trans. P. Remnant and J. Bennett. Cambridge: Cambridge University Press.

Leijenhorst, Cees. 2010. Bernadino Telesio (1509–1588): New Fundamental Principles of Nature. Trans. B. McNeil. In *Philosophers of the Renaissance*, ed. P.R. Blum, 168–180. Washington, DC: The Catholic University of America Press.

Leonelli, Sabina. 2016. *Data-Centric Biology: A Philosophical Study*. Chicago: University of Chicago.

Levine, Joseph. 1983. Materialism and Qualia: The Explanatory Gap. *Pacific Philosophical Quarterly* 64 (4): 354–361.

Lewis, C.S. 1960. *Studies in Words*. Cambridge: Cambridge University Press.

Lewis, C.I. 1991. *Mind and the World Order: Outline of a Theory of Knowledge*. Boston: Dover Publications.

Lichtenstein, Parker E. 1967. Psychological Systems: Their Nature and Function. *Psychological Record* 17 (3): 321–340.

Lilienfeld, Scott O. 2012. Public Skepticism of Psychology: Why Many People Perceive the Study of Human Behavior as Unscientific. *American Psychologist* 67 (2): 111–129.

Little, Kenneth. 2002. Pitu's Doubt: Entrée Clown Self-Fashioning in the Circus Tradition. In *Popular Theatre: A Sourcebook*, ed. J. Schechter, 138–148. London: Routledge.

Locke, John. 1841. *An Essay Concerning Human Understanding*. London: Thomas Tegg.

Lundin, Robert W. 1972 [1979]. *Theories and Systems of Psychology*. Toronto, Canada: D.C. Heath.

Mach, Ernst. 1897. *Contributions to the Analysis of the Sensations*, Trans. C.M. Williams. Chicago: The Open Court Publishing Co.

Macmillan, Malcolm, and Fred Crews. 1997. *Freud Evaluated: The Completed Arc*. Cambridge, MA: MIT Press.

Makkreel, Rudolf A. 2003. The Cognition-Knowledge Distinction in Kant and Dilthey and the Implications for Psychology and Self-Understanding. *Studies in History and Philosophy of Science Part A* 34 (1): 149–164.

Mandler, George. 1996. The Situation of Psychology: Landmarks and Choicepoints. *The American Journal of Psychology* 109 (1): 1–35.

Martin, Thomas L., and Duke Pesta. 2016. *The Renaissance and the Postmodern: A Study in Comparative Critical Values*. London: Routledge.

Marton, Ference. 1981. Phenomenography—Describing Conceptions of the World Around Us. *Instructional Science* 10 (2): 177–200.

———. 1986. Phenomenography—A Research Approach Investigating Different Understandings of Reality. *Journal of Thought* 21 (2): 28–49.

Marwick, Arthur. 1970. *What Is History and Why It Is Important*. London: McGraw-Hill/Open University Press.

———. 1993. "A Fetishism of Documents?" The Salience of Source-Based History. In *Developments in Modern Historiography*, ed. H. Kozicki, 107–138. London: Macmillan.

———. 2001. *The New Nature of History*. London: Palgrave.

Marx, Melvin Herman, and William A. Hillix. 1963. *Systems and Theories in Psychology*. New York: McGraw-Hill.

Maslow, Abraham H. 1943. A Theory of Human Motivation. *Psychological Review* 50 (4): 370–396.

———. 1968. *Toward a Psychology of Being*. New York: Van Nostrand Reinhold.

———. 1970a. The Farther Reaches of Human Nature. *Journal of Transpersonal Psychology* 1 (1): 1–9.

———. 1970b. *Motivation and Personality*. New York: Harper & Row.

Margolis, Joseph. 1984. *Philosophy of Psychology*. Upper Saddle River, NJ: Prentice Hall.

Maurer, Armand. 1978. Method in Ockham's Nominalism. *The Monist* 61 (3): 426–443.

———. 1999. *The Philosophy of William of Ockham: In the Light of its Principles.* Irving, TX: Pontifical Institute of Mediaeval Studies (PIMS).

Mayer, A., and J. Orth. 1901. Zur qualitativen untersuchung der associationen. *Zeitschrift für Psychologie* 26: 1–13.

Menn, Stephen. 1998. The Intellectual Setting. In *The Cambridge History of Seventeenth-Century Philosophy*, ed. D. Garber and M. Ayers, vol. I, 33–86. Cambridge: Cambridge University Press.

Metzger, Wolfgang. 1971. The Historical Background for National Trends in Psychology: German Psychology. In *Historical Perspectives in Psychology: Readings*, ed. V.S. Sexton and H. Misiak, 329–353. Pacific Gove, CA: Brooks Cole Publishing.

McDonald, Terrence J. 1996. Is Vice Versa? Historical Anthropologies and Anthropological Histories. In *The Historic Turn in the Human Sciences*, ed. T.J. McDonald, 17–52. Ann Arbor, MI: University of Michigan Press.

McGeoch, John A. 1933. The Formal Criteria of a Systematic Psychology. *The Psychological Review* 40 (1): 1–12.

Merleau-Ponty, Maurice. 2002. *Phenomenology of Perception.* London: Routledge Classics.

Merz, John T. 1965. *A History of European Thought in the Nineteenth Century.* New York: Dover.

Miller, George A. 2003. The Cognitive Revolution: A Historical Perspective. *Trends in Cognitive Sciences* 7 (3): 141–144.

Miller, Gregory A. 2010. Mistreating Psychology in the Decades of the Brain. *Perspectives on Psychological Science* 5 (6): 716–743.

Miller, Ted H. 2011. *Mortal Gods: Science, Politics, and the Humanist Ambitions of Thomas Hobbes.* University Park, PA: Penn State University Press.

Moes, Mark. 2000. *Plato's Dialogue Form and the Care of the Soul.* New York: Peter Lang.

Möhring, Maren. 2003. Performanz und historische Mimesis. In *Geschichtswissenschaft und "Performative Turn"*, ed. J. Martschukat and S. Patzold. Vienna: Böhlau Verlag.

Monod, Emmanuel. 2004. Einstein, Heisenberg, Kant: Methodological Distinction and Conditions of Possibilities. *Information and Organization* 14 (2): 105–121.

Moravcsik, Michael J. 1981. Creativity in Science Education. *Science Education* 65: 221–227.

de Mul, Elize. 2016. Existential Privacy and the Technological Situation of Boundary Regulation. In *Social Epistemology and Technology: Toward Public Self-Awareness Regarding Technological Mediation*, ed. F. Scalambrino, 69–79. London: Rowman & Littlefield International.

Mumford, Michael D. 2003. Where Have We Been, Were Are We Going? Taking Stock in Creativity Research. *Creativity Research Journal* 15: 107–120.

Murray, E.J. 1986. Possibilities and Promises of Eclecticism. In *Handbook of Eclectic Psychotherapy*, ed. J.C. Norcross, 398–415. New York: Brunner-Mazel.

Nagel, Thomas. 1974. What Is It Like To Be a Bat? *Philosophical Review* 83: 435–450.

Nancy, Jean-Luc, and Philippe Lacoue-Labarthe. 1992. *The Title of the Letter: A Reading of Lacan*. Trans. F. Raffoul and D. Pettigrew. Albany, NY: SUNY Press.

Newton, Isaac. 1964. *The Mathematical Principles of Natural Philosophy (Principia Mathematica)*. New York: Citadel Press.

Newmark, Peter. 1998. *More Paragraphs on Translation*. Toronto, Canada: Multilingual Matters.

Nichols, Shaun. 2004. The Folk Psychology of Free Will: Fits and Starts. *Mind & Language* 19 (5): 473–502.

Nietzsche, Friedrich. 1967. *The Birth of Tragedy Out of the Spirit of Music*. Trans. W. Kaufmann. New York: Vintage Books.

———. 1974. *The Gay Science*. Trans. W. Kaufmann. New York: Vintage Books.

———. 1977. Homer's Contest. Trans. W. Kaufmann. *The Portable Nietzsche*. London: Penguin.

———. 1979. On Truth and Lies in a Nonmoral Sense. In *Philosophy and Truth: Selections from Nietzsche's Notebooks of the Early 1870's*, ed. and trans. D. Breazeale, 79–97. Atlantic Highlands, NJ: Humanities Press.

———. 1989a. *Beyond Good & Evil: Prelude to a Philosophy of the Future*. Trans. W. Kaufmann. New York: Vintage Books.

———. 1989b. *On the Genealogy of Morals*. Eds. and Trans. W. Kaufmann and R.J. Hollingdale. New York: Vintage Books.

O'Brien, Denise. 1969. *Empedocles' Cosmic Cycle*. Cambridge: Cambridge University Press.

O'Callaghan, John P. 2003. *Thomist Realism and the Linguistic Turn: Toward a More Perfect Form of Existence*. South Bend, IN: Notre Dame University Press.

Ockham, William. 1990. *Philosophical Writings: A Selection*. Ed. S.F. Brown and Trans. P. Boehner. Indianapolis, IN: Hackett Publishing.

O'Donahue, William, Kyle E. Ferguson, and Amy E. Naugle. 2003. The Structure of the Cognitive Revolution: An Examination from the Philosophy of Science. *The Behavior Analyst* 26 (1): 85–110.

O'Keefe, Tim. 2005. *Epicurus on Freedom*. Cambridge: Cambridge University Press.

Olson, Michael J. 2014. The Camera Obscura and the Nature of the Soul: On a Tension Between the Mechanics of Sensation and the Metaphysics of the Soul. *Intellectual History Review* 25 (3): 279–291.

Ostenfeld, Erik. 1987. *Ancient Greek Psychology and the Modern Mind-Body Debate*. Aarhus: Aarhus University Press.

Owen, G.E.L. 1986. *'Tithenai ta Phainomena'. Logic, Science and Dialectic*, 239–251. London: Duckworth Publishing.

Panaccio, Claude. 2004. *Ockham on Concepts*. Aldershot: Ashgate.

Pandora, Katherine. 2002. *Rebels Within the Ranks: Psychologists' Critique of Scientific Authority and Democratic Realities in New Deal America*. Cambridge: Cambridge University Press.

Papineau, David. 2012. *Philosophical Devices: Proofs, Probabilities, Possibilities, and Sets*. Oxford: Oxford University Press.

Parkinson, G.H.R. 1982. The Internalization of Appearances. In *Leibniz: Critical and Interpretive Essays*, ed. M. Hooker. Minneapolis, MN: Minnesota University Press.

Paton, Herbert James. 1931. The Key to Kant's Deduction of the Categories. *Mind* 40 (159): 310–329.

———. 1997. *Kant's Metaphysic of Experience*. Vol. 1. Sterling, VA: Thoemmes Press.

Peirce, Charles Sanders. 1982. *Writings of Charles S. Peirce: 1857–1866*. Bloomington, IN: Indiana University Press.

Peregrin, Jaroslav. 2001. *Meaning and Structure: Structuralism of (Post)Analytic Philosophers*. Burlington, VT: Ashgate.

Perls, Frederick S., Ralph Hefferline, and Paul Goodman. 1994. *Gestalt Therapy: Excitement and Growth in the Human Personality*. Gouldsboro, ME: The Gestalt Journal Press.

Peters, F.E. 1967. *Greek Philosophical Terms*. New York: New York University Press.

Peters, Douglas P., and Stephen J. Ceci. 1980. A Manuscript Masquerade. *The Sciences* 20 (7): 16–19.

Petit, Philip. 1977. *The Concept of Structuralism: A Critical Analysis.* Berkeley, CA: University of California Press.

———. 2001. *A Theory of Freedom: From the Psychology to the Politics of Agency.* Oxford: Oxford University Press.

Phillips, John. 2006. Agencement/Assemblage. *Theory, Culture & Society* 23 (2–3): 108–109.

Place, U.T. 1956. Is Consciousness a Brain Process? *British Journal of Psychology* 47: 44–50.

Plato. 1860. *Philebus: A Dialog of Plato on Pleasure and Knowledge and Their Relations to the Highest Good.* Trans. E. Poste, Edward. London: John W. Parker and Son, West Strand.

———. 1997a. *Apology.* Trans. G.M.A. Grube. In John M. Cooper (Ed.), *Plato: Complete Works.* Indianapolis, IN: Hackett Publishing.

———. 1997b. *Meno.* Trans. G.M.A. Grube. In John M. Cooper (Ed.), *Plato: Complete Works.* Indianapolis, IN: Hackett Publishing.

———. 1997c. *Phaedo.* Trans. G.M.A. Grube. In *Plato: Complete Works*, ed. John M. Cooper. Indianapolis, IN: Hackett Publishing.

———. 1997d. *Phaedrus.* Trans. A. Nehamas and P. Woodruff. In *Plato: Complete Works*, ed. John M. Cooper. Indianapolis, IN: Hackett Publishing.

———. 1997e. *Republic.* Trans. G. M. A. Grube and Rev. C. D. C. Reeve. In *Plato: Complete Works*, ed. John M. Cooper. Indianapolis, IN: Hackett Publishing.

———. 1997f. *Symposium.* Trans. A. Nehamas and P. Woodruff. In *Plato: Complete Works*, ed. John M. Cooper. Indianapolis, IN: Hackett Publishing.

———. 1997g. *Timaeus.* Trans. D. J. Zeyl. In *Plato: Complete Works*, ed. John M. Cooper. Indianapolis, IN: Hackett Publishing.

Polansky, Ronald. 1983. *Energeia* in Aristotle's *Metaphysics* IX. *Ancient Philosophy* 3: 160–170.

———. 2010. *Aristotle's De Anima: A Critical Commentary.* Cambridge: Cambridge University Press.

Polybius. 1922. *The Histories.* Trans. W.R. Paton. London: William Heinemann.

Prochaska, James O., and Carlo C. DiClementi. 1986. The Transtheoretical Approach. In *Handbook of Eclectic Psychotherapy*, ed. J.C. Norcross, 163–200. New York: Brunner-Mazel.

Puntel, Lorenz B. 2001. Truth: A Prolegomenon to a General Theory. In *What Is Truth?* ed. R. Schantz. Berlin: Walter de Gruyter.

Putnam, H.. 1975. The Nature of Mental States. In *Mind, Language and Reality: Philosophical Papers*, vol. 2, 429–440. Cambridge: Cambridge University Press.

Pylyshyn, Zenon. 1984. *Computation and Cognition*. Cambridge, MA: MIT Press.

Rachlin, Howard. 1994. *Behavior and Mind: The Roots of Modern Psychology*. Oxford: Oxford University Press.

Raue, Charles G. 1889. *Psychology as a Natural Science Applied to the Solution of Occult Psychic Phenomena*. Philadelphia, PA: Porter & Coates.

Reeve, C.D.C. 2006. *Plato on Love*. Indianapolis, IN: Hackett Publishing.

Reid, Thomas. 1853. *Essays on the Intellectual Powers of Man*. London: Longmans and Company.

Rhine, Joseph B. 1973. *Exta-Sensory Perception*. Wellesley, MA: Branden Press.

Richards, Graham. 1987. Of What Is History of Psychology a History? *The British Journal for the History of Science* 20 (2): 201–211.

———. 2002. *Putting Psychology in its Place: A Critical, Historical Overview*. New York: Routledge.

Ricoeur, Paul. 1970. *Freud and Philosophy*. Trans. D. Savage. New Haven, CT: Yale University Press.

———. 1981. *Hermeneutics and the Human Sciences: Essays on Language, Action and Interpretation*. Trans. J.B. Thompson. Cambridge: Cambridge University Press.

Riskin, Jessica. 2002. *Science in the Age of Sensibility: The Sentimental Empiricists of the French Enlightenment*. Chicago: University of Chicago Press.

Robinson, Edward S. 1964. *Association Theory Today: An Essay in Systematic Psychology*. New York: Hafner Publishing Company.

Rockmore, Tom. 2011. *Kant and Phenomenology*. Chicago: University of Chicago Press.

Rogers, Carl R. 1961. *On Becoming a Person*. Boston: Houghton Mifflin.

———. 1963a. The Actualizing Tendency in Relation to "Motives" and to Consciousness. In *Nebraska Symposium on Motivation*, ed. M. Jones, 1–24. Lincoln, NE: University of Nebraska Press.

———. 1963b. The Concept of the Fully Functioning Person. *Psychotherapy: Theory, Research and Practice* 1 (1): 17–28.

———. 1964. Freedom and Commitment. *The Humanist* 24 (2): 37–40.

———. 1965. A Humanistic Conception of Man. In *Science and Human Affairs*, ed. R.E. Farson, 18–31. Palo Alto, CA: Science & Behavior Books.

———. 1979. Foundations of the Person-Centered Approach. *Education* 110 (2): 98–107.

———. 1995. *A Way of Being*. Boston: Houghton Mifflin.

Rommen, Heinrich A. 1998. *The Natural Law: A Study in Legal and Social History and Philosophy*. Trans. T.R. Hanley. Indianapolis, IN: Liberty Fund.

Rorty, Richard. 1979. *Philosophy and the Mirror of Nature*. Princeton, NJ: Princeton University Press.

———. 1984. The Historiography of Philosophy: Four Genres. In *Philosophy in History: Essays on the Historiography of Philosophy*, ed. R. Rorty, J.B. Schneewind, and Q. Skinner, 49–76. Cambridge: Cambridge University Press.

———. 1989. *Contingency, Irony, and Solidarity*. Cambridge: Cambridge University Press.

———, ed. 1992a. *The Linguistic Turn: Essays in Philosophical Method*. Chicago: University of Chicago Press.

———. 1992b. *Wittgenstein, Heidegger, and the Reification of Language. Essays on Heidegger and Others. Vol II of Philosophical Papers*, 50–66. Cambridge: Cambridge University Press.

———. 1999a. *Philosophy and Social Hope*. London: Penguin Books.

———. 1999b. *Solidarity or Objectivity? Objectivity, Relativism, and Truth. Vol. I of Philosophical Papers*, 21–34. Cambridge: Cambridge University Press.

Rottschaefer, William A. 1997. *The Biology and Psychology of Moral Agency*. Cambridge: Cambridge University Press.

Rousseau, Jean-Jacques. 2010. *Emile or On Education*. Trans. C. Kelly and A. Bloom. Hanover, NH: Dartmouth College Press.

Ruck, Carl A.P. 1986. Mushrooms and Mysteries: On Aristophanes and the Necromancy of Socrates. *Helios* 8 (2): 1–28.

Russell, Bertrand. 2010. *The Philosophy of Logical Atomism*. London: Routledge.

Rust, John. 1987. Is Psychology a Cognitive Science? *Journal of Applied Philosophy* 4 (1): 49–55.

Ryle, Gilbert. 1949. *The Concept of Mind*. Chicago: University of Chicago Press.

Sachs, Joe. 2001. *Aristotle's On the Soul and On Memory and Recollection*. St. Paul, MN: Green Lion Press.

Sahakian, William S. 1975. *History and Systems of Psychology*. London: Wiley.

Santas, Gerasimos. 1979. Plato's Theory of Eros in the *Symposium*: Abstract. *Noûs* 13 (1): 67–75.

Santayana, George. 2011. *The Life of Reason or The Phases of Human Progress*. Cambridge, MA: MIT Press.

Sarno, Ronald. 1969. Hesiod: From Chaos to Cosmos to Community. *The Classical Bulletin* 45 (5): 17–23.

Sartre, Jean-Paul. 1992. *Being and Nothingness*. Trans. H.E. Barnes. New York: Washington Square Press.

———. 1993. The Humanism of Existentialism. In *Essays in Existentialism*, 31–62. New York: Citadel Press.

de Saussure, Ferdinand. 2011. *Course in General Linguistics*. Eds. P. Meisel and H. Saussy, Trans. W. Baskin. New York: Columbia University Press.

Scalambrino, Frank. 2011. *Non-Being & Memory*. Doctoral Dissertation. Retrieved from ProQuest. (UMI: 3466382).

———. 2014. Review of *Perception Beyond Inference* by L. Albertazzi, G. J. van Tonder, D. Vishwanath, eds.. *Philosophical Psychology* 27(5), 764–768.

———. 2015a. *Full Throttle Heart: Nietzsche, Beyond Either/Or*. New Philadelphia, OH: The Eleusinian Press.

———. 2015b. Phenomenological Psychology. *Internet Encyclopedia of Philosophy*. http://www.iep.utm.edu/phen-psy/. Accessed 3 May 2017.

———. 2015c. The Temporality of Damnation. In *The Concept of Hell*, ed. R. Arp and B. McCraw, 66–82. New York: Palgrave Macmillan.

———. 2015d. The Vanishing Subject: Becoming Who You Cybernetically Are. In *Social Epistemology & Technology*, ed. F. Scalambrino, 197–206. London: Roman & Littlefield International.

———. 2015e. What Control? Life at the Limits of Power Expression. In *Social Epistemology & Technology*, ed. F. Scalambrino, 101–112. London: Roman & Littlefield International.

———. 2016a. *Meditations on Orpheus: Love, Death, and Transformation*. Pittsburgh, PA: Black Water Phoenix Press.

———. 2016b. Review of Jacques Lacan's *Seminar VIII* (On Transference). *Philosophy in Review* 36 (5): 211–214.

———. 2017. *Living in the Light of Death: Existential Philosophy in the Eastern Tradition, Zen, Samurai & Haiku*. Castalia, OH: Magister Ludi Press.

———. 2018a. Futurology in Terms of the Bioethics of Genetic Engineering: Proactionary and Precautionary Attitudes Toward Risk with Existence in the Balance. In *Social Epistemology and Futurology: Precautionary & Proactionary Perspectives*, ed. S. Fuller. London: Rowman and Littlefield International. (In Press).

———. 2018b. *Geisteswissenschaften*. In *The Wiley-Blackwell Encyclopedia of Social Theory*, eds. B. Turner, C. Kyung-Sup, C. Epstein, P. Kivisto, J.M. Ryan and W. Outhwaite, vol. II, 1st edn, 912–913. London: Wiley-Blackwell.

Schmidt, Claudia M. 2008. Kant's Transcendental and Empirical Psychology of Cognition. *Studies in History and Philosophy of Science Part A* 39 (4): 462–472.

Schneewind, J.B. 1998. *The Invention of Autonomy*. Cambridge: Cambridge University Press.

Schneider, Walter, and David J. Graham. 1992. Introduction to Connectionist Modeling in Education. *Educational Psychologist* 27 (4): 513–530.

Schopenhauer, Arthur. 2005. *Philosophical Writings*. Trans. W. Schirmacher. New York: Continuum.

Schrödinger, Erwin. 1926. An Undulatory Theory of the Mechanics of Atoms and Molecules. *Physical Review* 28 (6): 1049–1070.

Schwartz, Jeffrey, M. Henry, P. Stapp, and Mario Beauregard. 2005. Quantum Physics in Neuroscience and Psychology: A Neurophysical Model of Mind-Brain Interaction. *Philosophical Transactions of the Royal Society of London. Series B* 360 (1458): 1309–1327.

Seel, Norbert M. 2011. Gestalt Psychology of Learning. In *Encyclopedia of the Sciences of Learning*, ed. N.M. Seel, 1366–1371. New York: Springer.

Sellars, Wilfrid. 1956. Empiricism and the Philosophy of Mind. In *Minnesota Studies in the Philosophy of Science*, ed. H. Feigl and M. Scriven, vol. I, 253–329. Minneapolis, MN: University of Minnesota Press.

Serres, Michel. 1982. *Hermes: Literature, Science, Philosophy*. Trans. D.F. Bell. Baltimore, MD: The Johns Hopkins University Press.

Shannon, Claude E., and Warren Weaver. 1949. *The Mathematical Theory of Communication*. Urbana, IL: University of Illinois.

Sheed, Frank J. 1946. *Theology and Sanity*. New York: Sheed & Ward.

Shoemaker, Sydney. 1981. Some Varieties of Functionalism. *Philosophical Topics* 12: 93–119.

Silver, Burton, and Heather Busch. 2014. *Dancing with Cats*. San Francisco: Chronicle Books.

Simonton, Dean. 2004. *Creativity in Science: Chance, Logic, Genius, and Zeitgeist*. Cambridge: Cambridge University Press.

Sinatra, Maria. 2006. The Birth of Experimental Psychology in Germany Between Psychophysical Methods and Physiological Theories. *Physis; rivista internazionale di storia della scienza* 43: 91–131.

Singh, Arun K. 1999. *Comprehensive History of Psychology*. Jawahar Nagar, Delhi: Motilal Banarsidass.

Skinner, B.F. 1953. *Science and Human Behavior*. New York: Macmillan.

———. 1971. *Beyond Freedom and Dignity*. Indianapolis, IN: Hackett Publishing.

Skinner, Quentin. 1969. Meaning and Understanding in the History of Ideas. *History and Theory* 8: 3–53.

Skoll, Geoffrey R. 2014. *Dialectics in Social Thought: The Present Crisis*. New York: Palgrave Macmillan.

Slife, Brent D., Kari A. O'Grady, and Russell D. Kosits. 2017. Introduction to Psychology's Worldviews. In *The Hidden Worldviews of Psychology's Theory,*

*Research, and Practice*, ed. B.D. Slife, K.A. O'Grady, and R.D. Kosits, 1–8. New York: Routledge.

Smart, J.J.C. 1959. Sensations and Brain Processes. *The Philosophical Review* 68 (2): 141–156.

Smith, David L. 1999. *Freud's Philosophy of the Unconscious*. Dordrecht: Kluwer Academic Publishers.

Smith, Noel W. 2001. *Current Systems in Psychology: History, Theory, Research, and Applications*. Stamford, CT: Wadsworth Publishing.

Smith, Jonathan A., and Mike Osborn. 2003. Interpretative Phenomenological Analysis. In *A Practical Guide to Research Methods*, ed. J.A. Smith. London: Sage.

Sobociński, Bolesław. 1984. Leśniewski's Analysis of Russell's Paradox. In *Leśniewski's Systems: Ontology and Mereology*, ed. J.T.J. Srzednicki and V.F. Rickey, 11–44. The Hague: Martinus Nijhoff Publishers.

Sokal, Alan D. 1996. Transgressing the Boundaries: Towards a Transformative Hermeneutics of Quantum Gravity. *Social Text* (46/47): 217–252.

Sokal, Alan D., and Jean Bricmont. 1998. *Fashionable Nonsense: Postmodern Intellectuals' Abuse of Science*. New York: Picador.

Solomon, Robert C. 1974. Freud's Neurological Theory of Mind. In *Freud: A Collection of Critical Essays*, ed. R. Wollheim. Garden City, NY: Anchor Press.

———. 1987. *From Hegel to Existentialism*. Oxford: Oxford University Press.

Spiegel, Gabrielle M. 2005. Introduction. In *Practicing History: New Directions in Historical Writing After the Linguistic Turn*, ed. G.M. Spiegel, 1–32. London: Routledge.

Spinelli, Ernesto. 2005. *The Interpreted World: An Introduction to Phenomenological Psychology*. London: Sage.

Stephen, Daniel L. 1986. The Patient As Text: A Model of Clinical Hermeneutics. *Theoretical Medicine* 7: 195–210.

Stillman, Drake, and Trevor H. Levore. 1999. *Essays on Galileo and the History and Philosophy of Science*. Vol. I. Toronto: University of Toronto Press.

Stocking, George. 1968. On the Limits of 'Presentism' and 'Historicism' in the Historiography of the Behavioral Sciences. In *In Race, Culture, and Evolution: Essays in the History of Anthropology*. Chicago: University of Chicago Press.

Stump, Eleonore. 1989. *Dialectic and Its Place in the Development of Medieval Logic*. Ithaca, NY: Cornell University Press.

Sturm, Thomas. 2001. Kant on Empirical Psychology: How Not to Investigate the Human Mind. In *Kant and the Sciences*, ed. E. Watkins, 163–184. Oxford: Oxford University Press.

Suleiman, Susan R. 1990. *Subversive Intent: Gender, Politics, and the Avant-Garde*. Cambridge, MA: Harvard University Press.

Sulloway, Frank. 1992. *Freud, Biologist of the Mind: Beyond the Psychoanalytic Legend*. Cambridge, MA: Harvard University Press.

Svensson, Lennart. 1997. Theoretical Foundations of Phenomenography. *Higher Education Research & Development* 16 (2): 159–171.

Swindal, James. 2017. Faith and Reason. *Internet Encyclopedia of Philosophy*. http://www.iep.utm.edu/faith-re/. Accessed 7 Apr 2017.

Szasz, Thomas. 1988. *The Myth of Psychotherapy*. Syracuse, NY: Syracuse University Press.

———. 1997. The Healing Word: Its Past, Present, and Future. In *The Evolution of Psychotherapy The Third Conference*. Bristol, PA: Brunner/Mazel.

———. 1998. *Manufacture of Madness: A Comparative Study of the Inquisition and the Mental Health Movement*. Syracuse, NY: Syracuse University Press.

———. 2001. *Insanity: The Idea and Its Consequences*. Syracuse, NY: Syracuse University Press.

———. 2010. *The Myth of Mental Illness*. New York: Harper Perennial.

Thiel, Udo. 2011. *The Early Modern Subject: Self-Consciousness and Personal Identity from Descartes to Hume*. Oxford: Oxford University Press.

Thompson, Evan. 2007. *Mind in Life: Biology, Phenomenology, and the Sciences of Mind*. Cambridge, MA: Harvard University Press.

Titchener, Edward B. 1910. *A Textbook of Psychology*. New York: Macmillan.

———. 1914. On 'Psychology as the Behaviorist Views It. *American Philosophical Society* 53 (213): 1–17.

———. 1927. *Systematic Psychology: Prolegomena*. Ithaca, NY: Cornell University Press.

Tobias, Ashley. 2007. The Postmodern Theatre Clown. In *Clowns, Fools and Picaros: Popular Forms in Theatre, Fiction and Film*, ed. D. Robb, 37–56. Amsterdam: Rodopi.

Tosh, Nick. 2003. Anachronism and Retrospective Explanation: In Defense of a Present-Centered History of Science. *Studies in History and Philosophy of Science* 34 (3): 647–659.

Toulmin, Stephen. 1972. *Human Understanding*. Princeton, NJ: Princeton University Press.

Tracy, Theodore. 1982. Soul/Boatman Analogy in Aristotle's *De Anima*. *Classical Philology* 77 (2): 97–112.

Trevelyan, George M. 1949. *An Autobiography and Other Essays*. London: Longmans.

Tryon, Warren W. 2014. *Cognitive Neuroscience and Psychotherapy: Network Principles of a Unified Theory*. Oxford: Elsevier Science.

von Uexküll, Jakob. 2010. *A Foray Into the Worlds of Animals and Humans: With a Theory of Meaning*. Trans. J.D. O'Neil. Minneapolis, MN: Minnesota University Press.

Uždavinys, Algis. 2010. *Philosophy & Theurgy*. Kettering, OH: Angelico Press.

Valsiner, Jaan, and Alberto Rosa. 2007. *The Cambridge Handbook of Sociocultural Psychology*. Cambridge: Cambridge University Press.

VandenBos, Gary R. 2007. *APA Dictionary of Psychology*. Washington, DC: American Psychological Association.

Van Kaam, Adrian. 1966. *Existential Foundations of Psychology*. Pittsburgh, PA: Duquesne University Press.

Vaugh-Blount, Kelli, Alexandra Rutherford, David Baker, and Deborah Johnson. 2009. History's Mysteries Demystified: Becoming a Psychologist-Historian. *The American Journal of Psychology* 122 (1): 117–129.

Vico, Giambattista. 2002. *The First New Science*. Cambridge: Cambridge University Press.

Vidal, Fernando. 2011. *The Sciences of the Soul: The Early Modern Origins of Psychology*. Trans. S. Brown. Chicago: University of Chicago Press.

Vlieghe, Joris. 2016. How Learning to Read and Write Shapes Humanity: A Technosomatic Perspective on Digitization. In *Social Epistemology and Technology: Toward Public Self-Awareness Regarding Technological Mediation*, ed. F. Scalambrino, 127–136. London: Rowman & Littlefield International.

de Vogel, Cornelia J. 1955. The Present State of the Socratic Problem. *Phronesis* 1 (1): 26–35.

Walsh, Richard T., Thomas Teo, and Angelina Baydala. 2014. *A Critical History and Philosophy of Psychology: Diversity of Context, Thought, and Practice*. Cambridge: Cambridge University Press.

Wasson, R. Gordon, Albert Hofmann, and Carl A.P. Ruck. 2008. *The Road to Eleusis: Unveiling the Secret of the Mysteries*. Berkeley, CA: North Atlantic Books.

Watson, John B. 1913. Psychology as the Behaviorist Views It. *Psychological Review* 20 (2): 158–177.

Watson, Robert I. 1966. The Role and Use of History in the Psychology Curriculum. *Journal of the History of the Behavioral Sciences* 2 (1): 64–69.

———. 1967. Psychology: A Prescriptive Science. *American Psychologist* 22 (6): 435–443.

Waxman, Wayne. 1994. *Hume's Theory of Consciousness*. Cambridge: Cambridge University Press.

Wegner, Daniel M. 2003. *The Illusion of Conscious Will*. Cambridge, MA: MIT Press.

Wehrle, Walter E. 2000. *The Myth of Aristotle's Development and the Betrayal of Metaphysics*. London: Rowman & Littlefield.

Weimer, Walter B., and David S. Palermo. 1973. Paradigms and Normal Science in Psychology. *Science Studies* 3 (3): 211–244.

Weinert, Friedel. 2009. *Copernicus, Darwin, & Freud*. Hoboken, NJ: Wiley-Blackwell.

Whitehead, Alfred North. 1985. *Process and Reality*. New York: Free Press.

Wiener, Norbert. 1965. *Cybernetics, Or, the Control and Communication in the Animal and the Machine*. Cambridge, MA: MIT Press.

Wilhelmsen, Frederick D. 1956. *Man's Knowledge of Reality: An Introduction to Thomistic Epistemology*. Upper Saddle River, NJ: Prentice Hall.

Williams, Linda. 1981. *Figures of Desire: A Theory and Analysis of Surrealist Film*. Berkeley, CA: University of California Press.

Wittgenstein, Ludwig. 1969. *On Certainty*. Trans. G.E.M. Anscombe. New York: Harper & Row Publishers.

———. 1980. *Remarks on the Philosophy of Psychology*. Vol. 2. Chicago: University of Chicago Press.

———. 1982. Conversations on Freud; Excerpt from 1932–3 Lectures. In *Philosophical Essays on Freud*, ed. R. Wollheim and J. Hopkins. Cambridge: Cambridge University Press.

———. 2001. *Philosophical Investigations*. Trans. G.E.M. Anscombe, P.M.S. Hacker, and J. Schulte. Hoboken, NJ: Wiley-Blackwell.

Wolman, Benjamin B. 1960. *Contemporary Theories and Systems in Psychology*. New York: Harper & Brothers Publishers.

Wood, Robert E. 1990. *A Path into Metaphysics: Phenomenological, Hermeneutical, and Dialogical Studies*. Albany, NY: SUNY Press.

———. 2015. *The Beautiful, the True, and the Good: Studies in the History of Thought*. Washington, DC: The Catholic University of America.

Woodward, William R., and Mitchell G. Ash. 1982. Preface. In *The Problematic Science: Psychology in Nineteenth-Century Thought*, ed. W.R. Woodward and M.G. Ash, v–vi. New York: Praeger Publishing.

Worthen, Valerie. 1974. Psychotherapy and Catholic Confession. *Journal of Religion and Health* 13 (4): 275–284.

Wuellner, Bernard J. 1956. *Summary of Scholastic Principles*. Chicago: Loyola University Press.

Wundt, Wilhelm. 1904. *Principles of Physiological Psychology*. Trans. E.B. Titchener, vol. 1. New York: Macmillan.

———. 2014. *Lectures on Human and Animal Psychology*. Trans. J.E. Creighton and E.G. Titchener. New York: Routledge.

Yates, Frances A. 1964. *Giordano Bruno and the Hermetic Tradition*. Chicago: University of Chicago Press.

Yolton, John W. 1984. *Thinking Matter: Materialism in Eighteenth-Century Britain*. Minneapolis, MN: Minnesota University Press.

Zagzebski, Linda T. 1991. *The Dilemma of Freedom and Foreknowledge*. Oxford: Oxford University Press.

———. 2002. Recent Work on Divine Foreknowledge and Free Will. In *The Oxford Handbook of Free Will*, ed. R. Kane, 45–64. Oxford: Oxford University Press.

Zepf, Siegfried. 2016. Psychoanalysis as a Natural Science: Reconsidering Freud's 'Scientistic Self-Misunderstanding. *International Forum of Psychoanalysis* 25: 157–168.

Ziman, John. 1978. *Reliable Knowledge: An Exploration of the Grounds for Belief in Science*. Cambridge: Cambridge University Press.

Žižek, Slavoj. 1987. Why Lacan Is Not a Post-Structuralist. *Newsletter of the Freudian Field* 1 (2): 31–39.

Zuckert, Catherine H. 2009. *Plato's Philosophers: The Coherence of the Dialogues*. Chicago, IL: Chicago University Press.

# Index[1]

---

[1] Note: Page number followed by 'n' refer to notes.

© The Author(s) 2018
F. Scalambrino, *Philosophical Principles of the History and Systems of Psychology*,
https://doi.org/10.1007/978-3-319-74733-0